KNOWLEDGE DISCOVERY WITH
SUPPORT VECTOR MACHINES

T0350202

KNOWLEDGE DISCOVERY WITH SUPPORT VECTOR MACHINES

LUTZ HAMEL
University of Rhode Island

WILEY

A JOHN WILEY & SONS, INC., PUBLICATION

Library of Congress Cataloging-in-Publication Data:

Hamel, Lutz.
   Knowledge discovery with support vector machines / Lutz Hamel.
      p. cm. — (Wiley series on methods and applications in data mining)
   Includes bibliographical references and index.
   ISBN 978-0-470-37192-3 (cloth)
   1. Support vector machines.   2. Data mining.   3. Machine learning.   4. Computer algorithms.
   I. Title.
   Q325.5.H38 2009
   005.1–dc22   2009011948

10 9 8 7 6 5 4 3 2 1

To Natalie, Enzo, and Oliver
and in memory of Klaus

CONTENTS

PREFACE

Since their introduction in 1995, support vector machines have become one of the preeminent machine learning paradigms. Support vector machines are now employed routinely in areas that range from handwriting recognition to bioinformatics to the mining of very large databases. This book has been written to provide an introduction to this important class of machine learning algorithms with a minimum of technical background in order to make this material as widely accessible as possible. With the exception of some basic notions in calculus and probability theory, the book is completely self-contained. Important concepts in linear algebra and optimization theory are carefully motivated and introduced. Specifically, we have excluded any technical material that does not contribute directly to the understanding of support vector machines. Many other excellent textbooks are available today that develop support vector machines in much more technical detail than is provided here. These books should be accessible to the reader after reading this book. It is worth mentioning that we develop support vector machines from a computational perspective rather than from the traditional statistical perspective.

The book is aimed at upper-level undergraduate as well as beginning graduate students who want to learn more about support vector machines or who are pursuing research in machine learning and related areas. It should also prove a gentle tutorial on support vector machines for machine learning researchers and data analysts. The main objective of this book is to provide the necessary background to work with existing machine learning tool sets that include support vector machines as part of their suite of components. Once the material in this book has been mastered, the reader will be able to apply standard support vector machine learning algorithms to his or her problems with concrete insights as to what is going on "under the hood." To facilitate this goal, most chapters have short tutorial sections that provide guidance on how the learned material is applied in actual tool sets. In this book we chose two open-source programs, WEKA and R, for this purpose. We chose WEKA because it represents a prototypical, GUI-driven data analysis tool, and we chose R because it is the open-source reimplementation of the popular S-Plus statistical computing environment. The data analysis techniques used in WEKA and R are easily transferred to other tool sets.

The content of this book is based on a one-semester course given over a number of years to beginning graduate computer science students at the University of Rhode Island who want to conduct research in machine learning or to apply machine intelligence to other areas, such as computational chemistry, molecular biology, and forensic sciences. The book consist of three parts. Part I covers foundational issues such as the definition of machine learning, concepts from linear algebra such as vector spaces and decision surfaces, and simple learning methods including perceptron learning. Part II develops support vector machines are developed starting from the primal, linear setting and then continuing to the dual, nonlinear setting. Here we also cover implementation, model evaluation, and elements of statistical learning theory. In Part III the basic support vector machine model is extended in various ways. For instance, we develop approaches that extend the canonical binary support vector machine model to an arbitrary number of classes. We also investigate regression problems using support vector machines. A typical course offering at the University of Rhode Island would cover Part I and II with a selection of chapters from Part III as time permits.

ACKNOWLEDGMENTS

This book would not have been possible without the help of a number of people. First I would like to thank the series editor, Daniel Larose, for suggesting this project. I also want to thank Frank Corrano, whose encouragement and knowledge of the publishing industry were vital during the conception of the book. I would like to thank Michael Berry, Ute Schmid, David Brown, Christian Convey, Raghu Jayan, and the anonymous reviewers, who all provided valuable feedback on various versions of the draft. In particular, I want to thank my graduate student, Scott Pion, who read every chapter of the draft and provided detailed comments. Many thanks also to all the students who suffered through various incarnations of the draft over the years. The collective comments caught many inaccuracies and ambiguities and made this into a better book. Whatever errors remain are purely mine. I am grateful to the editorial team at Wiley: Paul Petralia, Anastasia Wasko, and Michael Christian. They answered questions in an expedient manner and made this entire process an enjoyable one. I also want to acknowledge the Department of Computer Science and Statistics at the University of Rhode Island, which provided me with the environment and freedom to pursue this project. Many thanks to Bob Frio, who kept me motivated with our weekly lunch meetings at Oatley's. A special thank you to my parents, who enabled me to take this journey. And finally, I am eternally grateful to my wife, Natalie, whose support, patience, love, and understanding made this all possible.

LUTZ HAMEL

Kingston, Rhode Island
November 2008

PART I

CHAPTER 1

WHAT IS KNOWLEDGE DISCOVERY?

Knowledge discovery is a semiautomated process of extracting useful information from collections of data that are too big to be investigated manually. By *semiautomated* we mean that we use computer-based tools for the discovery process but that guidance by an analyst is indispensable. The information retrieved by the discovery process usually takes on the form of actionable or explanatory patterns often referred to as *models*. There are many different types of models. For instance, we have models that are represented as *if–then–else* rules as well as models that implement artificial neural networks. All models have the desirable property that they tend to ignore unnecessary detail and summarize the major trends in data. A model can represent or summarize terabytes of data and therefore provides access to information or knowledge hidden in large amounts of data. In this book we deal with one particular type of model called a *support vector machine*. Support vector machines represent a powerful new class of models invented by Vladimir Vapnik in the early 1990s. They have been shown to be competitive with artificial neural networks and outperform them in many cases.

A term that is often associated with knowledge discovery is *data mining*. Data mining can be considered a specific kind of knowledge discovery process that aims at extracting information from databases. Data mining is often referred to as *knowledge discovery in databases* (KDD).

Knowledge discovery is a highly interdisciplinary undertaking ranging from domain analysis, data cleansing, and visualization to model evaluation and deployment (see Figure 1.1). However, at the core of the knowledge discovery process is a discovery algorithm that performs some kind of pattern recognition and constructs models of the data encountered. The discovery algorithms we are concerned with in

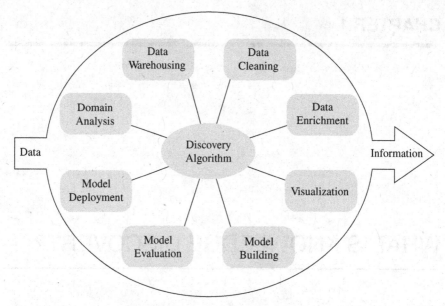

FIGURE 1.1 The knowledge discovery process: from data to information.

this book are based on *machine learning*. Let us start by defining what we mean by machine learning.

1.1 MACHINE LEARNING

Phenomena whose behavior we can observe exist all around us. Consider, for example, the orbits of the planets around the sun or the timing of the tides. The central question in machine learning is: *Can we use computers to discover and describe patterns based on these behaviors?* The answer to this question is a resounding "yes" and it is the topic of the remainder of the book.

Perhaps the easiest way to describe phenomena is through classification. Here, a particular object either belongs to a class of objects or it does not. When we see a cat, we easily recognize that it belongs to the class of mammals, and when we see a crow, we recognize that it belongs to the class of birds. Abstractly speaking, we can imagine that there exists some process in connection with some phenomenon that labels objects as *true* if they belong to the class in question or *false* if they do not belong to the class. In our case, we have *mammal*(cat) = *true* and *mammal*(crow) = *false*, as well as *bird*(cat) = *false* and *bird*(crow) = *true*. Here, *mammal* and *bird* are processes that provide the labels for any object according to the class of mammals and the class of birds, respectively. Typically, classifications are not as easy as mammals and birds, and in general we do not have access to the processes that label the objects. We can only observe the consequences of these processes: the observable labels for each object. The goal of machine learning then is to compute a suitable model for a labeling process that approximates the original process as closely as possible. The following definition states this more formally.

Definition 1.1 (Machine Learning)
Given:

- *A data universe X*
- *A sample set S, where $S \subset X$*
- *Some target function (labeling process) $f : X \rightarrow \{true, false\}$*
- *A labeled training set D, where $D = \{(x, y) \mid x \in S \text{ and } y = f(x)\}$*

Compute a function $\hat{f} : X \rightarrow \{true, false\}$ using D such that

$$\hat{f}(x) \cong f(x) \tag{1.1}$$

for all $x \in X$.

Let us take a look at this definition in more detail. The data universe X is the set of objects of interest. For example, this might be a set of celestial objects viewable in a photograph taken through a telescope; it could also be a set of persons who visited a particular web page; or it could be a collection of proteins whose function in the cell and three-dimensional structure are known. The sample set S is a subset of the data universe. In general, the sample set is necessary since most collections of objects we are interested in tend to be very large or perhaps infinite, and building models can be very slow for large data universes and impossible for infinite data universes. Therefore, the sample set S acts as a representative of the data universe in order to make the process of building models tractable. The target function f is the process that provides the observable labels. It is assumed that f is able to provide a suitable value in $\{true, false\}$ for any element in X when that element is observed. Thus, even though we have no direct access to the process itself, we are always able to observe the labels this process assigns to the elements in the data universe. For example, when we interpret a photograph, a target function f might label celestial objects viewable in the photograph according to whether or not they are stars. We use this property of the target function to construct the training set D by observing the labels for objects in the sample set S. As an aside, machine learning that makes use of labeled training data is referred to as *supervised learning*. There are other types of machine learning, referred to as *unsupervised learning*, that do not need labeled training data. Finally, equation (1.1) in our definition of machine learning formally states that learning can be viewed as computing the function $\hat{f}$ as an approximation to or a model of the original process f based on the training examples in D. That is, the result of machine learning is a model of the original labeling function. However, out of convenience we often say that $\hat{f}$ is a model of the training data D. This is compatible with the formal view expressed in (1.1) because the elements in the training set are input–output pairs of the original labeling function, $(x, y) \in f$ with $x \in S$ and $y = f(x)$, and this means that modeling the function f and modeling the training data D are one and the same.

The names of the labels in {*true, false*} are arbitrary; instead of *true* and *false* we could have used T and F, 0 and 1, or *blue* and *green*. The important fact is that this set contains two distinct labels: one for class membership and one for nonmembership. We can also consider classification problems with more than two possibilities. The only difference from our definition of machine learning above would be that the codomain of the original labeling process f and its model $\hat{f}$ is a set that includes an appropriate number of distinct labels.

Once we have a model of the original labeling process, two interesting things can be accomplished. First, we can use the model to compute or *predict* the label of an element in the data universe X without having to observe this element. Second, the model can provide some insight into the original labeling process. That is, a model possesses some *explanatory* ability. Consider the following scenario, where the data universe X represents all the customers of a bank. Now, assume that a model $\hat{f}$ classifies the customers according to who is likely to default on a mortgage (*true*) and who is not (*false*). The bank can now use this model to predict which of its customers are likely to default on their mortgage payments before the event is observable, and is able to take actions such as offering refinance or debt management options. The bank can also use the model to discover which features of the data universe X are most relevant to the prediction; that is, the model can tell the bank the characteristics of a bank customer who is likely to default. These characteristics can take on the form of multiple maxed-out credit cards or perhaps a large, high-interest home equity loan.

1.2 STRUCTURE OF THE UNIVERSE X

As varied as the objects in a data universe may be, they can usually be described by a collection of *features* or *attributes*. The most common way to represent a set of objects is as a table where each feature is given as a table column and each object is a row in the table. Table 1.1 is a table representing a subset S of the data universe X of all objects with legs. We have five objects in this set. Each object in S is described by four features:

1. *Legs*: the number of legs the object has
2. *Wings*: yes if the object has wings; otherwise, no
3. *Fur*: yes if the object has fur; otherwise, no
4. *Feathers*: yes if the object has feathers; otherwise, no

When we apply a labeling process such as *mammal* to an object in S (e.g., Cat), we actually apply the labeling process to the feature set of that object. The name of the object does not carry any information; it is the description or representation of that object that matters during classification. That is, *mammal*(Cat) is shorthand for *mammal*(4, no, yes, no). If we had called our cat "Jup," *mammal*(Jup) would still be shorthand for *mammal*(4, no, yes, no) because the nature of the object did not change. Therefore, we ignore the names of the objects and view our set S as a subset of the cross-product of our features; that is, S is a subset of all possible object descriptions

TABLE 1.1 Simple Feature Table for a Small Number of Objects

	Legs	Wings	Fur	Feathers
Cat	4	no	yes	no
Crow	2.	yes	no	yes
Frog	4	no	no	no
Bat	4	yes	yes	no
Barstool	3	no	no	no

that we can generate given our four features. In our case we have

$$S \subset \text{Legs} \times \text{Wings} \times \text{Fur} \times \text{Feathers}, \tag{1.2}$$

and the description of Cat is a member of S according to Table 1.1, $(4, \text{no}, \text{yes}, \text{no}) \in S$. Since we view S as a subset of our data universe X, it follows that

$$X \subseteq \text{Legs} \times \text{Wings} \times \text{Fur} \times \text{Feathers}. \tag{1.3}$$

Each object in our data universe X is described by four features.

We construct the training data set D by applying the target function *mammal* to each object in S:

$$mammal(4, \text{no}, \text{yes}, \text{no}) = true,$$
$$mammal(2, \text{yes}, \text{no}, \text{yes}) = false,$$
$$mammal(4, \text{no}, \text{no}, \text{no}) = false,$$
$$mammal(4, \text{yes}, \text{yes}, \text{no}) = true,$$
$$mammal(4, \text{no}, \text{no}, \text{no}) = false.$$

The training data can also be represented as a table and is shown in Table 1.2. Here we dropped the names of the objects from the table altogether since they do not add any information. It is typical that in this representation of the training data the class label is made into an additional feature often called the *dependent attribute*.

Looking at the training data we see an interesting pattern emerging, in that being a mammal seems to be highly correlated with having fur. So perhaps a reasonable model $\hat{f}$ for the labeling process *mammal* is

$$\hat{f}(legs, wings, fur, feathers) \equiv \textbf{if } fur = \text{ yes } \textbf{then } true \textbf{ else } false. \tag{1.4}$$

In other words, given any object in our data universe the model tests the input value *fur*, and if it is set to yes it will return *true*; otherwise, it will return *false*. If our training set is representative, our model will approximate the original labeling process over the entire data universe:

$$\hat{f}(x) \cong mammal(x) \tag{1.5}$$

TABLE 1.2   Training Data as a Table

Legs	Wings	Fur	Feathers	Mammal[a]
4	no	yes	no	*true*
2	yes	no	yes	*false*
4	no	no	no	*false*
4	yes	yes	no	*true*
3	no	no	no	*false*

[a]The label observed for each object in the table.

for all $x \in X$. Here we used a pattern found in the training set to construct a model and inferred that this model will approximate the labeling process *mammal* over the rest of the data universe. This type of reasoning is called *inductive learning*.

1.3   INDUCTIVE LEARNING

Our definition of machine learning (Definition 1.1) expresses an *inductive process* where, given a limited amount of data in the form of a training set, we try to induce a function that approximates the original labeling process over the entire data universe. That is, we *generalize* from specific instances in the training set D to the entire data universe X. We call this *inductive learning*. At the heart of inductive learning lies the assumption that the training set is an accurate representation of the entire universe. This assumption is formalized in the following hypothesis.

Inductive Learning Hypothesis *Any function found to approximate the target function well over a sufficiently large set of training examples will also approximate the target function well over unobserved examples.*

The intricacies of inductive learning can be illustrated by the *black swan problem*. Consider Figure 1.2. Here the set X denotes the universe of all possible swans (i.e., black and white swans) and the set D denotes the training set for a machine learning algorithm. From this training set a learning algorithm might infer a model in which all swans are white, or more formally,

$$\hat{f}(x) = white \qquad (1.6)$$

for all $x \in X$. This is clearly only an approximation to the original process,

$$f : X \rightarrow \{white, black\}, \qquad (1.7)$$

which labels most of the swans white but also labels some swans black. Our model $\hat{f}$ would be a poor choice for answering scientific questions on the color of swans. On the other hand, if 99% of the swans in the world are white, our model has an accuracy of 99% when evaluated over the entire data universe. This means that it is a pretty good model if we want an approximation of the color of swans.

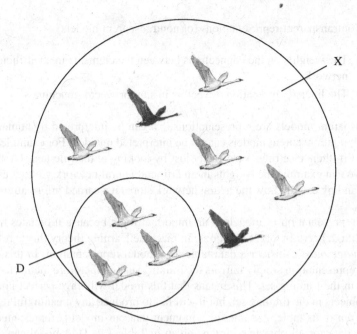

FIGURE 1.2   Data universe X and training set D for the *black swan problem*.

The question of inductive learning and whether or not a training set is a good representation of a data universe depends on the application of the ensuing models and is not a clear-cut proposition. It is desirable, however, to construct a training set as representative of the data universe as possible; that is, it is desirable to construct a training set that is "sufficiently large." In our case we should try to include at least one black swan in the training data set. Sophisticated techniques from statistical sampling theory can be used to ensure that the training data are "large enough." However, ultimately there will always be some uncertainty about the objects captured in our training set. We will study techniques that help us to evaluate some of this uncertainty and, with it, the generalization ability and expected accuracy of our models.

1.4   MODEL REPRESENTATIONS

Since we want the approximation $\hat{f}$ of the target function f to be computable, we are interested in appropriate representations of the models $\hat{f}$. Typically, we consider two types of model representations:

1. Transparent representations (or transparent models)

    a. If–then–else rules

    b. Decision trees

2. Nontransparent representations (or nontransparent models)

    a. The weights on the connections between the elements in an artificial neural network

    b. The linear combination of vectors in support vector machines

Transparent models are representations that can be interpreted by human beings unaided; nontransparent models cannot be interpreted unaided. For example, we can interpret if–then–else rules very easily just by looking at the rule text. On the other hand, we can examine the weights in an artificial neural network without ever fully understanding exactly how the neural network stores its learned information in these weights.

The representation of models is an important topic because it dictates how well we can model certain target functions. In machine learning theory this is referred to as *language bias*. Consider a data table as a model representation. In this case the model representation simply mirrors the training set and therefore memorizes all the objects in the training set. This means that this model will have perfect knowledge of the objects in the training set, but it will fail to produce any meaningful results for objects not in its table. Assume for a moment that our model is represented by the training data for all objects with legs given in Table 1.2. This model can certainly answer questions on objects, such as (4, yes, yes, no), that are in the table simply by looking up the object that matches the features of the query and returning the value stored in the dependent attribute as the answer:

$$(4, \text{yes}, \text{yes}, \text{no}) \mapsto true. \tag{1.8}$$

But this model cannot answer questions on objects that are not in its table. Consider

$$(2, \text{no}, \text{no}, \text{no}) \mapsto ? \tag{1.9}$$

This means that our model does not generalize beyond the objects found in its table and therefore is a poor choice as an approximation of the original labeling process over the data universe.

The limitations of this model are due to the fact that we chose the training data table as our model implementation. Now, consider another type of representation: The model consists of a constant. Regardless of what type of object the model is handed, it will always generate the same constant response. We have seen this above in the swan example, where the model always produces the response *white*. If we pick the constant to be the majority label in the training set, in our case the label *false*, this simple model will make mistakes on the training set. However, if the training set is an accurate representation of the data universe as a whole, we can expect that the model will have the same or similar accuracy on the data universe as for the training set. Thus, we can say that the model does generalize to a certain extent; it at least encodes the majority label in its simple structure and uses this single piece of information to assign labels to unobserved objects.

Model representations such as decision trees, neural networks, and support vector machines fall somewhere in between the two extremes above. The algorithms that give rise to more sophisticated model representations discover regularities that relate objects to their corresponding labels, and these regularities are then encoded in appropriate model representations.

In the previous discussion we have seen a simple decision rule model for our *mammal* target function that captured the regularity or pattern that being a mammal and having fur seems to be highly correlated. It is interesting to observe that, in general, transparent model representations lag in performance compared to nontransparent model representations. The constraint that a model is interpretable by people unaided seems to interfere with the modeling process, in that a transparent model is not able to classify certain phenomena as effectively as are nontransparent models.

EXERCISES

1.1 Explain in your own words what is meant by the statement *a model generalizes well*.

1.2 Briefly explain what *inductive learning* means.

1.3 Consider the training set given in Table 1.2. Write a program that will detect the perfect correlation between the *fur* attribute and the *mammal* labels and outputs this as a model along the lines of equation (1.4).

1.4 Write a program that can accept any training data set of the form given in Table 1.2 and that computes a majority label model. You can assume that the last attribute of the training table is always the dependent attribute.

1.5 Consider a large set of a variety of objects and make that your data universe X. Now consider the labeling function $bird : X \rightarrow \{true, false\}$ that labels each object in X as a bird (or not). Design a model $\hat{f} : X \rightarrow \{true, false\}$ that could be implemented on a computer that approximates the original function $bird$. What is your feature set? Now take a subset D of X as your training data. Analyze where and how your model makes mistakes when it is applied to D and/or to X.

1.6 Consider a naturally occurring phenomenon around you. Construct a classification model for it using machine learning. What is the data universe? What is the feature set? What are the labels? Can you estimate the accuracy of your model?

BIBLIOGRAPHIC NOTES

A readable introduction to machine learning from a computer science perspective is Mitchell's book [54]. Our definitions of machine learning and the inductive learning hypothesis closely follow Mitchell. A comprehensive and recent overview of the field of machine learning and pattern recognition is [10]. A more statistical view of machine learning can be found in books by Hastie et al. [36] and Gentle [34]. Quinlan's C4.5 and Breiman's et al. CART decision tree algorithms are described in detail in [62] and [16], respectively. An excellent description of neural networks is Bishop's book [9]. An older but interesting collection of papers dealing with the knowledge discovery process is [31]. A particularly gentle introduction to data mining is [2]. Data mining from the perspective of particular application areas such as customer support is discussed in [8]. Data preparation and data warehousing are discussed in [61] and [43], respectively. Perhaps the best known formalization of knowledge discovery and data mining is the CRISP methodology (http://www.crisp-dm.org). The earliest reference to the *black swan problem* we are aware of is [60].

CHAPTER 2

KNOWLEDGE DISCOVERY ENVIRONMENTS

A knowledge discovery environment or tool set must support the computational aspects of the discovery process. Here we take a look at some of the most commonly supported computational aspects of the knowledge discovery process, such as data manipulation and visualization as well as model construction and evaluation. We demonstrate these using two open-source systems: WEKA and R. The philosophies of each of these tool sets is very different, in that WEKA is GUI driven and R is based on a scripting language. Both environments incorporate the components necessary to accomplish sophisticated knowledge discovery tasks. We close the chapter with a very brief survey of alternative knowledge discovery environments.

2.1 COMPUTATIONAL ASPECTS OF KNOWLEDGE DISCOVERY

We mentioned in Chapter 1 that knowledge discovery is a semiautomated process; that is, it is a process that relies heavily on computational tools, but guidance by an analyst is indispensable. The analyst provides domain expertise and formulates the discovery task in such a way that it can be tackled using computational tools. Furthermore, the analyst makes decisions about when a model is appropriate and when it fails to summarize the data in any useful or insightful manner. The aspects that require analyst intervention, especially the domain analysis, are very difficult to formalize and automate, making cooperation between analyst and computer absolutely necessary for successful knowledge discovery projects. On the other hand, only computational tools make the analysis of large amounts of data possible. Here we take a brief look at these tools.

Knowledge Discovery with Support Vector Machines, by Lutz Hamel
Copyright © 2009 John Wiley & Sons, Inc.

To make the discussion more concrete, we demonstrate these aspects using WEKA and R. It will probably help to have access to either WEKA or R, or both. See the bibliographic notes at the end of the chapter on where and how to download these tools.

2.1.1 Data Access

Any knowledge discovery tool needs to provide an efficient way to access data. This might take on the form of a data table import mechanism or a way to pose SQL queries directly to a database or data warehouse. In some instances the knowledge discovery tools are embedded in the database engine to minimize data access issues. Here we concentrate on importing and exporting data tables.

A popular format for data tables is the *comma-separated value* (CSV) format . This is a text file in which each line represents a row of the original table and the fields of the table are separated by commas. For example, our training data from Table 1.2 can be encoded in a CSV file as follows:

```
Legs, Wings, Fur, Feathers, Mammal
4, no, yes, no, true
2, yes, no, yes, false
4, no, no, no, false
4, yes, yes, no, true
3, no, no, no, false
```

A useful convention in CSV files is that the first row is a list of the column names of the original table separated by commas. Analysts sometimes refer to the rows in the data table as *observations*. They often refer to the column that carries the mammal class labels as the *dependent attribute*, and the remaining columns are referred to as *independent attributes*. Go ahead and create a file called "mammals.csv" in your favorite text editor, as you will need it to experiment with the knowledge discovery tools.

WEKA WEKA is a GUI-driven knowledge discovery tool written in Java that is available for virtually every imaginable platform. When you start the WEKA tool set, it presents you with a choice of GUIs. For our purposes here you should always choose the *explorer* GUI. Choosing the explorer interface brings you to the explorer data access and preprocessing screen. To access a file, press the *Open file* button and in our case make sure that you select the CSV format option. Navigate to the file you would like to access and then press *Open*. Figure 2.1 shows the state of the interface after we have read in our CSV file containing the data for our mammal classification problem. The attributes of the objects in our CSV file are displayed in the *Attributes* panel. You can highlight each attribute in turn, and WEKA will display some basic statistics about this attribute, such as missing values, the number of distinct labels if it is a nominal attribute, or the mean if it is a numerical attribute. By default, WEKA selects the last attribute in the table as the dependent attribute. You can change this with the *Class* drop-down box, but for our purposes WEKA made the right selection.

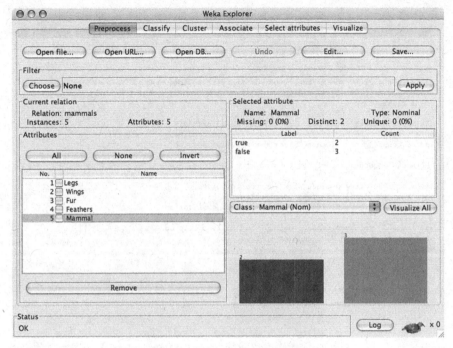

FIGURE 2.1 Accessing data files in WEKA.

WEKA offers alternative data access mechanisms besides reading CSV files. You can access data resources on the Web via the *Open URL* button, or you can pose an SQL query to a database via the *Open DB* button. WEKA also has an interactive data editor accessed by clicking the *Edit* button. Finally, you can save modified data sets by clicking *Save*.

R The R environment takes a very different approach from that of WEKA. Rather than being GUI driven, R exposes a command line interpreter for the R scripting language. Figure 2.2 shows the console window on MAC OS X. Everything you need to accomplish in your knowledge discovery project you can accomplish by issuing commands at the prompt. An interesting side effect of this is that you can write scripts for your discovery projects and execute these scripts on different data sets or with slightly different parameters. In effect, the scripts become an executable document of your discovery process. Let us assume that our "mammals.csv" file is in a folder called data sets, then we can read in the CSV file as follows:

```
> setwd("data sets")
> mammals.df <- read.csv("mammals.csv")
> mammals.df
```

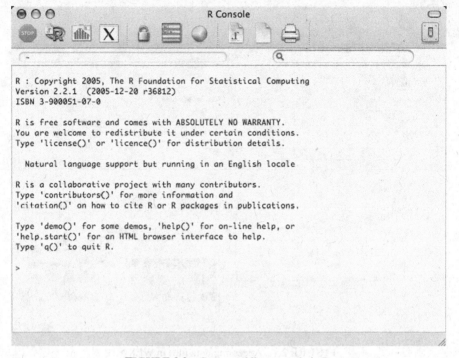

```
R : Copyright 2005, The R Foundation for Statistical Computing
Version 2.2.1  (2005-12-20 r36812)
ISBN 3-900051-07-0

R is free software and comes with ABSOLUTELY NO WARRANTY.
You are welcome to redistribute it under certain conditions.
Type 'license()' or 'licence()' for distribution details.

  Natural language support but running in an English locale

R is a collaborative project with many contributors.
Type 'contributors()' for more information and
'citation()' on how to cite R or R packages in publications.

Type 'demo()' for some demos, 'help()' for on-line help, or
'help.start()' for an HTML browser interface to help.
Type 'q()' to quit R.

>
```

FIGURE 2.2   Command line console in R.

```
  Legs Wings  Fur Feathers Mammal
1    4    no  yes      no   true
2    2   yes   no     yes  false
3    4    no   no      no  false
4    4   yes  yes      no   true
5    3    no   no      no  false
> summary(mammals.df)
      Legs         Wings      Fur      Feathers    Mammal
 Min.   :2.0    no :3     no :3     no :4     false:3
 1st Qu.:3.0    yes:2     yes:2     yes:1     true :2
 Median :4.0
 Mean   :3.4
 3rd Qu.:4.0
 Max.   :4.0
```

Here, we first set our working directory to data sets and then we use the function read.csv to read our "mammals.csv" file into the R *data frame* mammals.df. A data frame is R's representation of a data table, and we can see the contents of a data frame simply by typing the name of the data frame at the command line prompt as shown in the third line of the code snippet above. You can obtain basic statistics on the various attributes in your data frame with the summary command. R provides the appropriate statistics for each type of attribute; these include the minimum, maximum, and mean for numerical attributes and the frequency of the labels for nominal attributes. R also provides an interactive data editor,

```
> mammals.df <- edit(mammals.df)
```

To save a modified data frame, you can use the `write.csv` function,

```
> write.csv(mammals.df, "mammals.csv")
```

We should also mention that additional data connectivity, such as SQL adapters for various databases, is available as R packages. To install packages, you will need to access the R package manager and use it to download and install the desired packages. Pointers on how to accomplish this are given on the R Web page and in the help pages. A brief tutorial on the R scripting language is given in Appendix B.

2.1.2 Visualization

Data visualization is a powerful way to get to know your data. Most analysts use data visualization to "get a feel" for the data and also to establish the quality of the data. For example, an analyst might want to establish if the data have a lot of missing values or if perhaps some of the attribute values are skewed. Another interesting question that is often important in model building is whether some of the independent attributes are highly correlated, since in some cases, highly correlated independent attributes can reduce the effectiveness of the discovery algorithms. Many of these questions are easily answered using visualization.

WEKA   WEKA provides a number of ways to visualize data. For example, *scatterplots* are available in the *Visualize* tab on the top of the explorer screen. Figure 2.3 shows the scatterplots for our mammals data set. (You should probably open WEKA on your Computer for the following discussion since colors are not reproduced in the figures.) To make the plot more readable, you might have to experiment with the *PointSize* and *Jitter* (use the *Update* button after each alteration). The scatterplots are arranged in a matrix where the attribute names are listed in the columns as well as in the rows of the scatterplot matrix. This means that we can use the scatterplot matrix to assess the relationship of any attribute to all other attributes. The points with the color blue in the plots denote observations that belong to the class of mammals, and the color red denotes observations that do not belong to the class of mammals. The key is given in the *Class Colour* panel.

One way to use the scatterplots is to assess the relationship of the `Mammal` attribute to all the other attributes. The first row of the plot matrix does just that; it compares the `Mammal` attribute to all other attributes including the `Mammal` attribute itself. Working from left to right, we see that the `Mammal` attribute is first compared to the `Legs` attribute. There are a couple of things that we know about these two attributes. For instance, the `Mammal` attribute can take on only two values, *true* and *false*. If we

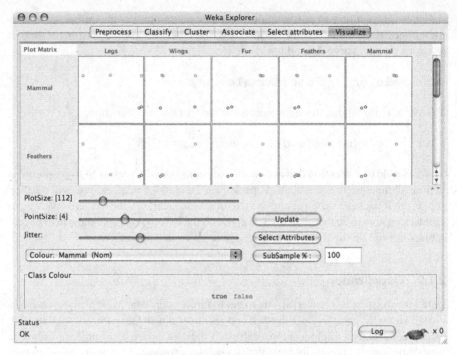

FIGURE 2.3   Scatterplots in WEKA.

project the observations onto the vertical axis, we see two groups, one for *true* (blue) and one for *false* (red). This is perhaps easier to see in the interactive version of this scatterplot, which is accessible by clicking on the scatterplot itself. Something a little bit more interesting happens when we project the observations onto the horizontal axis. We see that the observations fall into three groups: observations with two, three, and four legs, respectively, going from left to right on the axis. More precisely, we have one observation with two legs on the leftmost part of the axis. In the middle we have an observation with three legs, and finally, we have a group of observations with four legs. What is interesting is that the groups are no longer separated by mammal class membership. For example, the group of observations with four legs includes observations that are mammals and observations that are not mammals. It is exactly these types of relationships that analysts look for in visualizations.

Moving one scatterplot to the right, we see that the Mammal attribute is being compared to the Wings attribute. Again, projecting the observations onto the vertical axis we see that the observations are grouped by class membership. This is to be expected because we are still comparing the Mammal attribute to the other attributes. When we project the observations onto the horizontal axis, we see that they fall into two groups. One group denotes observations that have wings, and the other group denotes observations that do not have wings. We can clearly see that each group is heterogeneous in the sense that each group includes observations that are mammals and observations that are not mammals.

Considering the third plot, we compare the Mammal attribute to the attribute Fur. Projecting on the vertical axis remains the same as in the previous plots. However, something interesting happens when we project the observations onto the horizontal axis; they also group according to the mammal class! This scatterplot shows that the Fur attribute is perfectly correlated with the Mammal attribute. We already observed this in Chapter 1 and took advantage of it in order to build a very simple model for the *mammal* labeling process.

The fourth plot in the first row can be analyzed in a similar fashion. We leave this as an exercise for the reader. The last plot in the first row is the Mammal attribute again, and as we would expect, the Mammal attribute correlates perfectly with itself.

WEKA possesses another data visualization facility that is directly accessible from the data preprocessing screen in Figure 2.1 by clicking the button *Visualize All*. Before we do this, we have to overcome one difficulty with our data set. The Legs attribute is recognized by WEKA as a numerical attribute. This is technically correct, since the attribute only contains numbers, but we essentially use these numbers as labels. One way to see this is that by changing the values of the attribute such as 4 to a label, perhaps FOUR, does not change our classification problem. To force WEKA to recognize this attribute as a nominal attribute, we apply the *discretize filter* available in the *Filter* panel (see Figure 2.1). See Section 2.1.3 on how to transform this attribute from a numerical into a nominal attribute. Figure 2.4 shows the screen for the mammals data set with the Legs attribute treated as a nominal attribute. The information

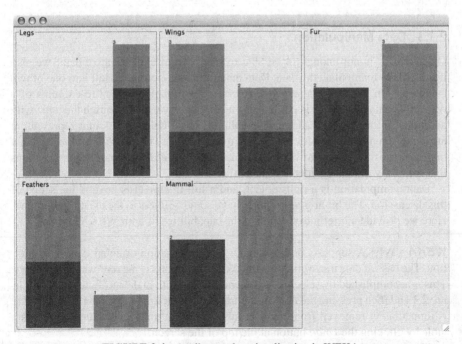

FIGURE 2.4 Attribute value visualization in WEKA.

displayed is very similar to the information displayed in the scatterplots, albeit in a more concise format. Here we see fields for all the attributes of the data set, and in each of the fields we see bar graphs for the corresponding values of the attributes. The class membership of the observations is also encoded to make it easy to spot correlations. For example, in the first field, which is the field for the Legs attribute, we see three bars, one for two legs, one for three legs, and one for four legs, respectively, from left to right. We can observe that the bars for two and three legs only contain observations that do not belong in the class of mammals (light gray). Conversely, we see that the bar for four legs has observations that belong to the class of mammals (dark gray) and has also observations that do not belong to the class of mammals (light gray). As before we can observe that the attribute Fur is perfectly correlated with class membership.

R   The R scripting language in conjunction with its flexible graphics engine allows an analyst to construct powerful visualizations. But the power comes at a price, in that detailed understanding of the scripting language is necessary to harness this power. An in-depth discussion of the scripting language and the graphics engine is beyond the scope of this brief introduction. Entire books have been written about the graphical capabilities of R. For more information refer to the bibliographic notes at the end of the chapter. However, having said that, a scatterplot matrix very similar to the scatterplot matrix in WEKA can be constructed with a single command,

```
> plot(mammals.df)
```

2.1.3 Data Manipulation

Of course, it is not enough to be able to read, write, and visualize data; we also need tools to manipulate the data. Data manipulation approaches fall into one of two categories. In the *attribute-oriented approach* we manipulate entire columns of a respective data table. This is particularly useful when we aim to enrich the table with additional information by adding data columns or for deleting columns representing attributes deemed not useful for the discovery process. In the *observation-oriented approach* we focus on the rows of data tables. This is useful for removing observations that are faulty or are considered to be outliers.

Data manipulation is a rich subject, and a full treatment is beyond the scope of this discussion. The bibliographic notes have some pointers to the existing literature. Here we provide a brief introduction to the capabilities of both WEKA and R.

WEKA   WEKA supports both attribute- and observation-oriented data manipulation. The easiest data transformation that WEKA supports is the removal of attributes. This is accomplished by selecting the unwanted attribute in the attribute panel in Figure 2.1 and then pressing the *Remove* button at the bottom of the screen. The attribute is immediately removed from the data table. You can undo this change to the data table by clicking the *Undo* button at the top of the screen.

More sophisticated data manipulations are available via *filters*. You can access filters via the *Choose* button, which provides you with a selection of both attribute- and observation-oriented filters. Note that WEKA calls observations *instances*. Filters are grouped into two categories: supervised and unsupervised. Supervised filters are data manipulations that need user intervention and guidance, whereas unsupervised filters are applied to the attributes or observations, with minimal user guidance.

To illustrate this, let us apply an attribute-oriented filter to our mammals data table. As pointed out above, in this data set we have the numerical attribute Legs. Although it is a numerical attribute, we are treating it as if it were a nominal attribute where the leg numbers 2, 3, and 4 are essentially labels. We can make our intentions clear by *discretizing* this attribute. To do so, we choose the filter

weka → filters → unsupervised → attribute → Discretize.

At this point the *Discretize* filter appears in the filter box with some default parameters. To change these parameters, click on the filter. This opens a dialog box that looks something like Figure 2.5. In our case we adjust the *attributeIndices* to point to the first attribute, Legs, and adjust the *bins* parameter to 3 (one bin for each number of legs). Click *OK* and then press *Apply* on the main screen. Now the type of the Legs attribute has changed from numerical to nominal and has three auto-generated labels.

R   The scripting language in R is a full-fledged programming language that supports scalar, vector, and matrix computations in addition to data frames. This makes data

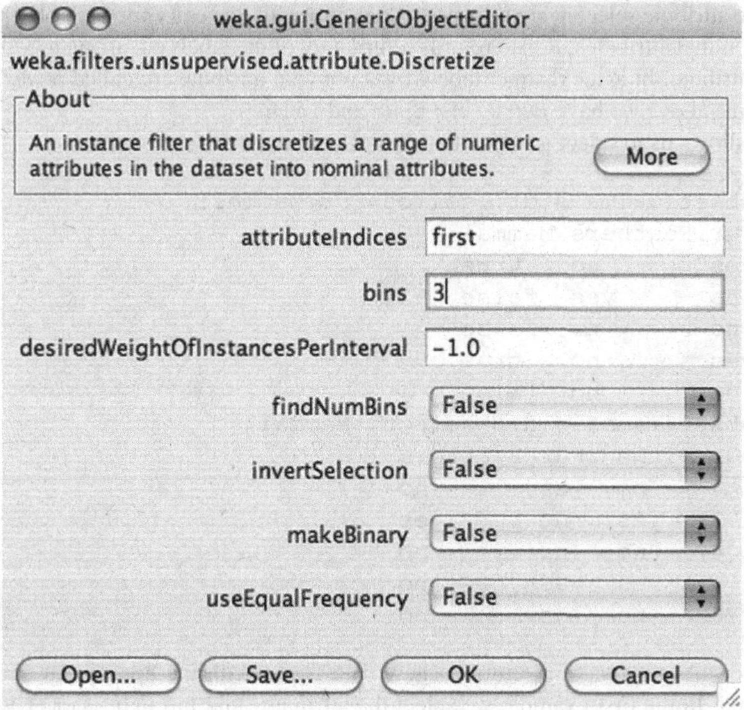

FIGURE 2.5   Attribute-oriented filter in WEKA.

manipulation in R infinitely more flexible and complex than the GUI-based data manipulation in WEKA. Here we provide a brief overview on how to manipulate attributes and observations in data frames. Recall that a data frame is a data table representation in R:

```
> mammals.df
  Legs Wings  Fur Feathers Mammal
1   4    no   yes      no   true
2   2   yes    no     yes  false
3   4    no    no      no  false
4   4   yes   yes      no   true
5   3    no    no      no  false
```

R provides a special notation that allows you to access individual attributes in a data frame:

```
> mammals.df$Legs
[1] 4 2 4 4 3
> mammals.df$Mammal
[1]  true   false  false   true   false
Levels:  false  true
```

We can access any attribute in the mammals data frame with the $ notation. The values for the attribute selected are returned as a vector with one entry for each observation. For nominal attributes, R also returns a summary of the labels occurring as values for that attribute. In R the distinct labels for a nominal attribute are called *levels*. In the example above we have two levels: true and false.

R allows us to select groups of attributes with the subset function:

```
> subset(mammals.df, select=Fur:Mammal)
  Fur Feathers Mammal
1 yes      no   true
2  no     yes  false
3  no      no  false
4 yes      no   true
5  no      no  false
> subset(mammals.df, select=-Mammal)
  Legs Wings  Fur Feathers
1   4    no   yes      no
2   2   yes    no     yes
3   4    no    no      no
4   4   yes   yes      no
5   3    no    no      no
```

The subset function returns a new data frame with the appropriate attributes selected. In the first example we select the attributes Fur through Mammal with the Fur:Mammal notation, and in the second example we select all attributes except for the attribute Mammal. In the latter, notice the minus sign before the Mammal attribute, indicating that it should be excluded from the resulting data frame.

We can also use the *subset* function for observation-oriented data manipulation. Let's assume that we want to construct a data frame that consists only of observations that have four legs. The following R command will accomplish that:

```
> subset(mammals.df, Legs == 4)
  Legs Wings  Fur Feathers Mammal
1    4    no  yes       no   true
3    4    no   no       no  false
4    4   yes  yes       no   true
```

Another, slightly more complicated example is the extraction of all observations that are mammals:

```
> mammal.levels <- levels(mammals.df$Mammal)
> mammal.levels
[1] "false" "true"
> true.level <- mammal.levels[2]
> subset(mammals.df, Mammal == true.level)
  Legs Wings Fur Feathers Mammal
1    4    no yes       no   true
4    4   yes yes       no   true
```

Here we first extract the levels used in the attribute Mammal with the levels function. We then extract the true level and use it in computing the observations that match this level.

This brief discussion only scratched the surface of what is possible with R. In R, vectors and matrices are very flexible objects to which vector- or matrix-based operations can be applied directly without having to execute any type of looping structure. This makes data manipulation very efficient, even for large data tables. Many domain-specific data manipulation routines are available as additional R packages. Therefore, if you are faced with a complex knowledge discovery task, it is worthwhile to peruse the R Web site for packages that might apply to your particular task.

2.1.4   Model Building and Evaluation

At the heart of the knowledge discovery process (Figure 1.1) we usually find two classes of discovery algorithms: machine learning algorithms and statistical techniques. Machine learning algorithms were developed in the field of artificial intelligence dating back to the late 1950s and were designed originally to provide intelligence to autonomous agents. Statistical techniques were developed in the context of probability and measure theory at the end of the nineteenth century. However, it was only in the late 1980s and early 1990s that researchers recognized that both areas were trying to solve very similar problems. With the advent of computational statistics, the borders between the two disciplines have all but disappeared and statistical techniques that are concerned with model building and inference are almost indistinguishable from machine learning, and vice versa. But there is still a difference between the two approaches that has to do mainly with the set of assumptions that one admits during analysis and model building. Most statistical techniques rely on the fact that there is some normal distribution of either the data or the modeling error. Machine learning algorithms, in general, do not make these assumptions and therefore are able to provide more accurate models in situations where normality assumptions are not warranted. On the other hand, new computational statistical techniques such as the bootstrap also dispense with many normality assumptions, again blurring the difference between machine learning and statistics.

Given this blurring of the differences between machine learning and statistical techniques, it is up to the user to pick the algorithm that works best for a particular problem domain. On the other hand, sometimes one of the approaches is forced upon the user by other, external constraints. For example, for the knowledge discovery task at hand, it might be of utmost importance that the models be transparent, that is, that the models can easily be read and understood by a human being, forcing the analyst to use something like decision trees or rule lists as models. Conversely, a detailed analysis of the modeling error and other statistics might be important in turn favoring more statistical approaches. Given this, it is perhaps no surprise that both WEKA and R support machine learning as well as statistical techniques. In this book we concentrate on machine learning with support vector machines at the heart of the knowledge discovery process.

WEKA   In WEKA we use the *Classify* screen to build models. The first thing we need to do is to select the type of model we would like to construct. To construct a support vector machine model, for instance, we press the classifier *Choose* button and select

weka → classifiers → functions → SMO.

SMO stands for *sequential minimal optimization* and is a particular implementation of support vector machines. For now, we leave all model parameters at their default values. For our simple mammals classification problem, the default parameters work just fine. We need to make sure that we are constructing our model with the appropriate dependent attribute. The drop-down box above the *Start* button indicates that the dependent attribute of the model is the nominal attribute Mammal and that is exactly what we want. We evaluate our model on the training data by selecting the first option in the *Test options* panel. This means that we will test the quality of the predictions of our model against the dependent attribute of the training set. We can now press the *Start* button to build a support vector machine model. Once we do that, WEKA will display model information in the *Classifier output* panel. Here WEKA tells us a little bit about the model building process, but most important, it tells us about how the model performed on the training data. It is reassuring to see that our model classified all our observations correctly. Figure 2.6 shows the state of the classify screen after the support vector machine model has been constructed.

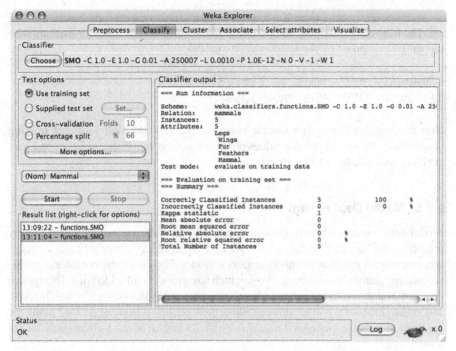

FIGURE 2.6 Model building and evaluation in WEKA.

R The R environment offers a host of different models that we could construct as part of our knowledge discovery process. Here we demonstrate how to construct support vector machines. To do this, you will have to download and install the package *e1071*. You can easily accomplish this with the *Package Installer*. Once you have installed the package, you will need to load it into the the current console environment with the command

```
> library(e1071)
```

Now we can construct a support vector machine model of our mammals data with the svm function:

```
> model<-svm(Mammal ~ .,data=mammals.df,kernel="linear")
```

The first argument to the svm function, 'Mammal ~ .,' is called a *formula* and tells the model building function that the attribute Mammal is the dependent attribute and that all other attributes are considered independent attributes. As in the case of WEKA, we accept all the default parameters with the exception of the kernel function, which we set to the linear kernel.

At this point we can evaluate our model by checking how it performs on the training set. The following statement compares the actual values of the Mammal attribute with the values computed by the support vector model:

```
> mammals.df$Mammal == fitted(model)
[1] TRUE TRUE TRUE TRUE TRUE
```

Here the function fitted returns the value computed by the model for each training observation. As we can see, the values predicted and the actual values for the Mammal attribute coincide for all five observations.

2.1.5 Model Deployment

Model deployment is highly domain dependent. In some cases this means simply predicting the value of the target attribute for a set of objects; in other cases it means constructing an entire application around a model. For the latter, consider a credit-scoring application at a mortgage bank which has a model embedded in it. In a typical scenario a bank employee enters a client's personal information, such as age, income, and other outstanding loan amounts, and then pushes a button. At this point the application uses the embedded model to predict whether or not a client qualifies for a mortgage.

WEKA WEKA does not supply any model deployment tools in its GUI. However, it does supply a Java version of its machine learning tools, and you are able to modify this Java library to suit your model deployment needs. This is not for the faint of heart, however.

R R takes a straightforward approach to model deployment via its predict function. Given a model and a data frame of objects for which the dependent attribute value is not known, we can apply the predict function to compute these values. The following is an example using our mammal model and the mammal data frame:

```
> independent.df <- subset(mammals.df, select=-Mammal)
> predict(model, independent.df)
     1      2      3      4      5
  true  false  false   true  false
Levels:  false   true
```

The first line deletes the target attribute Mammal from the mammals.df data frame and stores the result in a new data frame called independent.df. We do this, since we need a set of objects for which the Mammal attribute value is unknown. In the next line, we apply our support vector machine model to this new data frame with the predict function. Notice that the predict function returns a vector of computed Mammal attribute values, one for each object in the independent.df data frame. If we wanted to, we could now check whether these predictions are correct with respect to the original attribute values. This is left as an exercise for the reader.

2.2 OTHER TOOL SETS

A quick scan of the Web reveals many open-source knowledge discovery tools. Here we mention two other open-source projects that stand out in their completeness, ease of use, and support. The first one is *RapidMiner* (http://rapid-i.com), a GUI-driven tool set written in Java and very similar to WEKA. However, RapidMiner offers many more visualization tools and a much larger set of discovery algorithms than WEKA. The other open-source tool set is *Rattle* (http://rattle.togaware.com), which represents an interesting twist on R in that it implements a WEKA-like GUI for R which provides the essentials to accomplish knowledge discovery tasks. The GUI relieves the user from having to learn the intricacies of the R scripting language. On the other hand, by adopting the GUI, the user relinquishes some of the flexibility that the scripting language provides. The nice part about Rattle is that it does provide a fast way to harness some of the power the R environment provides, especially with respect to visualization.

On the commercial side, there are also many tool sets to choose from. Without any claim to being complete, we mention a few of them here in no particular order. Knowledge discovery tool sets that can be perceived as extensions of classical statistical computing environments include Clementine from SPSS (http://www.spss.com/clementine) and Enterprise Miner from SAS (http://www.sas.com/technologies/analytics/datamining/miner). A knowledge discovery environment along the lines of WEKA is the Insightful Miner (http://www.insightful.com/products/iminer), by the company that also produces a commercial version of R called *S-Plus*. A completely different approach to knowledge discovery tools is taken by Oracle (http://www.oracle.com/technology/products/bi/odm) and Microsoft (http://www.microsoft.com/sql/technologies/dm). Here, the discovery algorithms are implemented directly in the database, minimizing data access and transfer times. This is important for knowledge discovery projects that aim to extract information from very large data collections.

One interesting observation is that with the exception of the Oracle tool set and SAS, none of the commercial systems mentioned implement support vector machines as of the writing of this book (late 2008).

EXERCISES

2.1 In WEKA, load the iris data set. This data set is available in WEKA's data folder and is given in WEKA's native ARFF data format. Once loaded, try to answer the following questions:

(a) How many attributes are there?

(b) How many observations are there?

(c)   What are the levels in the dependent attribute `class`?

(d)   How many observations are there per level in the attribute `class`?

(e)   Find and report the basic statistics on each attribute.

(f)   Are any of the independent attributes highly correlated with each other? Try to determine this using WEKA's visualization screen.

2.2   Construct a support vector machine classifier for the iris data set using WEKA's SMO implementation. You can use all the default parameters. Does the model misclassify any observations if the model is evaluated on the training data?

2.3   In R, load the iris data set. The data set is available in R via the `data` command

```
> data(iris)
> iris[1:5,]
  Sepal.Length Sepal.Width Petal.Length
1          5.1         3.5          1.4
2          4.9         3.0          1.4
3          4.7         3.2          1.3
4          4.6         3.1          1.5
5          5.0         3.6          1.4
  Petal.Width Species
1         0.2  setosa
2         0.2  setosa
3         0.2  setosa
4         0.2  setosa
5         0.2  setosa
```

The data set is now available as the data frame `iris` in R. Try to answer the same questions as in Exercise 2.1 using the facilities that R provides. To build a simple support vector machine model, use the `svm` function available in the e1071 package using the parameter `kernel="linear"`.

2.4   Go to the UCI machine learning repository (see the bibliographic notes for details) and download a data set that deals with classification. Use WEKA and/or R to explore the data set. Try to build a support vector machine model using the SMO algorithm in WEKA and the `svm` function in R (use defaults). When the model is evaluated against the training set, does it make misclassification errors?

BIBLIOGRAPHIC NOTES

WEKA is available from the Web site http://www.cs.waikato.ac.nz/ml/weka, and R is available from http://www.r-project.org. The standard reference for WEKA is the book written by its developers, Witten and Frank [80]. The gentlest introduction to R that we know of is [24]. The de facto standard reference for R is the book by Venables and Ripley [76]. An accessible introduction and overview of R's graphics and visualization capabilities is [55]. One of the most extensive collections of data preparation techniques for knowledge discovery is [61]. An extensive review of the state of the art of machine learning and statistical techniques with respect to knowledge discovery is [36]. Computational statistics and the bootstrap are discussed in [34] and [29], respectively. Finally, if you are looking for data to experiment with, a good place to start is the UCI Machine Learning Repository (http://archive.ics.uci.edu/ml/). The repository contains about 160 academic as well as real-world data sets.

CHAPTER 3

DESCRIBING DATA MATHEMATICALLY

Our goal is to construct models of processes that label objects in a data universe according to class membership. That is, we are interested in building classifiers. To accomplish this effectively, we need to take a more mathematical approach to the description
of objects beyond the notion that an object is an element of the cross product of its
attributes. In particular, we need a quantitative way to talk about the similarities and
differences of the objects in our data universe. We also need a way to characterize
relationships between groups of objects. For instance, can two groups of objects
be separated easily, or is it very difficult to describe the differences between these
groups? The similarity and dissimilarity of objects as well as the separability of groups
of objects are central themes in the development of classifiers in general and in the
development of support vector machines in particular. In this chapter we look at some
of the foundations of linear algebra, such as vector spaces, dot products, and planes
that allow us to describe objects mathematically and construct classifiers effectively.

3.1 FROM DATA SETS TO VECTOR SPACES

Objects in a data universe are described by a common set of attributes. Since our
data universes tend to be very large, we usually consider only a subset of objects for
knowledge discovery tasks. We refer to these subsets as *training sets* or *data sets*. To
facilitate our mathematical development, we assume that all attributes that describe
our objects range over the real numbers, $\mathbb{R}$. We also assume that we are dealing
only with *binary classification* problems, that is, problems where each object can be

Knowledge Discovery with Support Vector Machines, by Lutz Hamel
Copyright © 2009 John Wiley & Sons, Inc.

TABLE 3.1 Simple Data Set for a Binary Classification Problem[a]

	Height	Weight	Age	Gender
Jane	25.4	32.7	2.5	F
Amanda	65.2	132.0	36.5	F
Paul	71.7	175.1	25.5	M
Mary	62.6	126.0	31.0	F
Gary	68.2	182.0	42.5	M
Betty	58.5	118.5	21.0	F
John	72.0	195.2	45.2	M

[a]The features of the objects are attributes that range over the real numbers, and each object can be labeled by only one of two labels.

labeled by only one of two possible labels. Table 3.1 depicts a small data set where the objects, a set of persons, are described by the attributes Height, Weight, and Age, which range over the real numbers. Here we assume that Age is a real-rather than an integer-valued attribute, in order to be able to express quantities such as an age of 2.5 years. In this data set the height is given in inches and the weight is given in pounds. Each object is labeled by a gender label of F or M. The data set can be visualized with a three-dimensional scatterplot as in Figure 3.1. We purposefully ignored the names of

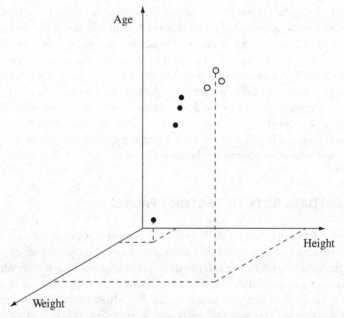

FIGURE 3.1 Three-dimensional scatterplot of the data set in Table 3.1. The filled circles represent the object labeled with F, and the open circles represent the objects labeled with M.

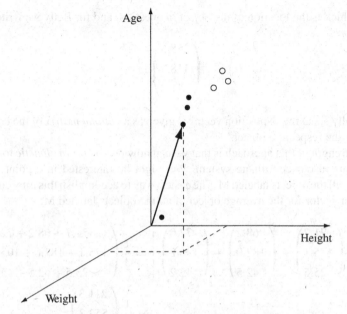

FIGURE 3.2 Position vector of the object Betty with Weight = 58.5, Height = 118.5, and Age = 21.0.

the persons in the plot, since a name constitutes a unique object identifier and does not give us any insights into the overall structure of the data. On the other hand, we use the gender labels to identify our objects in the plot as follows: The filled circles represent the objects labeled with F and the open circles represent the objects labeled with M.

An interesting observation is that by choosing to display our data set as a three-dimensional scatterplot, we essentially made each attribute a dimension in a coordinate system. That is, by treating each attribute as a dimension and by the fact that all our attributes range over the real values, we can visualize each object as a point in the three-dimensional coordinate system $\mathbb{R} \times \mathbb{R} \times \mathbb{R}$. This view is consistent with our previous view, where objects are members of the cross product of their attributes, but now we have the nice property that we can interpret our objects geometrically as points in a coordinate system. To achieve this, the only simplification we have made is that we assumed that all attributes range over $\mathbb{R}$. We often abbreviate the three-dimensional coordinate system as $\mathbb{R}^3$. For n-dimensional coordinate systems, we write $\mathbb{R}^n$.

Let us take this a little bit further by describing each point in our three-dimensional space with a *position vector*. We can visualize position vectors as arrows that are rooted in the origin $(0, 0, 0)$ of our coordinate system and point to the location of the object in our three-dimensional space. For example, the position vector for Betty starts at $(0, 0, 0)$ and ends at $(58.5, 118.5, 21.0)$, as in Figure 3.2. Since position vectors are always rooted at the origin, it is sufficient to just give simply the coordinates of their target, which is the location of the object in question, and for Betty we write

$$\begin{pmatrix} 58.5 \\ 118.5 \\ 21.0 \end{pmatrix}.$$

Technically speaking, a position vector is given as a *column matrix* of the coordinate values of the respective object.

The strength of this approach is that we can now use *vector arithmetic* to compute new points in our coordinate system. We might be interested in a point that best describes all the objects labeled M. The easiest way to accomplish this is by computing a position vector for the average object of all the objects labeled M:

$$\frac{1}{3}\left[\begin{pmatrix} 71.7 \\ 175.1 \\ 25.5 \end{pmatrix} + \begin{pmatrix} 68.2 \\ 182.0 \\ 42.5 \end{pmatrix} + \begin{pmatrix} 72.0 \\ 195.2 \\ 45.2 \end{pmatrix}\right] = \frac{1}{3}\begin{pmatrix} 71.7 + 68.2 + 72.0 \\ 175.1 + 182.0 + 195.2 \\ 25.5 + 42.5 + 45.2 \end{pmatrix}$$

$$= \frac{1}{3}\begin{pmatrix} 211.3 \\ 552.3 \\ 113.2 \end{pmatrix}$$

$$= \begin{pmatrix} \dfrac{211.3}{3} \\ \dfrac{552.3}{3} \\ \dfrac{113.2}{3} \end{pmatrix}$$

$$= \begin{pmatrix} 70.4 \\ 184.1 \\ 37.7 \end{pmatrix}.$$

To compute the position vector of this average object, we first add the position vectors of all the objects labeled M and then multiply this sum by the value 1/3 (since there are only three such objects). Notice that addition and multiplication is done *componentwise*: that is, the operation is done separately for each dimension.

By admitting such operations on our objects where the results of these operations can be viewed as members of our data universe, we have effectively converted our data universe into a *vector space*. Here, every object in our data universe can be viewed as a vector and we are able to compute new objects in our data universe using algebraic vector operations. Not only do vectors allow us to compute new points but they give us a convenient way to measure similarity between objects using dot products. In addition, the geometric interpretation of vectors is conceptually very powerful, as we will see when we look at machine learning in this setting. Let us formalize these vector concepts some more.

3.1.1 Vectors

We start with the definition of a vector.

Definition 3.1   *A directed line segment is called a* **vector**. *A vector has both a length and a direction. A vector of length* 1 *is called a* **unit vector**.

According to this definition, position vectors are clearly vectors that always start at the origin of the respective coordinate system. Going back to our data set in Table 3.1, consider the point describing Amanda with coordinates (65.2, 132.0, 36.5); then the corresponding position vector, say $\bar{a}$, is determined uniquely by the coordinates of that point and the origin (0, 0, 0). We write

$$\bar{a} = \begin{pmatrix} 65.2 \\ 132.0 \\ 36.5 \end{pmatrix},$$

where 65.2, 132.0, and 36.5 are called the *components* of vector $\bar{a}$. In this example we have considered only a three-dimensional coordinate system, but we can easily generalize this to an arbitrary n-dimensional coordinate system. Assume that we have such an n-dimensional coordinate system; then a point $Q = (q_1, q_2, \ldots, q_n)$ will be associated with a position vector, call it $\bar{q}$, where

$$\bar{q} = \begin{pmatrix} q_1 \\ q_2 \\ \vdots \\ q_n \end{pmatrix}. \tag{3.1}$$

We have exactly one component q_i for each dimension in our coordinate system. With respect to notation, rather than writing our vectors as column matrices as we have done above, we write them as row matrices, $\bar{q} = (q_1, q_2, \ldots, q_n)$, when there is no confusion. This makes for more compact text when discussing vectors. However, when you see a vector given as a row matrix, you will need to bear in mind that what is intended is the column matrix.

Given the components of some position vector in $\mathbb{R}^n$, say $\bar{p} = (p_1, p_2, \ldots, p_n)$, we can compute its *length*, written as $|\bar{p}|$ and defined formally as,

$$|\bar{p}| = \sqrt{p_1^2 + p_2^2 + \ldots + p_n^2}. \tag{3.2}$$

One of the reasons that we switched from a table representation to a vector representation is so that we can apply mathematical operations to the objects in the data set. Perhaps the easiest operation to formalize is equality. This operation allows us to determine whether or not two objects are the same.

Definition 3.2   *Let $\overline{a} = (a_1, a_2, \ldots, a_n)$ and $\overline{b} = (b_1, b_2, \ldots, b_n)$ be position vectors in $\mathbb{R}^n$, then $\overline{a}$ and $\overline{b}$ are **equal** if and only if the corresponding components of each vector are equal. Formally,*

$$\overline{a} = \overline{b} \; iff \; a_1 = b_1, a_2 = b_2, \ldots, a_n = b_n. \tag{3.3}$$

In other words, two position vectors are equal if and only if they point to the same point in the coordinate system. From a data set perspective, this means that two objects are equal if and only if they agree in all of their attribute values.

Next, let us take a look at vector addition. This is one of the operations we used to compute the average object to represent all the objects labeled M earlier in this section, and we already know that it is performed componentwise. Formally,

Definition 3.3   *Let $\overline{a} = (a_1, a_2, \ldots, a_n)$, $\overline{b} = (b_1, b_2, \ldots, b_n)$, and $\overline{c} = (c_1, c_2, \ldots, c_n)$ be position vectors in $\mathbb{R}^n$, then we define **vector addition** as*

$$\overline{c} = \overline{a} + \overline{b}, \tag{3.4}$$

such that $c_1 = a_1 + b_1$, $c_2 = a_2 + b_2$, $\ldots$, $c_n = a_n + b_n$.

We can associate the set of algebraic identities shown in Table 3.2 with vector addition. Here $\overline{a}$, $\overline{b}$, and $\overline{c}$ are position vectors in $\mathbb{R}^n$. Furthermore, the vector

$$\overline{0} = \underbrace{(0, 0, \ldots, 0)}_{n} \tag{3.5}$$

is called the *null vector*. This vector has zero length and can be considered the position vector of a point in the origin of an n-dimensional coordinate system. Finally, the vector $(-\overline{a})$ is the vector $\overline{a}$ with all of its components negated,

$$-\overline{a} = -(a_1, a_2, \ldots, a_n) = (-a_1, -a_2, \ldots, -a_n).$$

Given this, it is straightforward to show that the identities in Table 3.2 hold using the algebraic properties of scalar addition. For instance, we can show that the *identity*

TABLE 3.2   Algebraic Properties of Vector Addition

$\overline{a} + \overline{b} = \overline{b} + \overline{a}$	commutativity
$(\overline{a} + \overline{b}) + \overline{c} = \overline{a} + (\overline{b} + \overline{c})$	associativity
$\overline{a} + \overline{0} = \overline{a}$	identity
$\overline{a} + (-\overline{a}) = \overline{0}$	reciprocity

property holds as follows:

$$\begin{aligned}
\overline{a} + \overline{0} &= (a_1, a_2, \ldots, a_n) + (0, 0, \ldots, 0) \\
&= (a_1 + 0, a_2 + 0, \ldots, a_n + 0) \\
&= (a_1, a_2, \ldots, a_n) \\
&= \overline{a}.
\end{aligned}$$

To provide a geometric interpretation for vector addition, we need to introduce *vector translation*. Vector translation is important because it allows us to construct any arbitrary vector from an appropriate position vector simply by shifting the position vector to the desired location in the coordinate system without changing its length or orientation. It is clear that the resulting vector is parallel to and has the same length as the original position vector. Furthermore, the resulting vector is considered equivalent to the original position vector. Conversely, any vector can be turned into a position vector by a translation that roots its starting point in the origin of the coordinate system. Figure 3.3 illustrates vector translation. Note that we could interpret this figure in one of two ways. The first interpretation is that we have a position vector $\overline{v}$ that is translated into a vector, also called $\overline{v}$, not rooted at the origin. The second interpretation is that we have an arbitrary vector $\overline{v}$ that we translate into a position vector, also called $\overline{v}$.

We are now ready to tackle the geometric interpretation of vector addition. In Figure 3.4 we see that the vector $\overline{c} = \overline{a} + \overline{b}$ can be computed geometrically by translating the position vector $\overline{b}$ in such a way that its starting point coincides with the endpoint of position vector $\overline{a}$. Connecting the starting point of $\overline{a}$ with the endpoint of the translated vector $\overline{b}$ gives us our resulting sum vector $\overline{c}$. It is interesting to note

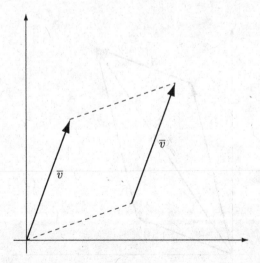

FIGURE 3.3   Translating a position vector into another vector with the same orientation and length.

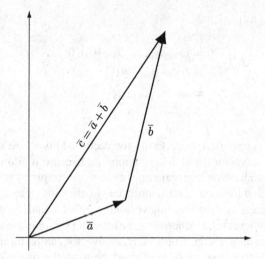

FIGURE 3.4 Vector addition.

that the algebraic entities in Table 3.2 can be shown to hold using purely geometric arguments based on vector translation. In Figure 3.5 we show that the commutativity identity holds for vector addition using our geometric interpretation. That is, it doesn't matter which vector we translate—we always wind up with the same result vector.

The last operation we discuss here is the multiplication of a vector by a scalar. This operation was the other operation used in the computation of the position vector of the average object of all the objects labeled M at the beginning of the chapter.

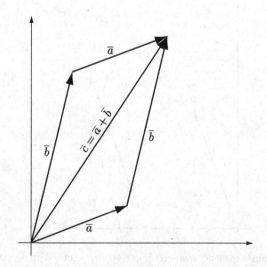

FIGURE 3.5 Vector addition is commutative.

TABLE 3.3 Algebraic Properties of Multiplying a Vector by a Scalar

$q(\bar{a}+\bar{b}) = q\bar{a}+q\bar{b}$	distributivity I
$(p+q)\bar{a} = p\bar{a}+q\bar{a}$	distributivity II
$p(q\bar{a}) = (pq)\bar{a}$	associativity
$1\bar{a} = \bar{a}$	identity

Definition 3.4 *Let* $\bar{a} = (a_1, a_2, \ldots, a_n)$ *be a position vector in* $\mathbb{R}^n$ *and let* $p \in \mathbb{R}$; *then we define* **multiplication by a scalar** *as*

$$p\bar{a} = (pa_1, pa_2, \ldots, pa_n). \tag{3.6}$$

This operation is also performed componentwise, in that each component of the vector is multiplied by the scalar of the multiplication. From the properties of scalar multiplication as well as scalar and vector addition, it is straightforward to show that the identities in Table 3.3 hold. Here p and q represent arbitrary scalars in $\mathbb{R}$ and $\bar{a}$ and $\bar{b}$ are position vectors in $\mathbb{R}^n$. Let us show that the *distributivity II* property holds:

$$(p+q)\bar{a} = ((p+q)a_1, (p+q)a_2, \ldots, (p+q)a_n)$$
$$= (pa_1+qa_1, pa_2+qa_2, \ldots, pa_n+qa_n)$$
$$= p\bar{a}+q\bar{a}.$$

Similar proofs exist for the other identities.

Geometrically, we can interpret vector multiplication by a scalar as a *scaling operation*; that is, the resulting vector will still have the same orientation and starting point as the original vector, but its length will have been modified. Consider the vector $\bar{a} = (a_1, a_2, \ldots, a_n)$ multiplied by some scalar value x; then from our definition (3.6), we have

$$x\bar{a} = (xa_1, xa_2, \ldots, xa_n).$$

The length of this new vector can be computed as

$$|x\bar{a}| = \sqrt{(xa_1)^2 + (xa_2)^2 + \cdots + (xa_n)^2}$$
$$= \sqrt{x^2a_1^2 + x^2a_2^2 + \cdots + x^2a_n^2}$$
$$= x\sqrt{a_1^2 + a_2^2 + \cdots + a_n^2}$$
$$= x|\bar{a}|.$$

This shows that the length of some vector that is multiplied by a scalar is simply the length of the original vector multiplied by that scalar.

3.1.2 Vector Spaces

Earlier we mentioned that by viewing objects in a data universe as vectors and admitting vector addition and scalar multiplication on these vectors, we essentially converted our data universe into a vector space. We made the basic assumption that when we apply vector addition and scalar multiplication to objects in our data set, we obtain new objects within our data universe. In other words, we assumed that the computed object is an object that can be represented in our coordinate system. In our case, where all attributes are real-valued, it should be clear that this assumption is valid, since any combination of real-valued coordinates gives rise to a position vector within our coordinate system $\mathbb{R}^n$. Another way of looking at this is that our real-valued coordinate system defines an infinite set of vectors to which we can apply vector addition and scalar multiplication and obtain vectors which themselves belong to this infinite set of vectors. A set of vectors that has this property is called *closed under vector addition and scalar multiplication* and is considered a *vector space*. We now define this in a more rigorous way.

Definition 3.5 *A nonempty set V of vectors in $\mathbb{R}^n$ is called a **real vector space** if vector addition and scalar multiplication are defined and closed over this set and satisfy the axioms given in Tables 3.2 and 3.3 with constants $p, q \in \mathbb{R}$.*

An interesting consequence of the closure property of vector spaces is that we can represent elements of a vector space by linear combinations of other vectors in that space. Formally:

Definition 3.6 *Let $\bar{a}_1, \bar{a}_2, \ldots, \bar{a}_m$ be vectors in some vector space V; then an expression of the form*

$$\bar{v} = \sum_{i=1}^{m} q_i \bar{a}_i = q_1 \bar{a}_1 + \cdots + q_m \bar{a}_m, \tag{3.7}$$

*where $q_i \in \mathbb{R}$, is called a **linear combination**, and from the closure properties of addition and multiplication, it follows that $\bar{v} \in V$.*

This leads to the following observations. A set of vectors $\bar{a}_1, \bar{a}_2, \ldots, \bar{a}_m \in V$ for some vector space V is called *linearly dependent* if at least one vector in this set can be represented as a linear combination of the others. The set is called *linearly independent* if none of the vectors in the set can be represented in terms of the others.

Consider the following: Let $\bar{a} = (1, 2, 3)$, $\bar{b} = (0, 0, 3)$, and $\bar{c} = (2, 4, 0)$ be a set of vectors in a vector space V. This set is linearly dependent because

$$\bar{a} = \bar{b} + \tfrac{1}{2}\bar{c}.$$

An important example of linear independence is the following in three-dimensional real vector space. Here the set $\bar{i} = (1, 0, 0)$, $\bar{j} = (0, 1, 0)$, and $\bar{k} = (0, 0, 1)$ is called *linearly independent* because none of the vectors can be represented as a linear combination of the others. The following expands the notion of linear independence and allows us to define what we mean by the dimension of a vector space.

Definition 3.7 *Let V be a real vector space and let B be a set of linearly independent vectors such that $B \subseteq V$ and any $\overline{v} \in V$ can be represented as a linear combination of the vectors in B, Then the set B is called a **basis** of V and the cardinality of B defines the **dimension of the vector space**.*

A familiar and important example of dimensionality is the following. Here, the unit vectors $\overline{i} = (1, 0, 0)$, $\overline{j} = (0, 1, 0)$, and $\overline{k} = (0, 0, 1)$ form the canonical basis of a three-dimensional real vector space. Any vector in this space can be represented uniquely as a linear combination of these three vectors. Since these three unit vectors form the basis set of any three-dimensional real vector space, they also form the basis of the vector space based on our data set in Table 3.1. This means that we can rewrite any vector of our data set in terms of a linear combination of these basis vectors. Consider the position vector for Amanda. We can rewrite it as

$$(65.2, 132.0, 36.5) = 65.2(1, 0, 0) + 132.0(0, 1, 0) + 36.5(0, 0, 1).$$

In our development of machine learning in general and support vector machines specifically, we always let V be the set of all possible vectors in the coordinate system $\mathbb{R}^n$ for n attributes. This means that the set V is infinite and closed under vector addition and scalar multiplication and therefore is clearly a vector space. Furthermore, the basis of this real vector space will have a cardinality of n. This is nice because it makes the intuitive notion of our training data as an n-dimensional data set coincide with the formal notion of the dimension of a vector space. Since our vector space V and the cross product $\mathbb{R}^n$ are isomorphic, that is, every point in $\mathbb{R}^n$ gives rise to a vector in V, and vice versa, we refer to the real vector space based on the n attributes of our data universe as $\mathbb{R}^n$ when there is no confusion.

3.2 THE DOT PRODUCT AS A SIMILARITY SCORE

The perspective of a data universe as a vector space not only allows us to perform arithmetic on objects but also gives us a convenient and quantitative way to measure similarity between objects using the dot product of two vectors. The dot product of two vectors computes a single scalar value, and this value can be interpreted as a similarity score between the two vectors. We can define the dot product in one of two ways: by an algebraic definition and by a geometric definition.

Definition 3.8 *Given two vectors $\overline{a} = (a_1, \ldots, a_n)$ and $\overline{b} = (b_1, \ldots, b_n)$ in an n-dimensional real vector space $\mathbb{R}^n$, we define the **dot product** $\overline{a} \bullet \overline{b}$ as*

$$\overline{a} \bullet \overline{b} = a_1 b_1 + \cdots + a_n b_n \quad \text{(algebraic)}$$
$$\overline{a} \bullet \overline{b} = |\overline{a}||\overline{b}| \cos \gamma \quad \text{(geometric)},$$

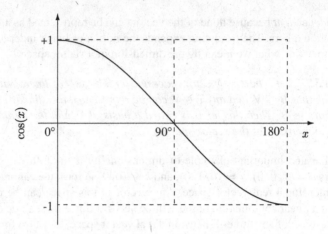

FIGURE 3.6 Values of the cosine function over the angles from 0° to 180°.

where $|\bar{a}|$ and $|\bar{b}|$ is the length of vector $\bar{a}$ and $\bar{b}$, respectively, and γ is the angle between the two vectors.

In the algebraic definition we sum the products of the respective components, which gives us a scalar value. In the geometric definition we compute the dot product by multiplying the product of the lengths of the two vectors by the cosine of the angle between them, which also gives us a scalar value. Using the *law of cosines*, it is possible to show that the algebraic and geometric definitions coincide (see Exercise 3.3).

That the dot product can be viewed as a similarity score between two vectors is immediately clear from the geometric interpretation of the dot product. Let $\bar{u}$ and $\bar{v}$ be unit vectors with $|\bar{u}| = 1$ and $|\bar{v}| = 1$; then the geometric interpretation of the dot product allows us to compute their dot product as

$$\bar{u} \bullet \bar{v} = |\bar{u}||\bar{v}| \cos \gamma = \cos \gamma.$$

The dot product of the two unit vectors is equal to the cosine of the angle between them. If this angle is close to 0°, the dot product is close to 1, indicating similarity; if the angle between the two vectors is close to 180°, the dot product is close to −1, indicating similarity but with opposite orientation; and finally, if the angle is close to 90°, we obtain 0 for the dot product, indicating, dissimilarity (Figure 3.6). This means that if two vectors have similar orientations or exactly opposite orientations, we consider them similar, and if two vectors have an angle close to 90° between them, we consider them dissimilar. The concept of dissimilar vectors is of such importance that we call two vectors that have an angle of exactly 90° between them *orthogonal vectors*. The following definition makes this precise.

Definition 3.9 *Two non-zero-length vectors are* **orthogonal** *if and only if their dot product is zero.*

Consider the following, given the unit vectors $\bar{i} = (1, 0, 0)$, $\bar{j} = (0, 1, 0)$, and $\bar{k} = (0, 0, 1)$ that form the basis of our three-dimensional vector space, then we have

$$\bar{i} \bullet \bar{j} = 1 \times 0 + 0 \times 1 + 0 \times 0 = 0,$$
$$\bar{j} \bullet \bar{k} = 0 \times 0 + 1 \times 0 + 0 \times 1 = 0,$$
$$\bar{k} \bullet \bar{i} = 0 \times 1 + 0 \times 0 + 1 \times 0 = 0.$$

All the dot products result in the value zero; that is, the basis vectors are pairwise orthogonal. Because of this property, we often call vector spaces that have a basis *orthogonal spaces*, and we call vector spaces that have a set of unit vectors as their basis *orthonormal* or *Euclidean spaces*. In particular, our vector space $\mathbb{R}^n$ is a Euclidean space.

To be able to utilize dot products as similarity measures in our vector spaces, we extend our notion of vector space by equipping a vector space with the dot product operation. This gives rise to the dot product space.

Definition 3.10   *A **dot product space** is a vector space where dot products are defined.*

In real vector spaces the dot product is always defined; therefore, real vector spaces can always be considered dot product spaces. This means that our real vector space $\mathbb{R}^n$ is also a dot product space, and this implies that we can use dot products to measure the similarity between objects in our data set.

Consider the data set in Table 3.1. We can compute the similarity score between the persons in the data set. For example, we can compare Amanda and Jane:

$$(25.4, 32.7, 2.5) \bullet (65.2, 132.0, 36.5) = 25.4 \times 65.2 + 32.7 \times 132.0 + 2.5 \times 36.5$$
$$= 6063.6.$$

We continue by comparing Amanda and Mary:

$$(65.2, 132.0, 36.5) \bullet (62.6, 126.0, 31.0)$$
$$= 65.2 \times 62.6 + 132.0 \times 126.0 + 36.5 \times 31.0$$
$$= 21,845.0.$$

As we can see, the similarity score between Amanda and Mary is much higher than the similarity score between Amanda and Jane, indicating that Amanda and Mary have much more in common than do Amanda and Jane. Looking at the data set, this is not surprising, since Jane is a toddler, whereas Amanda and Mary are women of similar height, weight, and age.

It is possible to show that the algebraic identities in Table 3.4 hold for the dot product. Here $\bar{a}, \bar{b}, \bar{c} \in \mathbb{R}^n$ and $p, q \in \mathbb{R}$. Of the four identities given, perhaps the *linearity* identity is the most nonintuitive. However, it becomes straightforward when

TABLE 3.4   **Algebraic Identities of the Dot Product**

$(p\overline{a} + q\overline{b}) \bullet \overline{c} = p\overline{a} \bullet \overline{c} + q\overline{b} \bullet \overline{c}$	linearity
$\overline{a} \bullet \overline{b} = \overline{b} \bullet \overline{a}$	symmetry
$\overline{a} \bullet \overline{a} \geq 0$	nonnegativity
$\overline{a} \bullet \overline{a} = 0 \text{ iff } \overline{a} = \overline{0}$	nondegeneracy

considering that a linear function over the vector space $\mathbb{R}^n$, say $f : \mathbb{R}^n \to \mathbb{R}^n$, has to satisfy the following two axioms:

$$f(\overline{a} + \overline{b}) = f(\overline{a}) + f(\overline{b}), \tag{3.8}$$

$$f(p\overline{a}) = pf(\overline{a}), \tag{3.9}$$

with $\overline{a}, \overline{b} \in \mathbb{R}^n$ and $p \in \mathbb{R}$. The linearity identity shown in Table 3.4 is simply a combination of these two axioms, with the dot product taking the place of the function f. The *symmetry* axiom states that the dot product operation is commutative. The last two axioms are interesting, since they state that computing a dot product of a vector with itself will always return a value greater or equal to zero, and if the dot product returns the value zero, the vector in question is the null vector. The fact that a dot product of a vector with itself will always return a positive value can easily be seen by the geometric interpretation of the dot product; a vector is maximally similar to itself. Also, from the geometric interpretation it can be seen that only the null vector can be maximally similar to itself and still return a similarity score of zero. The last two axioms together are often stated as *positive definiteness*.

In addition to the identities given in Table 3.4, we have the following identities, which are perhaps not as fundamental but nonetheless useful. The first is the relation between the length of a vector and the dot product of a vector with itself:

$$|\overline{a}| = \sqrt{\overline{a} \bullet \overline{a}}. \tag{3.10}$$

The next equation,

$$\cos \gamma = \frac{\overline{a} \bullet \overline{b}}{|\overline{a}||\overline{b}|}, \tag{3.11}$$

states that the cosine of the angle between two vectors can be computed by dividing the dot product of the two vectors by the product of their respective lengths.

3.3   LINES, PLANES, AND HYPERPLANES

One of our goals, as stated in the introduction to this chapter, is to describe the separability of groups of objects with different labels. A simple way to show that two groups of objects with respective different labels can be separated is to show that there exists a line, plane, or hyperplane (depending on the dimensionality of the data set) that separates the two groups. Here we lay the mathematical groundwork for these structures, and we will study them in more detail as decision surfaces in Chapter 4.

Assume that we are given a linear function in the familiar form

$$f(x) = y = -mx, \tag{3.12}$$

with $x, y, m \in \mathbb{R}$. We can interpret this function as a line with the set of points $(x, y) \in \mathbb{R}^2$ that satisfy the equation

$$mx + y = 0. \tag{3.13}$$

Here we consider $\mathbb{R}^2$ a two-dimensional dot product space. Generalizing this a bit with respect to the coefficients gives us

$$w_1 x + w_2 y = 0, \tag{3.14}$$

where $w_1 = m$ and $w_2 = 1$. We can now interpret the left side of (3.14) as the dot product of the two position vectors $\overline{w} = (w_1, w_2)$ and $\overline{x} = (x, y)$, such that

$$\overline{w} \bullet \overline{x} = w_1 x + w_2 y. \tag{3.15}$$

Plugging this equality back into (3.14), we obtain the identity

$$\overline{w} \bullet \overline{x} = 0. \tag{3.16}$$

The fact that the dot product between the two vectors is zero implies that $\overline{w}$ and $\overline{x}$ are orthogonal by Definition 3.9.

Since (3.16) is an alternative formulation of the line $w_1 x + w_2 y = mx + y = 0$, we should examine the components of this alternative formulation more closely. Here we can interpret the vector $\overline{x}$ as the position vector for any point (x, y) that lies on the line $mx + y = 0$. Furthermore, since this line goes through the origin of the coordinate system, it follows that the position vector $\overline{x}$ for any point on the line is parallel to the line. The vector $\overline{w}$ is orthogonal to the vector $\overline{x}$, and since $\overline{x}$ is parallel to the line $mx + y = 0$, it follows that $\overline{w}$ is also orthogonal to the line. Figure 3.7 illustrates these relationships. The vector $\overline{w}$ is called the *normal vector*.

So far we have only considered functions that go through the origin of the coordinate system. Let us consider a more general form that includes an offset term $b \in \mathbb{R}$,

$$f(x) = y = -mx + b. \tag{3.17}$$

By reasoning similar to that for a line through the origin, we may show that we can define an analogous formulation for the function above based on the dot product

$$\overline{w} \bullet \overline{x} = b, \tag{3.18}$$

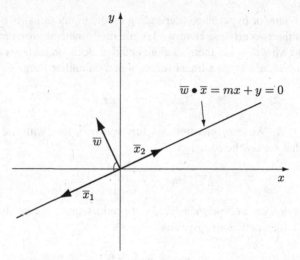

FIGURE 3.7 Relationship between the canonical definition of a line $mx + y = 0$ and its dot product equivalent, $\overline{w} \bullet \overline{x} = 0$, where $\overline{w}$ is the normal vector and $\overline{x}_1$ and $\overline{x}_2$ are position vectors of the points (x_1, y_1) (x_2, y_2) on the line, respectively.

where $\overline{w} = (m, 1)$ and $\overline{x} = (x, y)$. Figure 3.8 illustrates this construction. Note that the normal vector $\overline{w}$ and the position vector $\overline{x}$ are no longer orthogonal, indicating that the line does not run through the origin but crosses the y-coordinate at $(0, b/w_2)$. However, the vector $\overline{w}$ is still orthogonal to the line.

Now that we have an alternative way of specifying a line in (3.18) that does not depend explicitly on writing out linear combinations, we can easily extend our

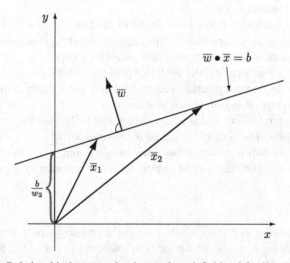

FIGURE 3.8 Relationship between the dot product definition of a line $\overline{w} \bullet \overline{x} = b$ and its constituent parts; $\overline{w} = (w_1, w_2)$ is the normal vector and $\overline{x}_1$ and $\overline{x}_2$ are position vectors of the points (x_1, y_1) and (x_2, y_2) on the line, respectively. The y-intercept is b/w_2.

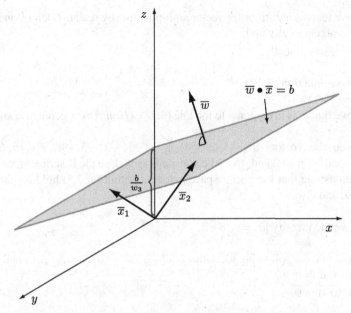

FIGURE 3.9 Relationship between the dot product definition of a plane $\overline{w} \bullet \overline{x} = b$ and its constituent parts; $\overline{w} = (w_1, w_2, w_3)$ is the normal vector and $\overline{x}_1$ and $\overline{x}_2$ are position vectors of the points (x_1, y_1, z_1) and (x_2, y_2, z_2) on the plane, respectively. The z-intercept is b/w_3.

notation to three-dimensional spaces. If we let $\overline{w} = (w_1, w_2, w_3)$ and $\overline{x} = (x, y, z)$, the equation

$$\overline{w} \bullet \overline{x} = b \tag{3.19}$$

describes a *plane* where $\overline{w}$ is the normal vector of that plane and $\overline{x}$ is the position vector of points on the plane (see Figure 3.9).

We can consider even higher-dimensional cases with $\overline{w} = (w_1, \ldots, w_n)$ and $\overline{x} = (x_1, \ldots, x_n)$, where

$$\overline{w} \bullet \overline{x} = b. \tag{3.20}$$

Here (3.20) defines a *hyperplane* in n-dimensional space, but notationally it does not differ from (3.18) and (3.19). Therefore, equation (3.20) is a convenient notation for planes in arbitrarily dimensioned spaces, including lines in two-dimensional spaces, and we make use of this notation in the remainder of the book.

EXERCISES

3.1 Prove that the identities for vector addition (Definition 3.3) hold
  (a) algebraically and,
  (b) geometrically.

3.2 Prove that the identities for vector multiplication by scalars (Definition 3.4) hold
   (a) algebraically and,
   (a) geometrically.

3.3 Derive equation (3.18).

3.4 Prove that $\overline{w}$ is orthogonal to the line (3.18). (*Hint*: Use a geometric argument.)

3.5 Given the vectors $\overline{a} = (1, 2, 3, 4), \overline{b} = (-1, -2, -3, -4), \overline{c} = (5, 6, 7, 8) \in \mathbb{R}^4$, and let $p = 2$ and $q = 3$ be constants in $\mathbb{R}$, Use the R scripting language to demonstrate that the vector space axioms (Definition 3.5) hold for the vectors $\overline{a}, \overline{b}$, and $\overline{c}$.

3.6 Prove the identity $|\overline{a}| = \sqrt{\overline{a} \bullet \overline{a}}$.

3.7 Show that the following identities hold with $\overline{a} = (a_1, a_2, \ldots, a_n)$ and $q \in \mathbb{R}$:
   (a) $0\,\overline{a} = \overline{0}$
   (b) $q\,\overline{0} = \overline{0}$
   (c) $(-1)\overline{a} = -\overline{a}$

3.8 [*challenging*] Show that the algebraic and geometric definitions of the dot product (Definition 3.8) coincide. To do this, use the law of cosines,

$$|\overline{c}|^2 = |\overline{a}|^2 + |\overline{b}|^2 - 2|\overline{a}||\overline{b}| \cos \gamma,$$

where the vectors $\overline{a}, \overline{b}$, and $\overline{c}$ form a triangle and γ is the angle between vectors $\overline{a}$ and $\overline{b}$. (*Hint* $\overline{v} \bullet \overline{v} = |\overline{v}|^2$.)

BIBLIOGRAPHIC NOTES

Linear algebra is a large and mature field in mathematics with many excellent text and reference books. Good places to start are Wikipedia (http://www.wikipedia.com) and MathWorld (http://mathworld.wolfram.com) by searching for the keywords *linear algebra*. Our own development follows the linear algebra section of Kreyszig's book [48] fairly closely. A very accessible and well-written treatment of vector spaces is [35]. A linear algebra textbook available online is [37]. A unique treatment of data analysis from a geometric perspective is Michael Kirby's book [44], which develops more fully the ideas sketched here.

CHAPTER 4

LINEAR DECISION SURFACES AND FUNCTIONS

One of the fundamental questions in binary classification problems is the separability of the two groups of objects. The most straightforward approach to answering this question is to construct a line, plane, or hyperplane (depending on the dimensionality of the data set) that separates the two groups as best as possible. In a binary classification problem, a line, plane, or hyperplane that separates the two groups of objects is called a *linear decision surface*. Constructing a linear decision surface for a particular training data set and then using this decision surface to classify other points in the data universe can be considered inductive learning, since we generalize from the separability of the instances in the training data to the separability of the entire data universe.

To make all this mathematically more convenient, we use decision functions rather than decision surfaces to assign labels to unlabeled points in the data universe. However, as we will see, decision functions themselves use decision surfaces in computing an appropriate label for the unlabeled objects. The decision functions can be seen as models or approximations of the labeling functions of our original classification problem.

4.1 FROM DATA SETS TO DECISION FUNCTIONS

Let us start with a binary classification problem where the objects of interest are labeled with $+1$ and -1. We assume these labels because they are mathematically convenient, and as we know from our discussion in Chapter 1, the names of labels do not really matter as long as we have an appropriate number of distinct labels—one label for each class in our classification problem. We also assume that all attributes of our objects range over the real numbers; that is, we can view each object in our data universe as a position vector in the n-dimensional dot product space $\mathbb{R}^n$, where n is the number of attributes.

Let us cast our classification problem into the machine learning framework developed in Chapter 1:

- Let the dot product space $\mathbb{R}^n$ be our data universe with vectors $\overline{x} \in \mathbb{R}^n$ as objects.
- Let S be a sample set such that $S \subset \mathbb{R}^n$.
- Let $f : \mathbb{R}^n \to \{+1, -1\}$ be the target function.
- Let $D = \{(\overline{x}, y) \mid \overline{x} \in S$ and $y = f(\overline{x})\}$ be the training set.

Compute a function $\hat{f} : \mathbb{R}^n \to \{+1, -1\}$ using D such that

$$\hat{f}(\overline{x}) \cong f(\overline{x}) \tag{4.1}$$

for all $\overline{x} \in \mathbb{R}^n$. The framework above is virtually identical to Definition 1.1 except that we replaced our general notion of a data universe with the dot product space $\mathbb{R}^n$, and we use the label set $\{+1, -1\}$ instead of *true* and *false*. Our aim is to construct a model $\hat{f}$ that approximates the original labeling function f. To accomplish this, we construct a line, plane, or hyperplane, depending on the value of n, that separates the classes $+1$ and -1 as best as possible. We then use this *linear decision surface* to construct our model $\hat{f}$. Notice that we have introduced a language bias into our machine learning problem: If a training set cannot be separated by a line, plane, or hyperplane, we are not able to construct a decision function for this machine learning problem. That is, we are biased toward constructing linear decision surfaces.

4.1.1 Linear Decision Surfaces Through the Origin

For illustration purposes, assume that our data universe is the two-dimensional dot product space $\mathbb{R}^2$. Also assume that our training data set is *linearly separable*; that is, we are guaranteed to find a line that separates the two classes in our training data perfectly. Finally, we assume that this line goes through the origin of our dot product space. Given these assumptions, we are guaranteed to be able to construct a line, say g,

$$g(\overline{x}) = \overline{w} \bullet \overline{x} = 0, \tag{4.2}$$

with $\overline{x}, \overline{w} \in \mathbb{R}^2$, that separates our training data perfectly. Since g separates the training data perfectly, we call it a *decision surface*. Figure 4.1a illustrates the decision surface for our two-dimensional dot product space $\mathbb{R}^2$, where the points shown as $+$ and $-$ are objects in the training set with labels $+1$ and -1, respectively. Notice that the normal vector $\overline{w}$ points into the direction of the points labeled with $+1$. We say that these points are *above* the decision surface and we say that the points labeled with -1 are *below* the decision surface.

Once we have a decision surface, we can use it to assign a label to any point in our data universe according to whether it falls above the decision surface or below it.

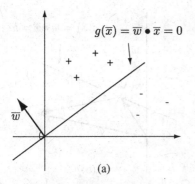
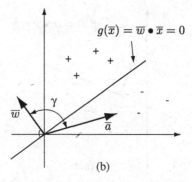

$$g(\overline{x}) = \overline{w} \bullet \overline{x} = 0$$

$$g(\overline{x}) = \overline{w} \bullet \overline{x} = 0$$

(a)   (b)

FIGURE 4.1 (a) Simple decision surface separating two classes; (b) classifying a point $\overline{a}$ using the decision surface.

Consider some point $\overline{a} \in \mathbb{R}^2$, where $\overline{a} \notin S$; that is, the point is an element of our data universe $\mathbb{R}^2$ but is not part of our training data set. If $\overline{a}$ falls above the decision surface, we assign it a $+1$ label, and if it falls below the surface, we assign it a -1 label. The reason that we had the normal vector of the decision surface point in the direction of the points labeled $+1$ is that this gives us a straightforward way to actually compute the label of our point $\overline{a}$. When we apply the decision surface g from (4.2) to the point $\overline{a}$,

$$g(\overline{a}) = \overline{w} \bullet \overline{a} = |\overline{w}||\overline{a}| \cos(\gamma) \doteq k, \tag{4.3}$$

it will produce a positive value k if $\overline{a}$ lies above the surface with $\gamma \leq 90°$ and a negative value k if $\overline{x}$ lies below the decision surface with $\gamma > 90°$. Here γ is the angle between the normal vector of the decision surface $\overline{w}$ and the position vector $\overline{a}$ (see Figure 4.1b). We can take advantage of this to construct the *decision function* $\hat{f}$ as follows:

$$\hat{f}(\overline{x}) = \begin{cases} +1 & \text{if } g(\overline{x}) \geq 0 \\ -1 & \text{if } g(\overline{x}) < 0 \end{cases} \tag{4.4}$$

for all $\overline{x} \in \mathbb{R}^2$. Our decision function will compute the label $+1$ for any points in our data universe that fall above the decision surface g, and it will compute the label -1 for any points below the decision surface. Since the decision function $\hat{f}$ will assign a label to any point in our data universe, we can view it as an approximation to the original labeling function f. It is an approximation because we used the separability of the training data as a way to infer the separability of the entire data universe. This is *inductive learning* in the sense that we rely on the fact that the instances in training data are an accurate representation of the entire data universe.

4.1.2 Decision Surfaces with an Offset Term

Let us relax our assumption that our decision surface has to go through the origin of our dot product space $\mathbb{R}^2$; that is, we now consider decision surfaces of the form

$$g(\overline{x}) = \overline{w} \bullet \overline{x} = b. \tag{4.5}$$

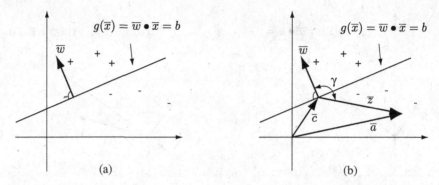

FIGURE 4.2 (a) Decision surface with an offset separating two classes; (b) classifying a point $\bar{a}$ using the decision surface.

We still only consider binary classification problems with labels $+1$ and -1, and the assumption that the training data set is linearly separable also still holds. Everything we discussed in Section 4.1.1 continues to apply in this situation: We have a decision surface such that training instances labeled $+1$ are considered to be above the surface, and training instances labeled -1 are below the surface (see Figure 4.2a). The only complication arises when we want to compute the label for some point, say $\bar{a} \in \mathbb{R}^2$, that is not part of our training set. In the case when the decision surface ran through the origin, the origin was a point on the decision surface and gave us a unique perspective in that both the normal vector of the decision surface and the position vector $\bar{a}$ were rooted here. Thus, taking the dot product $\bar{w} \bullet \bar{a}$ at the origin gave us an easy way to determine whether $\bar{a}$ was located above or below the surface. Unfortunately, simply assigning a label according to the value of the dot product no longer works when the decision surface does not run through the origin, since the origin is not a point on the decision surface and therefore lost its unique perspective. However, we can recreate this unique perspective by picking some arbitrary point, say $\bar{c}$, on the decision surface itself, that is,

$$g(\bar{c}) = \bar{w} \bullet \bar{c} = b, \tag{4.6}$$

and letting $\bar{z}$ be the vector such that $\bar{a} = \bar{c} + \bar{z}$, or

$$\bar{z} = \bar{a} - \bar{c}. \tag{4.7}$$

Finally, we translate the normal vector $\bar{w}$ such that it is rooted in point $\bar{c}$. This gives us the setup illustrated in Figure 4.2b. If we consider the vector $\bar{z}$ to be the "position vector" of point $\bar{a}$ with respect to point $\bar{c}$, our point $\bar{c}$ offers almost the same perspective as the origin did in the case when the decision surface ran through the origin: The vectors $\bar{w}$ and $\bar{z}$ are both rooted here and the dot product

$$\bar{w} \bullet \bar{z} = |\bar{w}||\bar{z}| \cos(\gamma) = k \tag{4.8}$$

produces a positive value k if the point $\overline{a}$ is above the decision surface with $\gamma \leq 90°$ and a negative value k if it is below the decision surface with $\gamma > 90°$, with γ being the angle between the normal vector $\overline{w}$ and the vector $\overline{z}$.

By substituting (4.5), (4.6), and (4.7) into (4.8), we obtain a more convenient formulation of that dot product in terms of the actual point $\overline{a}$ to be labeled and our decision surface g:

$$
\begin{aligned}
\overline{w} \bullet \overline{z} &= \overline{w} \bullet (\overline{a} - \overline{c}) && \text{using (4.7)} \\
&= \overline{w} \bullet \overline{a} - \overline{w} \bullet \overline{c} && \text{by linearity} \\
&= \overline{w} \bullet \overline{a} - b && \text{using (4.6)} \\
&= g(\overline{a}) - b && \text{using (4.5)}
\end{aligned}
$$

That is, the necessary dot product for point $\overline{a}$ can be computed by applying our decision surface g to $\overline{a}$ and then subtracting the offset term b. Notice that the point $\overline{c}$ that we used for our perspective on the decision surface vanishes in this formulation. Generalizing this to any arbitrary point in the dot product space, we can construct our decision function as

$$
\hat{f}(\overline{x}) = \begin{cases} +1 & \text{if } g(\overline{x}) - b \geq 0 \\ -1 & \text{if } g(\overline{x}) - b < 0 \end{cases} \tag{4.9}
$$

for all $\overline{x} \in \mathbb{R}^2$. As required, our decision function will assign a $+1$ label to points above the decision surface and a -1 label to points below the decision surface. When we consider decision surfaces through the origin with $b = 0$, the decision function in (4.9) degenerates to the decision function (4.4) and we can therefore view decision surfaces that run through the origin as a special case of more general decision surfaces that include an offset term.

Here we developed the structure of the decision surfaces and functions based on the dot product space $\mathbb{R}^2$. However, a closer look at the derivation reveals that there is nothing that would prevent us from developing the same structure for decision surfaces and functions in higher-dimensional spaces. Thus, for some decision surface $\overline{w} \bullet \overline{x} = b$ in an n-dimensional dot product space $\mathbb{R}^n$, we can always construct the decision function

$$
\hat{f}(\overline{x}) = \text{sgn}(\overline{w} \bullet \overline{x} - b), \tag{4.10}
$$

with $\overline{w}, \overline{x} \in \mathbb{R}^n, b \in \mathbb{R}$, and

$$
\text{sgn}(k) = \begin{cases} +1 & \text{if } k \geq 0 \\ -1 & \text{if } k < 0 \end{cases} \tag{4.11}
$$

for all $k \in \mathbb{R}$.

4.2 SIMPLE LEARNING ALGORITHM

Let us look at an algorithm that actually constructs a decision function given an appropriate training set. That is, given a linearly separable training set

$$D = \{(\overline{x}_1, y_1), (\overline{x}_2, y_2), \ldots, (\overline{x}_l, y_l)\}, \qquad (4.12)$$

with $\overline{x}_i \in \mathbb{R}^2$ and $y_i \in \{+1, -1\}$, we first construct a decision surface of the form (4.5) by computing the normal vector $\overline{w}$ and the offset term b from the training set. We then use this decision surface to construct a decision function of the form given in equation (4.10).

Step 1   We start by computing the average objects or means of the two respective classes in our training set D. We denote the mean for the class labeled $+1$ with $\overline{c}_+$ and the mean for the class labeled -1 with $\overline{c}_-$. We can compute these means as

$$\overline{c}_+ = \frac{1}{l_+} \sum_{(\overline{x}_i, +1) \in D} \overline{x}_i, \qquad (4.13)$$

$$\overline{c}_- = \frac{1}{l_-} \sum_{(\overline{x}_i, -1) \in D} \overline{x}_i, \qquad (4.14)$$

where

$$l_+ = |\{(\overline{x}, y) \mid (\overline{x}, y) \in D \text{ and } y = +1\}|, \qquad (4.15)$$

$$l_- = |\{(\overline{x}, y) \mid (\overline{x}, y) \in D \text{ and } y = -1\}|, \qquad (4.16)$$

where l_+ denotes the number of elements in D labeled $+1$ and l_- denotes the number of elements in D labeled -1. The means are computed analogously to the average object of all the objects labeled M (see Section 3.1). Figure 4.3a illustrates the construction of the class means.

Step 2   Next, we construct the vector $\overline{d}$ such that $\overline{c}_+ = \overline{c}_- + \overline{d}$, or

$$\overline{d} = \overline{c}_+ - \overline{c}_-. \qquad (4.17)$$

See Figure 4.3b.

Step 3   In this step we compute the mean, call it $\overline{c}$, between the two class means $\overline{c}_+$ and $\overline{c}_-$ as

$$\overline{c} = \tfrac{1}{2}(\overline{c}_+ + \overline{c}_-). \qquad (4.18)$$

We can see this construction in Figure 4.3c.

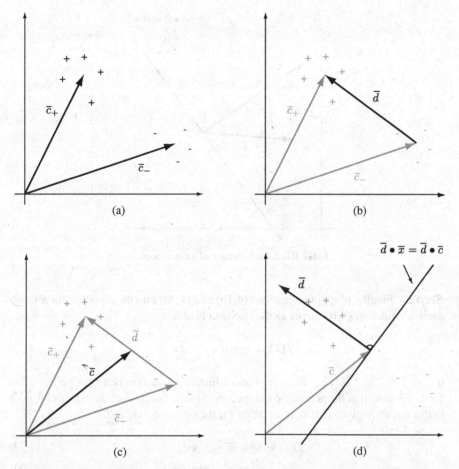

FIGURE 4.3   Geometric constructions for the simple learning algorithm: (a) the means $\overline{c}_+$ and $\overline{c}_-$ of the two classes; (b) the difference vector $\overline{d}$; (c) the midpoint $\overline{c}$ between the two means; (d) the decision surface $\overline{d} \bullet \overline{x} = \overline{d} \bullet \overline{c}$.

Step 4   We translate the vector $\overline{d}$ so that it is rooted in the average object $\overline{c}$, and we construct a line perpendicular to $\overline{d}$ through $\overline{c}$ (see Figure 4.3d). We can now interpret this line as a decision surface, and using equation (4.5) with

$$\overline{w} = \overline{d}, \tag{4.19}$$

$$b = \overline{d} \bullet \overline{c}, \tag{4.20}$$

we obtain the following equation for this decision surface:

$$\overline{d} \bullet \overline{x} = \overline{d} \bullet \overline{c}. \tag{4.21}$$

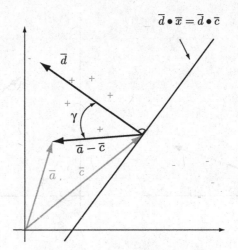

FIGURE 4.4 Labeling of unseen point $\bar{a}$.

Step 5 Finally, plugging equations (4.19) and (4.20) into the equation for a linear decision function (4.10) gives us the decision function

$$\hat{f}(\overline{x}) = \mathrm{sgn}(\overline{d} \bullet \overline{x} - \overline{d} \bullet \overline{c}) \tag{4.22}$$

for all $\overline{x} \in \mathbb{R}^2$. Applying the dot product linearity and symmetry properties from Table 3.4 as well as the geometric interpretation of the dot product from Definition 3.8 to this equation gives us a new equation for the decision function,

$$\hat{f}(\overline{x}) = \mathrm{sgn}((\overline{x} - \overline{c}) \bullet \overline{d}) \tag{4.23}$$

$$= \mathrm{sgn}(|\overline{x} - \overline{c}||\overline{d}| \cos \gamma), \tag{4.24}$$

which has a nice geometric interpretation. The value of the decision function for some point $\overline{x}$ is computed by taking the dot product between the vector $\overline{x} - \overline{c}$, the "position vector" of the point $\overline{x}$ with respect to $\overline{c}$, and the normal vector of the decision surface $\overline{d}$. If the angle γ between those two vectors is less than 90°, the point $\overline{x}$ is above the decision surface, and if γ is greater than 90°, it is below the surface. Figure 4.4 illustrates this for the unlabeled point $\overline{a}$.

We can take this one step further by deriving a purely algebraic expression for the decision function in terms of the class means by plugging equations (4.17) and (4.18) into (4.23):

$$\hat{f}(\overline{x}) = \mathrm{sgn}((\overline{x} - \overline{c}) \bullet \overline{d})$$

$$= \mathrm{sgn}\left(\left[\overline{x} - \tfrac{1}{2}(\overline{c}_+ + \overline{c}_-)\right] \bullet (\overline{c}_+ - \overline{c}_-)\right). \tag{4.25}$$

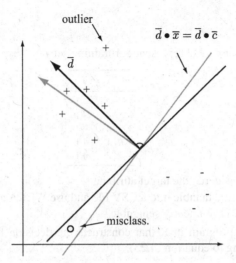

FIGURE 4.5 Outliers can distort the orientation of the decision surface, which leads to misclassification errors.

We can see that the value of the decision function for any point $\bar{x}$ can be computed directly from the class means.

4.3 DISCUSSION

We have developed a mathematical view of decision surfaces and functions and put them to use in a simple learning algorithm. In this algorithm every point in the data set contributes equally to computation of the respective class means. This can be problematic if the training set contains outliers, points that are unlike any other points in the data set. Outliers can distort the orientation of the decision surface, which can lead to misclassifications of points not part of the training set. This can be seen in Figure 4.5 for a single outlier in the class labeled $+1$. When this outlier is ignored, the decision surface is given as the construction with the gray lines, and we see that the point labeled with the circle is above the decision surface. However, when the outlier is not ignored, the decision surface is distorted, as shown by the dark-lined construction in Figure 4.5 and we see that in this case the point labeled with the circle falls below the decision surface. Here, the point labeled with the circle represents a point in our data universe that is not part of the training set.

One way to rectify this is to ignore outliers and only use points that truly represent the classes for our construction. We will see that more sophisticated algorithms such as perceptron learning and support vector machines solve this problem and that the influence of outliers on decision surfaces is minimized.

EXERCISES

4.1 Let the following table represent our training set D:

x_1	x_2	y
1	2	-1
1	4	-1
3	4	-1
3	1	$+1$
4	2	$+1$

where y is considered the target attribute.

   (a) Copy this data table into a CSV file and use WEKA and/or R to visualize the data. Is D linearly separable?

   (b) Write a program in R that constructs the decision function $\hat{f}$ using D according to equation (4.25).

   (c) Use the function $\hat{f}$ to classify the point $\overline{x} = (x_1, x_2) = (2, 2)$.

4.2 Let the data set in Table 3.1 be our training set D.

   (a) Write a program in R that constructs the decision function $\hat{f}$ using D according to equation (4.25).

   (b) Apply your decision function $\hat{f}$ to the objects in D and compare the labels given in D with the labels computed by your decision function. Explain your observations.

   (c) If necessary, what steps would you take to construct a better decision function?

4.3 Clinical data characterizing two types of cardiovascular diseases in terms of systolic blood pressure and the count of white blood cells of patients are presented in the table below. If we can construct a decision function $\hat{f}$ on these data, then given the systolic blood pressure and the white blood cell count of any patient with heart disease will enable us to predict which disease we need to treat without further diagnostics. Let the following table represent our training set D:

Systolic Blood Pressure	White Blood Count	Diagnosis
110	13,000	Myocardial infarction
90	12,000	Myocardial infarction
85	18,000	Myocardial infarction
120	8,000	Myocardial infarction
130	18,000	Myocardial infarction
180	5,000	Angina
200	7,500	Angina
165	6,000	Angina
190	6,500	Angina

where *Diagnosis* is considered the dependent attribute.

(a) Copy this data table into a CSV file and use WEKA and/or R to visualize the data. Is D linearly separable?

(b) Write a program in R that constructs the decision function $\hat{f}$ using D according to equation (4.25).

(c) How accurate is your decision function on the training data?

BIBLIOGRAPHIC NOTES

Decision surfaces are developed as decision boundaries in [36]. A more statistical point of view of decision functions is developed in virtually every elementary statistics textbook in the context of estimation theory (e.g., [39, 78]). Our simple learning algorithm was inspired by the development in [65, pp. 4, ff]. The data set in Exercise 4.3 is based on data published in [21].

CHAPTER 5

PERCEPTRON LEARNING

The *perceptron* can be thought of as the predecessor to the modern artificial neural network. It consists of a single neuron that computes a binary decision function based on a linear decision surface. Learning in the perceptron is accomplished by estimating the normal vector and offset term for the decision surface from the training data via a training algorithm. Once a perceptron has been trained, it can be used to classify any instance of the associated data universe.

The standard training algorithm for perceptrons is a heuristic[1] that searches the space of all possible normal vectors and offset terms for a decision surface that separates a linearly separable training set. An interesting property of the perceptron is that in addition to the standard training algorithm, we can also formulate a dual training algorithm. This algorithm searches over a set of coefficients that represent the amount of influence that each training data point has on the position of the decision surface. Together with the offset term, these influence coefficients characterize the decision surface. This is in contrast to the original or primal approach, where the decision surface is determined by the traditional normal vector and offset term. It is remarkable that in the dual formulation of perceptron training it becomes very explicit which training points are the constraints on the decision surface and which are not. This foreshadows some of the structures we will see in support vector machines.

---

[1]A *heuristic* is an algorithm that uses rules of thumb and approximations to find *some* solution to a given problem rather than an optimal solution.

Knowledge Discovery with Support Vector Machines, by Lutz Hamel
Copyright © 2009 John Wiley & Sons, Inc.

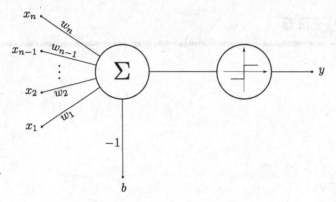

FIGURE 5.1   Architecture of a perceptron.

5.1   PERCEPTRON ARCHITECTURE AND TRAINING

In Chapter 4 we saw that we can compute a decision surface together with the corresponding decision function based on the means of the two respective classes in a binary classification problem. A completely different approach to finding a decision function was proposed by Frank Rosenblatt in the 1950s. He proposed a machine—the *perceptron*—whose architecture encodes the structure of a decision function directly based on an underlying linear decision surface. Today we recognize this architecture as an artificial neuron consisting of two computational components: an aggregation function and a transfer function. The structure of a perceptron's neuron is illustrated in Figure 5.1. The perceptron collects n weighted input signals, denoted by $x_1, \ldots, x_n$ with corresponding weights $w_1, \ldots, w_n$, and sums them together in the *aggregation component*. Note that the summation also has a bias term b with a constant weight of -1. This sum is then passed to the *transfer function*, which is a step filter that returns -1 if its input is negative and $+1$ if its input is positive. In other words, the step filter implements the sgn function (4.11). If we view each input x_k as a component of some input vector $\overline{x} = (x_1, \ldots, x_n)$ and each weight w_k as a component of a vector $\overline{w} = (w_1, \ldots, w_n)$, it is not difficult to see that the perceptron computes the following function:

$$y = \text{sgn}\left(\left[\sum_{k=1}^{n} w_k x_k\right] + (-1)b\right) = \text{sgn}(\overline{w} \bullet \overline{x} - b). \qquad (5.1)$$

Shifting our perspective slightly we can view the weight vector as the normal vector and the bias term as the offset term of some decision surface. Furthermore, the sgn function extracts the appropriate object label from this decision surface. This means that the perceptron represents a decision function of the form

$$\hat{f}(\overline{x}) = y = \text{sgn}(\overline{w} \bullet \overline{x} - b), \qquad (5.2)$$

Algorithm 5.1

let $D = \{(\overline{x}_1, y_1), (\overline{x}_2, y_2), \ldots, (\overline{x}_l, y_l)\} \subset \mathbb{R}^n \times \{+1, -1\}$
let $0 < \eta < 1$
$\overline{w} \leftarrow \overline{0}$
$b \leftarrow 0$
$r \leftarrow \max\{|\overline{x}| \mid (\overline{x}, y) \in D\}$
repeat
    for $i = 1$ to l
        if $\operatorname{sgn}(\overline{w} \bullet \overline{x}_i - b) \neq y_i$ then
            $\overline{w} \leftarrow \overline{w} + \eta y_i \overline{x}_i$
            $b \leftarrow b - \eta y_i r^2$
        end if
    end for
until $\operatorname{sgn}(\overline{w} \bullet \overline{x}_j - b) = y_j$ with $j = 1, \ldots, l$
return $(\overline{w}, b)$

based on a linear decision surface with normal vector $\overline{w}$ and offset term b. We call $\overline{w}$ and b the *free parameters* of the decision function in the sense that $\overline{w}$ and b are the parameters to be determined from the training data.

Rather than using a statistical approach to computing the free parameters of the decision function, Rosenblatt used a search heuristic that computes appropriate parameter values based on local refinements until a decision surface is found. Let us assume that our linearly separable training data has the form

$$D = \{(\overline{x}_1, y_1), (\overline{x}_2, y_2), \ldots, (\overline{x}_l, y_l)\}, \tag{5.3}$$

with $\overline{x}_i \in \mathbb{R}^n$ and $y_i \in \{+1, -1\}$. Then the training algorithm with many of the details left out can be given as follows:

Initialize $\overline{w}$ and b to random values.
repeat
    for each $(\overline{x}_i, y_i) \in D$ **do**
        if $\hat{f}(\overline{x}_i) \neq y_i$ **then**
            Update $\overline{w}$ and b incrementally.
        end if
    end for
until D is perfectly classified.
return $\overline{w}$ and b

Notice that the algorithm tests the perceptron decision function $\hat{f}$ on each element in the training set, and if a test fails, it adjusts the free parameters incrementally. This process continues until all elements in the training set are perfectly classified. Our assumption of linear separability is important in the context of training a perceptron, since the algorithm is guaranteed to converge only if the training data set is linearly separable. That is, when the training data are not linearly separable, the test of the decision function will always fail for some subset of training points, regardless of the adjustments we make to the free parameters, and the algorithm will loop forever.

Technically speaking, the training algorithm constitutes a *greedy search heuristic* through $\overline{w}$-b-space, where the values of the weight vector and the offset term are adjusted until a suitable decision surface is found. We call it a greedy search heuristic because it never backtracks to an earlier solution to explore alternative values but always uses the current state of the search to explore more of the search space. In the same vein as the perceptron architecture foreshadowed modern neural networks, the perceptron training algorithm foreshadowed the training algorithms of modern multilayer neural networks, such as backpropagation, in that these training algorithms are also greedy heuristic searches that use the errors produced by the network to guide the search.

Algorithm 5.1 shows the perceptron learning algorithm with more details filled in. The quantity r is called the *radius* of the training data set and can be considered the radius of the hypersphere centered at the origin of our coordinate system that encloses all the points of the data set. In our case, where the data universe is $\mathbb{R}^n$, this is simply the position vector length of the training set point located farthest from the origin. The quantity η, called the *learning rate*, controls the convergence speed of the search heuristic. At the heart of the algorithm are two *update rules*,

$$\overline{w} \leftarrow \overline{w} + \eta y_i \overline{x}_i, \tag{5.4}$$
$$b \leftarrow b - \eta y_i r^2. \tag{5.5}$$

The intuition behind these two rules is that in case of a misclassified point, they attempt to correct the position of the decision surface in such a way that the point is no longer misclassified.

Consider a training data set point $(\overline{x}_i, y_i)$ with $y_i = +1$. If this point is misclassified by the current decision surface, it receives a label of -1 instead of the required label $+1$. The first rule (5.4) attempts to correct this misclassification by *rotating* the decision surface in the direction of $\overline{x}_i$. The rotation is accomplished by adding a scaled version of the position vector $\overline{x}_i$ to the normal vector. The scaling factor is the learning rate η. This is easily seen by rewriting the update rule (5.4) as

$$\overline{w} \leftarrow \overline{w} + \eta \overline{x}_i, \tag{5.6}$$

with $y_i = +1$. The updated normal vector is computed by adding a scaled version of the position vector $\eta \overline{x}_i$ to the normal vector $\overline{w}$. The effect of this update rule on a decision surface in $\mathbb{R}^2$ is shown in Figure 5.2. Here, the training point $\overline{x}_i$ is below the original decision surface (light gray) and above the rotated decision surface (black). That is, the training point $\overline{x}_i$ with label $+1$ is misclassified by the original decision surface, but after the decision surface has been rotated it is no longer misclassified. An analogous computation can be performed for a misclassified point with a label -1. In this case the adjustment term will be subtracted from the normal vector, causing rotation in the opposite direction.

The second rule (5.5) attempts to correct a misclassification by *translating* the decision surface. Notice that this rule will translate the decision surface in the opposite direction of the class indicated by the desired class label y_i. This becomes obvious if

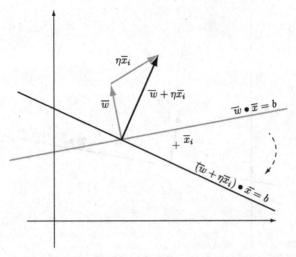

FIGURE 5.2 Effect of the perceptron update rule, which changes the normal vector of a decision surface.

we rewrite the rule as

$$b \leftarrow b + (-y_i)\eta r^2. \tag{5.7}$$

To see that this is appropriate, consider a decision surface that misclassifies the point $(\overline{x}_i, y_i)$, with $y_i = +1$. This means that the misclassified point is below the decision surface. To correct this misclassification, we need to translate the decision surface in the direction opposite to the normal vector; in other words, we need to translate it *away* from the class with objects labeled $+1$. The amount of translation is governed by the learning rate and the radius of the training data set. Figure 5.3 illustrates the effects of this update rule on a decision surface in $\mathbb{R}^2$. Here the training set point $\overline{x}_i$ with label $y_i = +1$ is misclassified by the original decision surface (light gray), and it is classified correctly by the translated decision surface (black).

The overall effect of the two update rules is illustrated in Figure 5.4 for a data universe $\mathbb{R}^2$. Here we have a decision surface at time step t that misclassifies one point: the circled point with label -1. This misclassification forces the perceptron learning algorithm to apply the update rules to this decision surface. The resulting rotated and translated surface is shown as the decision surface at time step $t + 1$. Notice that the update rules overcompensated, so this decision surface now misclassifies the circled point with the $+1$ label. This misclassification in turn forces the perceptron algorithm to apply the update rules in the opposite direction during the next iteration, leading to the decision surface at time step $t + 2$. The decision surface at time step $t + 2$ classifies all points correctly and the perceptron learning algorithm terminates.

Some reflection on this brief discussion perhaps highlights that most of the applications of the update rules will occur to points at the boundary between the two classes,

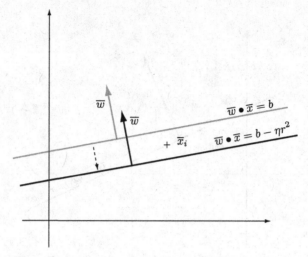

FIGURE 5.3   Effect of the perceptron update rule that changes the offset term of a decision surface.

since these are the most difficult points to separate and classify. Another way of looking at this is that the final decision surface has to be close to the boundary between the two classes, and that points that are close to this boundary will be misclassified much more often during perceptron training than points that lie far away from the boundary. Therefore, points close to the boundary between the classes contribute to the rotation and translation of the decision surface during the training phase much more often than do points that lie far away from the boundary. This is very different

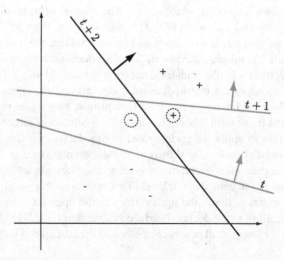

FIGURE 5.4   Perceptron algorithm at work; decision surfaces at time steps t, $t + 1$, and $t + 2$.

from the simple learning algorithm in Chapter 4, where each point in the training set contributed equally to the location of the decision surface by being part of the respective class mean. Interestingly, this insight—that points close to the boundary between the classes contribute more to the search for an appropriate decision surface than the other points—gives rise to an alternative or *dual formulation* of the perceptron training algorithm.

5.2 DUALITY

We know that the perceptron training algorithm (Algorithm 5.1) loops until no more classification mistakes are made. If we consider the normal vector update rule (5.4), then each time through the loop we add the term $\eta y_i \overline{x}_i$ to $\overline{w}$ if the training set point $\overline{x}_i$ is misclassified. From our earlier discussion and from Figure 5.2, we know that the normal vector update rule effects a rotation of the decision surface. Now, if some training point $\overline{x}_i$ is a particularly difficult point to classify, we might have to apply the normal vector update rule (5.4) multiple times until our decision surface is rotated enough to classify the point $\overline{x}_i$ correctly. The same holds for the translation rule (5.5), where we might have to translate the decision surface multiple times until it classifies the point $\overline{x}_i$ correctly. This means that points that are particularly difficult to classify typically contribute more to the computation of the final decision surface than points that are easy to classify.

Now, suppose that we introduce a counter that keeps track of how many times each point in the training set was misclassified. We would expect that points that are difficult to classify receive a high counter value and points that are easy to classify receive either a zero count or something close to zero. Let the vector $\overline{\alpha} = (\alpha_1, \ldots, \alpha_l)$ be our counter variable where each component of this vector corresponds to a training set data point. That is, component α_i will keep track of the number of times that training set point $\overline{x}_i$ was misclassified. With this we modify our perceptron learning algorithm as follows:

> Initialize $\overline{\alpha}$ and b to 0.
> **repeat**
>   **for each** $(\overline{x}_i, y_i) \in D$ **do**
>   **if** $\hat{f}(\overline{x}_i) \neq y_i$ **then**
>   Increment α_i by 1.
>   Update b.
>   **end if**
>   **end for**
> **until** D is perfectly classified
> **return** $\overline{\alpha}$ and b

Notice that in the innermost loop of the algorithm we replaced the normal vector update rule with a rule that increments the component α_i for the corresponding misclassified training set point $\overline{x}_i$. This looks reasonable, with the exception of the decision function $\hat{f}$. We no longer compute the normal vector necessary to specify the decision function directly, i.e., our new algorithm does not compute one of the free parameters necessary for our decision function. However, it is possible to recover the normal vector from the counter vector $\overline{\alpha}$. Going back to the insight that the normal vector $\overline{w}$ is a linear combination of the scaled versions of misclassified training set points (see Figure 5.2) gives us the following:

$$\overline{w} = \sum_{i=1}^{l} \eta \alpha_i y_i \overline{x}_i$$

$$= \eta \sum_{i=1}^{l} \alpha_i y_i \overline{x}_i. \tag{5.8}$$

Only misclassified points will have a nonzero α-value. Therefore, equation (5.8) does express the linear combination of misclassified points only, as intended. In this formulation the learning rate η is simply a scaling constant of the resulting normal vector and since we are interested primarily in the orientation of the decision surface, it is customary to drop this constant. This gives us the following identity for the construction of the normal vector from the counter $\overline{\alpha}$ and the labeled training set points:

$$\overline{w} = \sum_{i=1}^{l} \alpha_i y_i \overline{x}_i, \tag{5.9}$$

with

$$\alpha_i \approx 0 \text{ for "easy" points,}$$
$$\alpha_i \gg 1 \text{ for "difficult" points.}$$

Based on this, we can construct our perceptron decision function $\hat{f}$ as

$$\hat{f}(\overline{x}) = \text{sgn}(\overline{w} \bullet \overline{x} - b)$$

$$= \text{sgn}\left(\sum_{j=1}^{l} \alpha_j y_j \overline{x}_j \bullet \overline{x} - b \right). \tag{5.10}$$

This new decision function is a function with the free parameters $\overline{\alpha}$ and b, and the algorithm sketch above tries to find suitable values for these two free parameters.

With this new algorithm we have turned the problem of finding $\overline{w}$ and b into a problem of estimating the values for $\overline{\alpha}$ and b. Our search problem formulated in terms of $\overline{w}$ is called the *primal search problem* with the *primal variable* $\overline{w}$. Our search problem formulated in terms of $\overline{\alpha}$ is called the *dual search problem* with the *dual variable* $\overline{\alpha}$. Since we can use the dual variable to reconstruct a solution to the primal problem, it is clear that we can use either algorithm to find an appropriate

Algorithm 5.2

> let $D = \{(\overline{x}_1, y_1), (\overline{x}_2, y_2), \ldots, (\overline{x}_l, y_l)\} \subset \mathbb{R}^n \times \{+1, -1\}$
> let $0 \leq \eta < 1$
> $\overline{\alpha} \leftarrow \overline{0}$
> $b \leftarrow 0$
> $r \leftarrow \max\{|\overline{x}| \mid (\overline{x}, y) \in D\}$
> **repeat**
>   **for** $i = 1$ **to** l
>   **if** $\text{sgn}(\sum_{j=1}^{l} \alpha_j y_j \overline{x}_j \bullet \overline{x}_i - b) \neq y_i$ **then**
> $\alpha_i \leftarrow \alpha_i + 1$
> $b \leftarrow b - \eta y_i r^2$
>   **end if**
>   **end for**
> **until** $\text{sgn}(\sum_{j=1}^{l} \alpha_j y_j \overline{x}_j \bullet \overline{x}_k - b) = y_l$ with $k = 1, \ldots, l$
> **return** $(\overline{\alpha}, b)$

decision function. The dual algorithm with many of the details spelled out appears as Algorithm 5.2. As expected, we find two update rules,

$$\alpha_i \leftarrow \alpha_i + 1, \tag{5.11}$$

$$b \leftarrow b - \eta y_i r^2, \tag{5.12}$$

at the core of the algorithm. The first update rule increments the appropriate component α_i for each misclassification. The offset term update rule remains unchanged from the previous version of the algorithm.

In summary, the primal approach to perceptron training searches through $\overline{w}$-b-space and finds a representation of the underlying decision surface in terms of a normal vector and an offset term (Figure 5.5a). In the dual approach the training algorithm searches through $\overline{\alpha}$-b-space and constructs decision surfaces using the training set

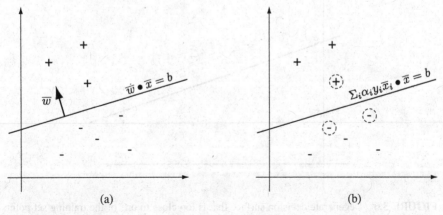

FIGURE 5.5 Decision surface representation in perceptron learning: (a) primal representation; (b) dual representation.

point coefficients $\overline{\alpha}$ and the offset term b (Figure 5.5b). Notice that in the dual representation it becomes very clear which training set points exert the most constraints on the decision surface. These are the points that are most difficult to separate and classify and typically have α-values $\gg 1$ and are indicated as points with circles around them in the illustration.

Duality, or the dual approach to classification, has interesting implications for algorithm design, since switching to the dual often brings to light hidden constraints of the classification problem. In our case we found that the dual solution is dominated by the constraints represented by the points close to the class boundaries. Therefore, duality is a powerful algorithm design tool that allows one to explore different algorithmic alternatives. This will prove extremely important during the development of support vector machines.

5.3 DISCUSSION

It is clear that the perceptron solves the problem of outliers in the training set encountered in Chapter 4, since only points close to the class boundaries have an influence on the decision surface. However, a consequence of the fact that both the primal and the dual perceptron learning algorithms are heuristics is that the decision surface search stops as soon as some decision surface is found that separates the training set. This can lead to degenerate decision surfaces that are positioned unnecessarily close to training set points. Considering that the training data set is only an approximate representation of the rest of the data universe, such degenerate solutions can lead to misclassifications of unseen points. Figure 5.6 illustrates a decision surface (gray)

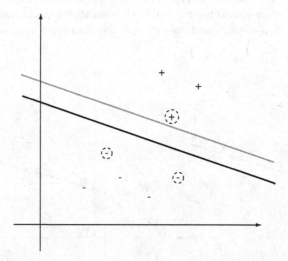

FIGURE 5.6 Degenerate decision surface that is too close to one of the training set points (gray), and an alternative decision surface placed midway between the training set points of opposite classes with the highest α-values (black).

that is placed very close to a training set point even though there is plenty of space for alternative positioning. Intuitively, we would expect a decision surface (black) that generalizes well to be placed midway between the training points from opposite classes with the highest α-values. Maximum-margin classifiers solve this problem in that the associated learning algorithm is guaranteed to find the decision surface that lies midway between the two class boundaries. Maximum-margin classifiers are the topic of Chapter 6.

EXERCISES

5.1 Use R to implement the primal and dual perceptron learning algorithms given above: Algorithms 5.1 and 5.2, respectively. Train your perceptrons with the data set from Exercise 4.1.

   (a) Do the perceptrons converge? If so, do they converge on the same decision surface?

   (b) In the dual form, identify the "difficult" and "easy" points in the training set by inspecting the α-values.

   (c) For both the primal and dual forms, construct a decision function and classify the point $\overline{x} = (2, 2)$.

5.2 Use R to implement the primal and dual perceptron learning algorithms given above: Algorithms 5.1 and 5.2, respectively. Train your perceptrons with the data set given in Table 3.1.

   (a) Do the perceptrons converge? If so, do they converge on the same decision surface?

   (b) In the dual form, identify the "difficult" and "easy" points in the training set by inspecting the α-values.

5.3 Implement the following learning algorithms in R:

   1. Simple learning given in equation (4.25)

   2. Perceptron learning, Algorithm 5.1.

   and train them with the training set from Exercise 4.1.

   (a) Plot the data set together with the induced decision surface for each algorithm.

   (b) What can you say about the differences in the respective induced decision surfaces?

   (c) For each of the learning algorithms above, use the respective decision function $\hat{f}$ and classify the point $\overline{x} = (2, 2)$.

5.4 [*challenging*] Install the "WEKA Classification Algorithm" plug-in (available on Sourceforge). Use the perceptron classifier to train a perceptron on the data given in Exercise 4.3. Evaluate your model.

BIBLIOGRAPHIC NOTES

The perceptron was first published in Rosenblatt's groundbreaking paper [64]. Discussions on perceptrons can also be found in neural network and machine learning books (e.g., [9, 51, 54]). Primal and dual representations of perceptron learning are developed in [23] and [38]. Minsky and Papert investigate the computational power of perceptrons in [53]. The dual representation of the perceptron, often referred to as the kernel-perceptron, was introduced by Freund and Schapire [32].

CHAPTER 6

MAXIMUM-MARGIN CLASSIFIERS

The learning approaches to binary classification problems of the preceding chapters can lead to decision surfaces that imply possible misclassification of data points that are not part of the training set. For the simple learning algorithm of Chapter 4, distortions of the decision surface can arise due to outliers. These distortions can lead to misclassifications. In the perceptron learning of Chapter 5, the training algorithm will terminate as soon as a decision surface is found for the training set. The underlying heuristic provides no guarantees that the decision surface constructed generalizes well from the training set to the data universe at large, implying possible misclassifications of points not in the training set.

Here we introduce a new approach that tries to avoid such shortcomings. This approach is based on searching for a decision surface that is equidistant to the class boundaries where the two classes are closest to each other. It also maximizes the distances to these class boundaries. By placing the decision surface right in the middle between the two class boundaries and by maximizing the distances from the class boundaries, this new approach reduces the probability of misclassification. We call such models *maximum-margin classifiers*.

The fact that we are searching for a decision surface with an optimality criterion such as the "maximum distance" implies an optimization problem, and as we will see, constructing a maximum-margin classifier is indeed a convex optimization problem that can be solved via quadratic programming techniques. The training set points that represent the heaviest constraints on the position of such an optimal decision surface, called *support vectors*, are related to the points with large α-values in the dual representation of the perceptron.

6.1 OPTIMIZATION PROBLEMS

Optimization problems are problems in which we want to select the best solution from a number of possible or feasible solutions. Typically, the feasible solutions are ranked by an objective function and the goal is to find the feasible solution that minimizes (or maximizes) the value of this function. In most optimization problems we also have a set of constraints that limit the solution space; that is, the constraints place limits on what constitutes a feasible solution and what does not. We can express optimization problems formally as

$$\min_{\overline{x}} \phi(\overline{x}), \tag{6.1}$$

such that

$$h_i(\overline{x}) \geq c_i, \tag{6.2}$$

with $i = 1, \ldots, l$ and for all $\overline{x} \in \mathbb{R}^n$. Here the function $\phi : \mathbb{R}^n \to \mathbb{R}$ is the *objective function*, and each function $h_i : \mathbb{R}^n \to \mathbb{R}$ is called a *constraint* with *bound* c_i. Any value $\overline{x} \in \mathbb{R}^n$ that satisfies the constraints is called a *feasible solution*. The optimization aims to find the feasible solution, $\overline{x}^*$, that minimizes the objective function such that for any other feasible solution $\overline{q} \in \mathbb{R}^n$, we have

$$\phi(\overline{x}^*) \leq \phi(\overline{q}). \tag{6.3}$$

If it is clear over which variable the optimization ranges, we often drop the subscript of the optimization operator.

We have stated optimization problems only in terms of minimization. This is not a limitation since we can turn any maximization problem into a minimization problem using one of the following identities:

$$\max \phi(\overline{x}) = \min -\phi(\overline{x}), \tag{6.4}$$

$$\max \phi(\overline{x}) = \min \frac{1}{\phi(\overline{x})} \tag{6.5}$$

as long as $1/\phi(\overline{x})$ is well-defined. Optimization problems are classified according to the properties of their corresponding objective functions and constraints. For example, a linear optimization problem has both a linear objective function and linear constraints. By this we mean that both the objective function and the constraints represents lines, planes, or hyperplanes in the appropriate dot product spaces.[1] When the objective function or the constraints are not linear, the optimization problem is considered to be nonlinear.

---

[1]Alternatively, a function is linear if it satisfies equations (3.8) and (3.9) when its graph is translated so that it goes through the origin of the dot product space.

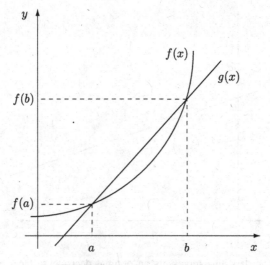

FIGURE 6.1 Convex function.

Here we are concerned with *convex optimization problems*. A convex optimization problem has a convex objective function and linear constraints. Optimization problems that are convex are particularly well behaved in that the objective function has a global minimum and the function surface is smooth in the sense that we can draw a line from one point on the function surface to any other point on the surface without crossing the surface itself. To illustrate this, consider the function $f : \mathbb{R} \to \mathbb{R}$ in Figure 6.1. Let $a, b \in \mathbb{R}$ be any values with $a < b$, and let $g : \mathbb{R} \to \mathbb{R}$ be a linear function such that $g(a) = f(a)$ and $g(b) = f(b)$. That is, g is a line that intersects the graph of function f at points $(a, f(a))$ and $(b, f(b))$. We say that the function f is convex if $f(x) \le g(x)$ for all values $x \in \mathbb{R}$ such that $a < x < b$. For a convex function f, the line g can touch the graph of the function for any interval $[a, b]$ in $\mathbb{R}$ but cannot cross it.

Simple examples of convex functions are functions that raise their argument to some positive, even integer power [e.g., $f(x) = x^2$]. Efficient algorithms exist that take advantage of the convexity of an objective function in order to solve a convex optimization problem. One such technique is quadratic programming, which we discuss in Section 6.4.

6.2 MAXIMUM MARGINS

Given a linearly separable training set for a binary classification problem, it is perhaps intuitive that the optimal decision surface is equidistant from the class boundaries. Informally, we can justify this by arguing that the training set is only an approximate representation of the data universe, and placing the decision surface equidistant from the respective class boundaries will increase the probability of correctly classifying

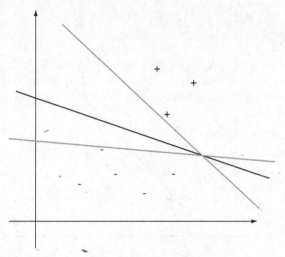

FIGURE 6.2 The dark line represents an optimal decision surface, and the light lines represent suboptimal decision surfaces in a binary classification problem.

points not in the training set. Maximizing the distances from the decision surface to the class boundaries will increase this probability even further.[2] In Figure 6.2 we illustrate this in $\mathbb{R}^2$-space, where the dark line is considered a better decision surface than either one of the light gray lines. To construct such optimal decision surfaces, we need a couple of additional concepts.

Definition 6.1   *A hyperplane supports a class if it is parallel to a (linear) decision surface and all points of its respective class are either above or below. We call such a hyperplane a **supporting hyperplane**.*

One way to think of a supporting hyperplane is as the translation of a copy of the decision surface to a point where it just touches the boundary of its respective class. In binary classification problems we typically have two supporting hyperplanes: one that is translated in the direction of the class with the $+1$ label and one that is translated in the direction of the class with the -1 label.

The second concept we need is the margin, which is crucial in this approach to constructing an optimal decision surface.

Definition 6.2   *In a binary classification problem the distance between the two supporting hyperplanes is called a **margin**.*

With these two concepts we can state our optimality criterion for a decision surface in more quantitative terms.

---

[2]We state this here without proof. Later we'll see that this fact holds when we talk about VC-dimensions in the context of statistical learning theory.

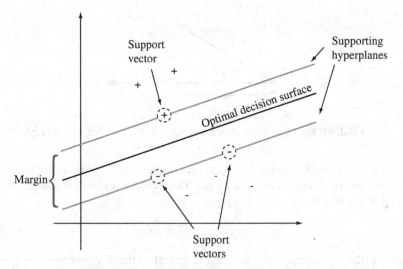

FIGURE 6.3 Optimal separating plane with its two supporting planes.

Definition 6.3 *A decision surface for a binary classification problem is* **optimal** *if it is equidistant from the two supporting hyperplanes and maximizes their margin.*

This means that our optimization problem involves finding a decision surface that allows the supporting hyperplanes to be translated as far as possible, thereby maximizing the margin and keeping the decision surface equidistant to the two supporting hyperplanes. Figure 6.3 puts all these concepts together. We have the two supporting hyperplanes translated so they just touch their respective class boundaries. The distance between the hyperplanes is the margin, and the optimal decision surface is located at the center of the margin. Notice that the size of the margin is constrained by the circled points in each class, called *support vectors*. If a supporting hyperplane were to cross a support vector of its respective class, it would no longer be considered a supporting hyperplane because members of its respective class would appear on both sides of the hyperplane. Also notice that the margin is at its maximum. Any rotation or translation of the decision surface would result in a smaller margin. Therefore, the goal in the maximum-margin classifier approach is to find the position of the decision surface that maximizes the margin, as shown here.

6.3 OPTIMIZING THE MARGIN

Finding a decision surface that maximizes the margin between the two supporting hyperplanes is an optimization problem where the feasible solutions are all possible decision surfaces with their associated supporting hyperplanes. Given these feasible solutions, the objective function for this optimization problem computes the size of the margin for each decision surface, and we maximize the objective function to find

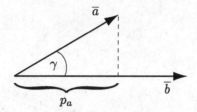

FIGURE 6.4   The value p_a is the projection of $\overline{a}$ in the direction of $\overline{b}$.

the maximum margin. The constraints in this case are the positions of the supporting hyperplanes, which are not allowed to cross their respective class boundaries. We can state this formally as

$$m^* = \max \phi(\overline{w}, b), \tag{6.6}$$

subject to the supporting hyperplane constraints. Here the objective function $\phi(\overline{w}, b)$ computes the margin of a given decision surface $\overline{w} \bullet \overline{x} = b$. The maximum margin m^* is due to some optimal decision surface, call it $\overline{w}^* \bullet \overline{x} = b^*$.

To make this optimization problem computable, we need to derive a suitable expression for the objective function ϕ. It is possible to derive our objective function, with a geometric argument, and to construct our geometric derivation we need the notion of a projection.

Definition 6.4   *Let $\overline{a}$ and $\overline{b}$ be vectors in $\mathbb{R}^n$ that form an angle γ between them; then we say that p_a is the **projection** of $\overline{a}$ in the direction of $\overline{b}$ such that*

$$p_a = |\overline{a}| \cos \gamma = \frac{\overline{a} \bullet \overline{b}}{|b|}. \tag{6.7}$$

Figure 6.4 shows this projection construction. Here p_a is a scalar that denotes the magnitude of $\overline{a}$ projected in the direction of $\overline{b}$.

We are now in a position to derive our objective function. Let us assume that we have a linearly separable training set

$$D = \{(\overline{x}_1, y_1), (\overline{x}_2, y_2), \ldots, (\overline{x}_l, y_l)\} \subseteq \mathbb{R}^n \times \{+1, -1\}. \tag{6.8}$$

Let us also assume that we have the optimal decision surface,

$$\overline{w}^* \bullet \overline{x} = b^*, \tag{6.9}$$

for this training set. Since this decision surface is optimal, the following identities hold:

$$m^* = \phi(\overline{w}^*, b^*) = \max \phi(\overline{w}, b). \tag{6.10}$$

Our maximum margin m^* is computed by the objective function ϕ given the parameters $\overline{w}^*$ and b^* of the optimal decision surface. Furthermore, finding the parameters

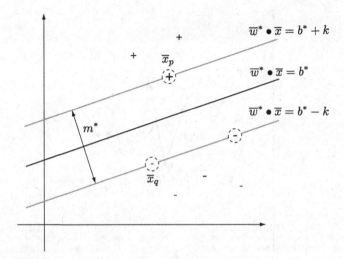

FIGURE 6.5   Margin m^* of the optimal decision surface $\overline{w}^* \bullet \overline{x} = b^*$.

for the optimal decision surface is an optimization problem, as we noted in equation (6.6). Now let us continue with our derivation of ϕ. Since the decision surface in equation (9.9) is a maximum-margin decision surface, we have two supporting hyperplanes equidistant from this surface: say,

$$\overline{w}^* \bullet \overline{x} = b^* + k, \tag{6.11}$$

$$\overline{w}^* \bullet \overline{x} = b^* - k. \tag{6.12}$$

The first hyperplane is the supporting hyperplane for the $+1$ class and is above the decision surface, and the second hyperplane is the supporting hyperplane for the -1 class and is below the decision surface (see Figure 6.5). In addition, since decision surface (9.9) is an optimal decision surface, the supporting hyperplanes are constrained by respective support vectors. Let the point $(\overline{x}_p, +1) \in D$ be a support vector for the $+1$ class with

$$\overline{w}^* \bullet \overline{x}_p = b^* + k. \tag{6.13}$$

That is, the support vector lies on the supporting hyperplane (6.11). Similarly, let $(\overline{x}_q, -1) \in D$ be a support vector for the -1 class with

$$\overline{w}^* \bullet \overline{x}_q = b^* - k. \tag{6.14}$$

This support vector lies on the supporting hyperplane (6.12). See Figure 6.5 for an illustration of this.

By definition, the distance between the two supporting planes is the margin m^*. We can compute this distance as the projection of the vector $\overline{x}_p - \overline{x}_q$ in the direction of $\overline{w}^*$. That is, we can compute the margin as the projection of the difference between

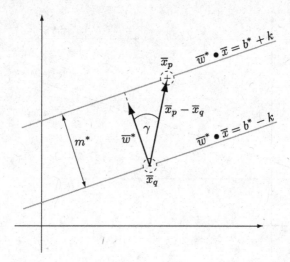

FIGURE 6.6   Computing the margin m^* between two supporting planes.

the two support vectors in the direction of the normal vector of the decision surface. See Figure 6.6 for this construction. In algebraic terms,

$$m^* = |\overline{x}_p - \overline{x}_q| \cos \gamma \qquad \text{by (6.7)}$$

$$= \frac{\overline{w}^* \bullet (\overline{x}_p - \overline{x}_q)}{|\overline{w}^*|} \qquad \text{by (6.7)}$$

$$= \frac{\overline{w}^* \bullet \overline{x}_p - \overline{w}^* \bullet \overline{x}_q}{|\overline{w}^*|} \qquad \text{by linearity in Table 3.4}$$

$$= \frac{(b^* + k) - (b^* - k)}{|\overline{w}^*|} \qquad \text{by (6.13) and (6.14)}$$

$$= \frac{2k}{|\overline{w}^*|}. \qquad\qquad\qquad\qquad (6.15)$$

Here γ is the angle between the vectors $\overline{w}^*$ and $\overline{x}_p - \overline{x}_q$. This gives us the optimization expression,

$$m^* = \max \frac{2k}{|\overline{w}|}. \qquad\qquad\qquad (6.16)$$

However, we want to express our maximization problem as a minimization problem. We do so by rewriting equation (6.16):

$$m^* = \max \frac{2k}{|\overline{w}|}$$

$$= \min \frac{|\overline{w}|}{2k}$$

$$= \min \frac{|\overline{w}|^2}{2k}$$

$$= \min \frac{1}{2k} \overline{w} \bullet \overline{w}$$

$$= \min \frac{1}{2} \overline{w} \bullet \overline{w}. \qquad (6.17)$$

Here the first step is justified by the identity (6.5) which states that a maximization problem can be viewed as a minimization of the reciprocal of the original objective function. The second step is justified since optimization over the positive values $|\overline{w}|$ is invariant under the transformation with the square function. The square function preserves the order-theoretic properties of its domain; that is, $x_1 \le x_2$ if and only if $x_1^2 \le x_2^2$ for $x_1, x_2 \ge 0$. This is another way of saying that x^2 is a monotonic function for $x \ge 0$ and that optimizing over x^2 is therefore the same as optimizing over x. The third step is the application of equation (3.10). The last step is justified since optimization is invariant under scaling with a constant. This means that we are free to pick a convenient value for k, and in our case we chose $k = 1$. This completes the derivation of our objective function as

$$\phi(\overline{w}, b) = \frac{1}{2} \overline{w} \bullet \overline{w}. \qquad (6.18)$$

It is perhaps peculiar that the objective function itself does not have a term b to be optimized. The offset term will, however, play a role in the constraints.

Now let us shift our focus to the constraints of the optimization problem. The notion is that the supporting hyperplanes for the respective classes need to stay supporting hyperplanes during the optimizations. That is, the supporting hyperplanes are not allowed to cross their respective class boundaries. Formally, this means that for our optimal supporting hyperplanes (6.11) and (6.12), the following identities have to hold, respectively:

$$\overline{w}^* \bullet \overline{x}_i \ge b^* + k \qquad \text{for all } (\overline{x}_i, y_i) \in D \text{ s.t. } y_i = +1, \qquad (6.19)$$

$$\overline{w}^* \bullet \overline{x}_i \le b^* - k \qquad \text{for all } (\overline{x}_i, y_i) \in D \text{ s.t. } y_i = -1. \qquad (6.20)$$

In other words, all the training points labeled $+1$ need to lie on or above the first supporting hyperplane, and all the training points labeled -1 need to lie on or below the second supporting hyperplane (see Figure 6.5). Thus, each point in the training data set is a constraint on its respective supporting hyperplane—the supporting hyperplane is not allowed to move beyond it. What needs to hold for the optimal supporting hyperplanes also needs to hold for all supporting hyperplanes for any decision surface. Generalizing and taking to our choice of $k = 1$ into account gives us

$$\overline{w} \bullet \overline{x}_i \ge 1 + b \qquad \text{for all } (\overline{x}_i, y_i) \in D \text{ s.t. } y_i = +1, \qquad (6.21)$$

$$\overline{w} \bullet (-\overline{x}_i) \ge 1 - b \qquad \text{for all } (\overline{x}_i, y_i) \in D \text{ s.t. } y_i = -1. \qquad (6.22)$$

We can write these constraints in a more compact way,

$$\overline{w} \bullet (y_i \overline{x}_i) \geq 1 + y_i b \qquad \text{for all } (\overline{x}_i, y_i) \in D. \tag{6.23}$$

In this formulation it is perhaps most obvious that *all* training set points give rise to constraints. The constraints also define the feasible region in that only decision surfaces where the margin fulfills these constraints are considered during optimization. The following proposition on computing an optimal decision surface with a maximum margin summarizes all this, making use of (6.18) and (6.23).

Proposition 6.1 (Maximum-Margin Classifier)   *Given a linearly separable training set*

$$D = \{(\overline{x}_1, y_1), (\overline{x}_2, y_2), \dots, (\overline{x}_l, y_l)\} \subseteq \mathbb{R}^n \times \{+1, -1\},$$

we can compute a maximum-margin decision surface $\overline{w}^* \bullet \overline{x} = b^*$ with an optimization

$$\min \phi(\overline{w}, b) = \min_{\overline{w}, b} \tfrac{1}{2} \overline{w} \bullet \overline{w} \tag{6.24}$$

subject to the constraints

$$\overline{w} \bullet (y_i \overline{x}_i) \geq 1 + y_i b \qquad \text{for all } (\overline{x}_i, y_i) \in D. \tag{6.25}$$

6.4 QUADRATIC PROGRAMMING

It is easy to see that our objective function in (6.24) is a convex function,

$$\phi(\overline{w}, b) = \tfrac{1}{2} \overline{w} \bullet \overline{w} = \tfrac{1}{2}(w_1^2 + \dots + w_n^2) \tag{6.26}$$

for $\overline{w} = (w_1, \dots, w_n)$. The objective function is shown in Figure 6.7 for the two-dimensional space $\mathbb{R}^2$. Convexity implies that we are able to find the global minimum of our objective function. In other words, given a set of feasible solutions, we will be able to find the one that will produce the smallest value of our objective function.

An efficient way to solve convex optimization problems of the form given here is via *quadratic programming*. Most quadratic program solvers are functions of the form

$$\overline{w}^* = \text{solve}(\mathbf{Q}, \overline{q}, \mathbf{X}, \overline{c}), \tag{6.27}$$

which represent the general convex optimization problem, also referred to as a *quadratic program*,

$$\overline{w}^* = \underset{\overline{w}}{\text{argmin}} \left(\tfrac{1}{2} \overline{w}^{\mathsf{T}} \mathbf{Q} \, \overline{w} - \overline{q} \bullet \overline{w} \right), \tag{6.28}$$

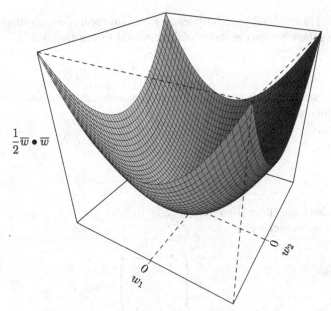

FIGURE 6.7   Objective function $\frac{1}{2}\overline{w} \bullet \overline{w}$ in $\mathbb{R}^2$-space.

subject to the constraints

$$\mathbf{X}^{\mathrm{T}}\overline{w} \geq \overline{c}. \tag{6.29}$$

Here $\mathbf{Q}$ is an $n \times n$ matrix, $\mathbf{X}$ is an $l \times n$ matrix, the vectors $\overline{w}^*, \overline{w}, \overline{q}$ are n-dimensional vectors, and the vector $\overline{c}$ is an l-dimensional vector. The operation $\overline{a}^{\mathrm{T}}$ denotes the transpose of some vector $\overline{a}$, and $\mathbf{M}^{\mathrm{T}}$ denotes the transpose of a matrix $\mathbf{M}$. We can transform this general optimization problem into a form that resembles our margin optimization in Proposition 6.1 if we let $\mathbf{Q}$ be the identity matrix $\mathbf{I}$ and $\overline{q} = \overline{0}$,

$$\overline{w}^* = \underset{\overline{w}}{\mathrm{argmin}} \left(\tfrac{1}{2}\overline{w}^{\mathrm{T}}\mathbf{I}\,\overline{w} - \overline{0} \bullet \overline{w} \right) = \underset{\overline{w}}{\mathrm{argmin}} \left(\tfrac{1}{2}\overline{w} \bullet \overline{w} \right), \tag{6.30}$$

with $\overline{w}^{\mathrm{T}}\mathbf{I}\,\overline{w} = \overline{w} \bullet \overline{w}$. The big difference between our formulation of margin optimization and the approach using a quadratic program solver is the fact that quadratic program solvers return the argument that minimizes the objective function rather than the minimized value of the objective function (whence the operator argmin rather than min). This does not pose a problem, however, since we can always reconstruct the optimal margin by plugging the optimized normal vector $\overline{w}^*$ into equation (6.15).

Now that we have the objective function of the quadratic program in a suitable form, let us turn our attention to the constraints. In contrast to our original margin optimization problem, the constraints in quadratic program solvers are expressed in matrix form [equation (6.29)]. However, by manipulating the constraints of our original margin optimization problem slightly, we can bring them into a form suitable for quadratic program solvers. Consider the following form of our constraints obtained by applying the symmetry property of dot products to equation (6.25):

$$(y_i \overline{x}_i) \bullet \overline{w} \geq 1 + y_i b \tag{6.31}$$

for all $(\overline{x}_i, y_i) \in D$ with $i = 1, \ldots, l$ and $\overline{x}_i = (x_i^1, \ldots, x_i^n)$. Given this, we can construct the matrix $\mathbf{X}$ as

$$\mathbf{X} = \begin{pmatrix} y_1 x_1^1 & \cdots & y_i x_i^1 & \cdots & y_l x_l^1 \\ \vdots & & \vdots & & \vdots \\ y_1 x_1^n & \cdots & y_i x_i^n & \cdots & y_l x_l^n \end{pmatrix}. \tag{6.32}$$

In other words, the ith column of $\mathbf{X}$ is equal to the vector $y_i \overline{x}_i = (y_i x_i^1, \ldots, y_i x_i^n)$. We construct the vector $\overline{c}$ as

$$\overline{c} = \begin{pmatrix} 1 + y_1 b \\ 1 + y_2 b \\ \vdots \\ 1 + y_l b \end{pmatrix}. \tag{6.33}$$

With these two constructions, it is now straightforward to show that the matrix format of the constraints in (6.29) is a compact representation of the constraint equations (6.31).

Notice that our construction of the vector $\overline{c}$ introduced the free variable b into the quadratic program, so we need to take this free variable into account in our optimization problem. That is, our optimization has to minimize the objective function over both $\overline{w}$ and b. The following proposition summarizes these constructions and expresses a maximum-margin optimization in terms of a optimization problem solvable via quadratic programming,

Proposition 6.2 *Given the linearly separable training set*

$$D = \{(\overline{x}_1, y_1), (\overline{x}_2, y_2), \ldots, (\overline{x}_l, y_l)\} \subseteq \mathbb{R}^n \times \{+1, -1\},$$

we can compute a maximum-margin decision surface $\overline{w}^* \bullet \overline{x} = b^*$ with a quadratic programming approach that solves the generalized optimization problem

$$(\overline{w}^*, b^*) = \underset{\overline{w}, b}{\operatorname{argmin}} \left(\tfrac{1}{2} \overline{w}^{\mathrm{T}} \mathbf{Q}\, \overline{w} - \overline{q} \bullet \overline{w} \right). \tag{6.34}$$

subject to the constraints

$$\mathbf{X}^{\mathrm{T}} \overline{w} \geq \overline{c}, \tag{6.35}$$

with $\mathbf{Q} = \mathbf{I}$, $\overline{q} = \overline{0}$, and where $\mathbf{X}$, and $\overline{c}$ are constructed according to (6.32) and (6.33), respectively.

Algorithm 6.1

let $D = \{(\overline{x}_1, y_1), (\overline{x}_2, y_2), \ldots, (\overline{x}_l, y_l)\} \subset \mathbb{R}^n \times \{+1, -1\}$
$r \leftarrow \max\{|\overline{x}| \mid (\overline{x}, y) \in D\}$
$q \leftarrow 1000$
let $\overline{w}^*$ and b^* be undefined
Construct **X** according to (6.32) using D.
for each $b \in [-q, q]$ **do**
    Construct $\overline{c}$ according to (6.33) using b.
    $\overline{w} \leftarrow solve(\mathbf{I}, \overline{0}, \mathbf{X}, \overline{c})$
    if ($\overline{w}$ is defined **and** $\overline{w}^*$ is undefined) **or**
       ($\overline{w}$ is defined **and** $|\overline{w}| < |\overline{w}^*|$) **then**
       $\overline{w}^* \leftarrow \overline{w}$
       $b^* \leftarrow b$
    end if
end for
if $\overline{w}^*$ is undefined **then**
    stop constraints not satisfiable
else if $|\overline{w}|^* > q/r$ **then**
    stop bounding assumption of $|\overline{w}|$ violated
end if
return $(\overline{w}^*, b^*)$

Algorithm 6.1 illustrates how a decision surface with a maximum margin is computed using a quadratic program solver. Here the function *solve* is assumed to be of the form (6.27). Most quadratic program solvers will return an *undefined* value for $\overline{w}$ if they cannot find a solution that satisfies all the constraints. Therefore, we see repeated tests in the algorithm as to whether or not the solver was successful in finding a solution. The quantity r represents the radius of the training set D. The constant q defines the size of the search interval for offset term values, and we set it to 1000. However, the precise value for q is highly data dependent and needs to be determined experimentally. We discuss this further below. The optimal normal vector $\overline{w}^*$ and offset term b^* are left undefined initially. Notice that $\overline{w}^*$ and b^* will remain undefined until the algorithm finds a solution that satisfies all the constraints.

Since the offset term b is a free variable, we need to pick appropriate values for b to be passed to the solver as part of the constraints. To determine a reasonable interval of values for b during optimization, consider the representation of a decision surface by the equation

$$b = \overline{w} \bullet \overline{x}. \tag{6.36}$$

This can be rewritten as

$$b = |\overline{w}||\overline{x}| \cos \gamma, \tag{6.37}$$

where γ is the angle between the vectors $\overline{w}$ and $\overline{x}$. With $0 \leq \gamma \leq \pi$ we have

$$-|\overline{w}||\overline{x}| \leq b \leq |\overline{w}||\overline{x}|. \tag{6.38}$$

We only consider points that lie within a hypersphere of radius r; that is, we only consider points with $|\overline{x}| \leq r$:

$$-|\overline{w}|r \leq b \leq |\overline{w}|r. \tag{6.39}$$

Unfortunately, $|\overline{w}|$ is unbounded, making the bound on b as stated useless. We can show this by considering that in a training set with radius r the largest possible margin is $2r$. Plugging this observation into equation (6.15), we obtain

$$\frac{2}{|\overline{w}|} \leq 2r. \tag{6.40}$$

We assume a value of $k = 1$, as before. This gives us a lower bound for $\overline{w}$:

$$\frac{1}{r} \leq |\overline{w}|. \tag{6.41}$$

This means that $|\overline{w}| = 1/r$ for the largest possible margin and $|\overline{w}| > 1/r$ for margins smaller than that. In fact, we have $|\overline{w}| \to \infty$ for infinitesimally small margins. However, we are interested in maximizing the margin; that is, decision surfaces with margins smaller than a certain threshold are not interesting enough to be considered part of the feasible solutions. To express this, we bound the values of $|\overline{w}|$ as follows:

$$\frac{1}{r} \leq |\overline{w}| \leq \frac{q}{r}, \tag{6.42}$$

where q is a bounding constant that bounds the value of $|\overline{w}|$ to a multiple of the maximum margin $1/r$. If we pick $q = 1000$ as it appears in the algorithm, the narrowest margin we consider a solution is 1000 times narrower than the maximum margin possible in a training set with radius r. Plugging (6.42) into (6.39) gives us

$$-q \leq b \leq q, \tag{6.43}$$

the bound for b as it appears in the algorithm.

The algorithm can fail to compute a decision surface on two accounts. The first type of failure arises when the solver cannot satisfy all the given constraints for any b in the given interval. The second type of failure arises when our bounding assumption for $|\overline{w}|$ is violated. Since we assumed a linearly separable training set, we are guaranteed to find a solution, and the failures imply that our bounding assumptions on b are not correct and the interval of values for b needs to be increased.

6.5 DISCUSSION

By defining the maximum margin as an optimality criterion for decision surfaces, we have achieved our goal of preventing degenerate decision surfaces from being considered as models for binary classification problems. However, when actually computing such maximum-margin classifiers using quadratic program solvers, we found that our solutions depend heavily on how we pick the free offset term parameter. Even though we have given some guidelines on how to search for the value of the offset term that leads to a maximum margin, the precise value can only be determined through experimentation. Searching for an optimal value of a free model parameter is not unusual in machine learning. Many complex learning algorithms have free parameters that need to be estimated via experimentation with the training set. Consider the optimal topology in artificial neural networks or the optimal pruning constant in decision tree learning algorithms. A marked exception is the dual of the maximum-margin algorithm we considered here. This dual algorithm also constructs a maximum-margin classifier but has no free parameters. We call this dual algorithm a *linear support vector machine*, and we develop this algorithm in Chapter 7.

EXERCISES

6.1 Write a program in R that implements the algorithm given in Algorithm 6.1 and apply it to your favorite linearly separable data set that represents a binary classification problem. (Use the quadratic program solver provided in the package *quadprog*.)

6.2 Implement the following learning algorithms in R:
1. Simple learning given in equation (4.25)
2. Perceptron learning, Algorithm 5.1
3. Maximum margin classifier, Algorithm 6.1

and train them with the training set from Exercise 4.1.

(a) Plot the data set together with the induced decision surface for each algorithm.

(b) What can you say about the differences in the respective induced decision surfaces?

(c) For each of the learning algorithms above, use the respective decision function $\hat{f}$ and classify the point $\overline{x} = \langle 2, 2 \rangle$.

6.3 [*challenging*] Optimal decision surfaces can also be developed via convex hulls of the respective classes in a linearly separable binary classification setting. Briefly, the optimal decision surface bisects the minimum distance of the two respective convex hulls at a right angle (see [5] and [6]).

(a) Write an algorithm that computes the optimal decision surface based on convex hulls.

(b) Show graphically that the decision surfaces computed by the convex hull algorithm and the maximum margin algorithm in Algorithm 6.1 coincide.

(c)   Show that the data points in the training set giving rise to the minimum distance between the respective hulls are the same points that are considered support vectors in the maximum-margin algorithm.

BIBLIOGRAPHIC NOTES

Maximum-margin decision surfaces are discussed in [10] and [26]. Many books on convex functions and optimization theory exist (e.g., [7, 56, 63]). One book that is particularly accessible is [14]. This book also has detailed descriptions of a number of algorithms that can be used to implement quadratic program solvers. Our geometric derivation of the objective function was inspired by a discussion in [65, pp. 189 ff].

PART II

CHAPTER 7

SUPPORT VECTOR MACHINES

Here we develop support vector machines. Fundamentally, support vector machines can be viewed as the dual to the maximum-margin classifiers developed in Chapter 6. The dual is obtained by applying Lagrangian optimization theory to the maximum-margin classifier optimization problem. This dual view of maximum-margin classifiers has interesting consequences. One such consequence is that linear classifiers based on support vector machines can easily be extended to nonlinear classifiers, thereby broadening the applicability of support vector machines tremendously. At the heart of this generalization from linear to nonlinear classifier is the notion of kernel functions. By applying what is referred to as the *kernel trick* to a linear support vector machine, we obtain a nonlinear classifier. What is remarkable is that nonlinear support vector machines retain the efficiency of finding linear decision surfaces but now allow us to apply these classifiers to training sets that are not linearly separable.

Toward the end of this chapter we generalize support vector machines even further by allowing the underlying maximum-margin classifier to make mistakes on the training set. This is accomplished through the introduction of slack variables. It might seem counterintuitive that we allow a classifier to make mistakes, but consider the fact that real-world training sets are not perfect and contain noise. Noise might give rise to an extremely complicated boundary between the classes of a classification problem. A classifier that is not allowed to make mistakes would have to model this complicated boundary flawlessly, giving rise to an extremely complicated decision surface. By assuming that the training set points that force the decision surface to be complicated are due to noise, and by essentially allowing the classifier to ignore these points, we can compute a much simpler decision surface. This is very attractive, since

Knowledge Discovery with Support Vector Machines, by Lutz Hamel
Copyright © 2009 John Wiley & Sons, Inc.

simple decision surfaces have a much higher probability of classifying points correctly that are not part of the training set than do complicated decision surfaces. In other words, simple decision surfaces tend to generalize better. We call maximum-margin classifiers that incorporate slack variables *soft-margin classifiers*. We often refer to maximum-margin classifiers that do not incorporate slack variables as *hard-margin classifiers*.

We begin the chapter by introducing Lagrangian optimization theory and the Lagrangian dual in more general terms. We then apply this theory to derive support vector machines. We conclude the chapter by looking at actual support vector machine implementations in both WEKA and R.

7.1 THE LAGRANGIAN DUAL

In optimization theory, deriving the dual of an optimization problem often yields new insights into the optimization problem at hand. These new insights can lead to new techniques for solving the optimization problem or, as we will see in the case of support vector machines, can lead to entirely new classes of optimization algorithms. A particularly convenient technique to derive the dual of an optimization problem is the *Lagrangian dual*.

Assume that we have an optimization problem of the form

$$\min_{\overline{x}} \phi(\overline{x}), \tag{7.1}$$

such that

$$g_i(\overline{x}) \geq 0 \tag{7.2}$$

for all $\overline{x} \in \mathbb{R}^n$ with $i = 1, \ldots, l$. Here we assume that ϕ is a convex objective function and we also assume that the constraints g_i are linear. As before, linear constraints are constraints that form lines, planes, or hyperplanes in $\mathbb{R}^n$. This formulation of an optimization problem is identical to our original formulation (6.1) if we take the constraints to be $g_i(\overline{x}) = h_i(\overline{x}) - c_i$. We often refer to this formulation as the *primal optimization problem*.

We can now construct a new optimization problem, called the *Lagrangian optimization problem*, based on our primal problem:

$$\max_{\overline{\alpha}} \min_{\overline{x}} L(\overline{\alpha}, \overline{x}) = \max_{\overline{\alpha}} \min_{\overline{x}} \left(\phi(\overline{x}) - \sum_{i=1}^{l} \alpha_i g_i(\overline{x}) \right), \tag{7.3}$$

such that

$$\alpha_i \geq 0 \tag{7.4}$$

for $i = 1, \ldots, l$ and $\overline{x} \in \mathbb{R}^n$. The new objective function $L(\overline{\alpha}, \overline{x})$ is called the *Lagrangian* and incorporates the original objective function ϕ together with a linear combination of the constraints g_i. The values $\alpha_1, \ldots, \alpha_l$ are called the *Lagrangian multipliers*, and when convenient we write them as the vector

$$\overline{\alpha} = (\alpha_1, \alpha_2, \ldots, \alpha_l). \tag{7.5}$$

We have exactly one Lagrangian multiplier α_i for each constraint g_i. We call $\overline{x}$ the *primal variable* and $\overline{\alpha}$ the *dual variable*.

This newly derived optimization problem has the unusual feature of two nested optimization operators with opposing optimization objectives. One way to view this is that each optimization operator returns a partially evaluated function to be optimized by the other optimization operator. Assume that we fix the vector $\overline{x}$ to the value $\overline{x}^*$; then the optimization problem becomes the maximization problem

$$\max_{\overline{\alpha}} L(\overline{\alpha}, \overline{x}^*) = \max_{\overline{\alpha}} \left(\phi(\overline{x}^*) - \sum_{i=1}^{l} \alpha_i g_i(\overline{x}^*) \right). \tag{7.6}$$

Conversely, if we fix $\overline{\alpha}$ to the value $\overline{\alpha}^*$, we obtain the minimization problem

$$\min_{\overline{x}} L(\overline{\alpha}^*, \overline{x}) = \min_{\overline{x}} \left(\phi(\overline{x}) - \sum_{i=1}^{l} \alpha_i^* g_i(\overline{x}) \right). \tag{7.7}$$

Solutions to the Lagrangian optimization (7.3) are points that both maximize the function $L(\overline{\alpha}, \overline{x})$ with respect to the dual variable $\overline{\alpha}$ and minimize it with respect to the primal variable $\overline{x}$. This implies that the solutions are *saddle points* on the graph of the function $L(\overline{\alpha}, \overline{x})$. Since we assume that the primal objective function $\phi(\overline{x})$ is convex and the constraints $g_i(\overline{x})$ are linear, we have a unique saddle point. Because the saddle point represents a solution, L will be minimal with respect to $\overline{x}$ and the partial derivative of L with respect to $\overline{x}$ at this point has to be zero:

$$\frac{\partial L}{\partial \overline{x}} = \overline{0}. \tag{7.8}$$

Let $\overline{x}^*$ be the value of $\overline{x}$ at the saddle point of L. Then evaluating the partial derivative of L with respect to $\overline{x}$ at that point gives us the identity

$$\frac{\partial L}{\partial \overline{x}}(\overline{\alpha}, \overline{x}^*) = \overline{0}. \tag{7.9}$$

Here the point $\overline{x}^*$ represents an optimum of L with respect to $\overline{x}$.

One of the interesting, and for us crucial, properties of Lagrangian optimization is that under certain conditions a solution to the Lagrangian is also a solution to our primal optimization problem. To see this, let $\overline{\alpha}^*$ and $\overline{x}^*$ be a solution to the

Lagrangian such that

$$\max_{\overline{\alpha}} \min_{\overline{x}} L(\overline{\alpha}, \overline{x}) = L(\overline{\alpha}^*, \overline{x}^*) = \phi(\overline{x}^*) - \sum_{i=1}^{l} \alpha_i^* g_i(\overline{x}^*). \qquad (7.10)$$

Then $\overline{x}^*$ is a solution to the primal objective function if and only if the following conditions hold:

$$\frac{\partial L}{\partial \overline{x}}(\overline{\alpha}^*, \overline{x}^*) = \overline{0}, \qquad (7.11)$$

$$\alpha_i^* g_i(\overline{x}^*) = 0, \qquad (7.12)$$

$$g_i(\overline{x}^*) \geq 0, \qquad (7.13)$$

$$\alpha_i^* \geq 0 \qquad (7.14)$$

for $i = 1, \ldots, l$. The most interesting of these conditions is perhaps equation (7.12), which states that each constraint g_i evaluated at $\overline{x}^*$ and multiplied by its corresponding Lagrangian multiplier α_i^* has to result in a value zero. That this is necessarily so can easily be seen from equation (7.10). Here the term $\sum_{i=1}^{l} \alpha_i^* g_i(\overline{x}^*)$ has to vanish so that $L(\overline{\alpha}^*, \overline{x}^*) = \phi(\overline{x}^*)$. The remaining conditions are straightforward. Equation (7.11) ensures that the value $\overline{x}^*$ lies on the saddle point, and equations (7.13) and (7.14) are the original constraints of the primal and Lagrangian optimization problems, respectively, and ensure that the points $\overline{\alpha}^*$ and $\overline{x}^*$ lie in the respective feasible regions. These conditions are collectively referred to as the *Karush–Kuhn–Tucker conditions* (KKT conditions). Because of its singular importance, equation (7.12) is often referred to as the *KKT complementarity condition*.

Solving a Lagrangian optimization problem where the primal objective function is convex can be simplified by taking advantage of the fact that the optimum $\overline{x}^*$ has to lie on the unique saddle point of the Lagrangian. Therefore, solving equation (7.9) for $\overline{x}^*$ allows us to construct an expression that will enable us to reformulate our original optimization problem in terms of its dual variable only, $L(\overline{\alpha}, \overline{x}^*) = \phi'(\overline{\alpha})$, and we can find the optimum with respect to the dual variable as the Lagrangian optimization,

$$\max_{\overline{\alpha}} \phi'(\overline{\alpha}), \qquad (7.15)$$

subject to

$$\alpha_i \geq 0 \qquad (7.16)$$

for $i = 1, \ldots, l$. We call the function ϕ' the *Lagrangian dual* (sometimes also called the Wolfe dual). This means that we can solve our primal optimization problem using the Lagrangian dual,

$$\max_{\overline{\alpha}} \phi'(\overline{\alpha}) = \phi'(\overline{\alpha}^*) = L(\overline{\alpha}^*, \overline{x}^*) = \phi(\overline{x}^*), \qquad (7.17)$$

where $\overline{x}^*$ and $\overline{\alpha}^*$ have to satisfy the KKT conditions.

Before moving on, let us illustrate these concepts by working through an example where we start with a primal optimization problem that we convert to its Lagrangian and then solve via the Lagrangian dual. Consider the convex optimization problem

$$\min \phi(x) = \min \tfrac{1}{2}x^2, \qquad (7.18)$$

subject to the linear constraint

$$g(x) = x - 2 \geq 0, \qquad (7.19)$$

with $x \in \mathbb{R}$. Here the standard technique of finding the minimum by taking the derivative of ϕ with respect to x and setting it to zero,

$$\frac{d\phi}{dx} = 0, \qquad (7.20)$$

fails because the value $x = 0$ that gives rise to the minimum is not part of the feasible region since it does not satisfy the constraint $x - 2 \geq 0$. Therefore, we need to find a value of x that lies in the feasible region and that minimizes the objective function. In this simple optimization problem it is easy to see that the value of x that satisfies the constraint and that minimizes the objective function is $x = 2$, as illustrated in Figure 7.1. Here the gray region represents all points (x, y) that satisfy the constraint $x - 2 \geq 0$; therefore, only the part of the objective function ϕ that falls into this region can be considered for optimization.

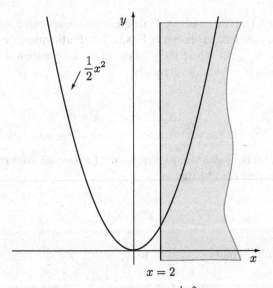

FIGURE 7.1 Plot of the objective function $\phi(x) = \tfrac{1}{2}x^2$. The gray area represents all the points (x, y) that satisfy the constraint $x - 2 \geq 0$.

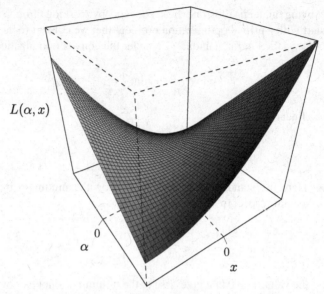

FIGURE 7.2 Graph of the Lagrangian $L(\alpha, x) = 1/2\, x^2 - \alpha(x - 2)$.

To solve this optimization problem using the Lagrangian dual, we first construct the Lagrangian using equation (7.3):

$$L(\alpha, x) = \tfrac{1}{2}x^2 - \alpha(x - 2). \tag{7.21}$$

As expected for a convex objective function, we have a unique saddle point in the graph of the Lagrangian, as shown in Figure 7.2. Furthermore, we know that this saddle point has to occur where the gradient of the Lagrangian with respect to the variable x is equal to zero; more precisely,

$$\frac{\partial L}{\partial x}(\alpha, x^*) = x^* - \alpha = 0. \tag{7.22}$$

Here x^* represents the value that minimizes the Lagrangian with respect to x at the saddle point. Solving for x^* gives us

$$x^* = \alpha. \tag{7.23}$$

Now, plugging (7.23) into (7.21) gives us

$$L(\alpha, x^*) = \tfrac{1}{2}\alpha^2 - \alpha^2 + 2\alpha = 2\alpha - \tfrac{1}{2}\alpha^2. \tag{7.24}$$

This Lagrangian no longer has any dependencies on the variable x, and we can therefore rewrite it as the Lagrangian dual optimization with $\phi'(\alpha) = L(\alpha, x^*)$,

$$\max_{\alpha} \phi'(\alpha) = \max_{\alpha} \left(2\alpha - \tfrac{1}{2}\alpha^2 \right), \tag{7.25}$$

subject to

$$\alpha \geq 0. \tag{7.26}$$

Now, we know that $L(\alpha, x)$ has a unique saddle point, and this implies that the function $\phi'(\alpha) = L(\alpha, x^*)$ has a unique maximum. This unique maximum has to occur where the slope of the Lagrangian dual is equal to zero. We can compute the value α^* at that unique maximum as

$$\frac{d\phi'}{d\alpha}(\alpha^*) = 2 - \alpha^* = 0. \tag{7.27}$$

Solving for α^* gives us the solution to the Lagrangian dual $\alpha^* = 2$. Then, according to (7.23), we have $x^* = \alpha^* = 2$. This solution coincides with the solution that we gleaned from Figure 7.1.

We can formally show that the solution to the primal optimization problem and to the Lagrangian dual must coincide by showing that the KKT complementarity condition (7.12) is satisfied:

$$\alpha^* g(x^*) = \alpha^*(x^* - 2) = 2(2 - 2) = 0.$$

7.2 DUAL MAXIMUM-MARGIN OPTIMIZATION

As we noted in the introduction to this chapter, support vector machines can be seen as the dual to maximum-margin classifiers. Here we derive this dual by applying the technique of the Lagrangian dual to maximum-margin classifiers. Assume that we are given a linearly separable training set of the form

$$D = \{(\overline{x}_1, y_1), (\overline{x}_2, y_2), \ldots, (\overline{x}_l, y_l)\} \subseteq \mathbb{R}^n \times \{+1, -1\}. \tag{7.28}$$

Recall our maximum-margin optimization problem from Proposition 6.1, with the constraints rewritten in a form appropriate for Lagrangian optimization,

$$\min_{\overline{w}, b} \phi(\overline{w}, b) = \min_{\overline{w}, b} \tfrac{1}{2} \overline{w} \bullet \overline{w}, \tag{7.29}$$

subject to the constraints

$$g_i(\overline{w}, b) = y_i(\overline{w} \bullet \overline{x}_i - b) - 1 \geq 0 \tag{7.30}$$

for $i = 1, \ldots, l$. We construct the corresponding Lagrangian as

$$L(\overline{\alpha}, \overline{w}, b) = \phi(\overline{w}, b) - \sum_{i=1}^{l} \alpha_i \, g_i(\overline{w}, b)$$

$$= \frac{1}{2} \overline{w} \bullet \overline{w} - \sum_{i=1}^{l} \alpha_i (y_i(\overline{w} \bullet \overline{x}_i - b) - 1)$$

$$= \frac{1}{2} \overline{w} \bullet \overline{w} - \sum_{i=1}^{l} \alpha_i \, y_i \overline{w} \bullet \overline{x}_i + b \sum_{i=1}^{l} \alpha_i \, y_i + \sum_{i=1}^{l} \alpha_i. \tag{7.31}$$

This gives us the Lagrangian optimization problem for maximum-margin classifiers,

$$\max_{\overline{\alpha}} \min_{\overline{w}, b} L(\overline{\alpha}, \overline{w}, b), \tag{7.32}$$

subject to

$$\alpha_i \geq 0 \tag{7.33}$$

for $i = 1, \ldots, l$. Now, let $\overline{\alpha}^*$, $\overline{w}^*$, and b^* be a solution to the Lagrangian optimization problem such that

$$\max_{\overline{\alpha}} \min_{\overline{w}, b} L(\overline{\alpha}, \overline{w}, b) = L(\overline{\alpha}^*, \overline{w}^*, b^*). \tag{7.34}$$

Then, since ϕ is convex and the constraints g_i are linear, the solution $\overline{\alpha}^*$, $\overline{w}^*$, and b^* will satisfy the following KKT conditions:

$$\frac{\partial L}{\partial \overline{w}}(\overline{\alpha}^*, \overline{w}^*, b^*) = \overline{0}, \tag{7.35}$$

$$\frac{\partial L}{\partial b}(\overline{\alpha}^*, \overline{w}^*, b^*) = 0, \tag{7.36}$$

$$\alpha_i^* (y_i(\overline{w}^* \bullet \overline{x}_i - b^*) - 1) = 0, \tag{7.37}$$

$$y_i(\overline{w}^* \bullet \overline{x}_i - b^*) - 1 \geq 0, \tag{7.38}$$

$$\alpha_i^* \geq 0 \tag{7.39}$$

for $i = 1, \ldots, l$. Equations (7.35) and (7.36) assure that $\overline{w}^*$ and b^* lie on the saddle point of the Lagrangian. The complementarity condition (7.37) implies that $\overline{w}^*$ and b^* are also solutions for our primal optimization problem,

$$\max_{\overline{\alpha}} \min_{\overline{w}, b} L(\overline{\alpha}, \overline{w}, b) = L(\overline{\alpha}^*, \overline{w}^*, b^*) = \phi(\overline{w}^*, b^*). \tag{7.40}$$

That is, we can use Lagrangian optimization to compute our maximum margin. And finally, equations (7.38) and (7.39) make sure that the solution falls into the respective feasible regions.

To solve the Lagrangian optimization, we construct the Lagrangian dual. As a first step we construct the points $\overline{w}^*$ and b^*. We know that these points have to lie on the saddle point of the Lagrangian. Applying the first KKT condition (7.35), we take the partial derivative of our Lagrangian L with respect to the primal variable $\overline{w}$, evaluate it at the saddle point $\overline{w}^*$, and set it to zero:

$$\frac{\partial L}{\partial \overline{w}}(\overline{\alpha}, \overline{w}^*, b) = \overline{w}^* - \sum_{i=1}^{l} \alpha_i y_i \overline{x}_i = \overline{0}. \tag{7.41}$$

It follows that

$$\overline{w}^* = \sum_{i=1}^{l} \alpha_i y_i \overline{x}_i. \tag{7.42}$$

Then, using the second KKT condition (7.36), we take the partial derivative of L with respect to the primal variable b, evaluate it at the saddle point b^*, and set it to zero:

$$\frac{\partial L}{\partial b}(\overline{\alpha}, \overline{w}, b^*) = \sum_{i=1}^{l} \alpha_i y_i = 0. \tag{7.43}$$

Interestingly, the partial derivative of L with respect to b does not yield an expression for b^* but instead, provides us with the constraint that at the saddle point b^* the expression $\sum_{i=1}^{l} \alpha_i y_i = 0$ has to hold. However, we can recover a value for b^* from the structure of our training data D and the fact that we know the optimal rotation $\overline{w}^*$ of our decision surface. Consider that in a maximum-margin classifier the supporting hyperplane for the $+1$ class has to go through some point $\overline{x}_p$, $+1$ closest to the class boundary (see Figure 6.5). This allows us to compute the offset b^+ of the supporting hyperplane for class $+1$ as

$$b^+ = \overline{w}^* \bullet \overline{x}_p. \tag{7.44}$$

We can be even more specific by recognizing that for a given rotation $\overline{w}^*$, the point $\overline{x}_p$ closest to the class boundary will produce the smallest offset; that is, we can compute b^+ as an optimization as follows:

$$b^+ = \min\{\overline{w}^* \bullet \overline{x} \mid (\overline{x}, y) \in D \text{ with } y = +1\}. \tag{7.45}$$

Applying similar reasoning to the class -1 gives us the equation

$$b^- = \max\{\overline{w}^* \bullet \overline{x} \mid (\overline{x}, y) \in D \text{ with } y = -1\}. \tag{7.46}$$

Now, in maximum-margin classifiers the decision surface is located right between the two supporting hyperplanes. This insight allows us to compute b^* as

$$b^* = \frac{b^+ + b^-}{2}. \tag{7.47}$$

It is noteworthy that both $\overline{w}^*$ and b^* can be expressed in terms of the dual variable $\overline{\alpha}$ by repeated use of equation (7.42). This means that our optimal decision surface $\overline{w}^* \bullet \overline{x} = b^*$ is completely determined by the value of $\overline{\alpha}$, and finding a solution $\overline{\alpha}^*$ will give us our decision surface. We find the solution $\overline{\alpha}^*$ by solving the Lagrangian dual.

We are now ready to construct our Lagrangian dual. Substituting (7.42) into (7.31) and applying the constraint (7.43) gives us

$$\phi'(\overline{\alpha}) = L(\overline{\alpha}, \overline{w}^*, b^*) = \sum_{i=1}^{l} \alpha_i - \frac{1}{2} \sum_{i=1}^{l} \sum_{j=1}^{l} \alpha_i \alpha_j y_i y_j \overline{x}_i \bullet \overline{x}_j. \tag{7.48}$$

This gives rise to the Lagrangian dual optimization for maximum-margin classifiers stated in the following proposition.

Proposition 7.1 (Maximum-Margin Lagrangian Dual) *Given the maximum-margin optimization as in Proposition 6.1, the Lagrangian dual optimization for maximum-margin classifiers is*

$$\max_{\overline{\alpha}} \phi'(\overline{\alpha}) = \max_{\overline{\alpha}} \left(\sum_{i=1}^{l} \alpha_i - \frac{1}{2} \sum_{i=1}^{l} \sum_{j=1}^{l} \alpha_i \alpha_j y_i y_j \overline{x}_i \bullet \overline{x}_j \right), \tag{7.49}$$

subject to the constraints

$$\sum_{i=1}^{l} \alpha_i y_i = 0, \tag{7.50}$$

$$\alpha_i \geq 0 \tag{7.51}$$

with $i = 1, \ldots, l$.

Given a solution $\overline{\alpha}^*$ to the Lagrangian dual optimization, it is interesting to look at the KKT complementarity condition (7.37) in more detail. This equation can be satisfied for each $i = 1, \ldots, l$ only if either $\alpha_i^* = 0$ or $y_i(\overline{w}^* \bullet \overline{x}_i - b^*) - 1 = 0$. Consider the case where we have $\alpha_j^* > 0$ for some point $(\overline{x}_j, y_j) \in D$. This means that to satisfy the complementarity condition we have $y_j(\overline{w}^* \bullet \overline{x}_j - b^*) - 1 = 0$, or

$$\overline{w}^* \bullet \overline{x}_j = b^* + 1 \quad \text{if } y_j = +1, \tag{7.52}$$

$$\overline{w}^* \bullet \overline{x}_j = b^* - 1 \quad \text{if } y_j = -1. \tag{7.53}$$

But these two equations are the equations of the supporting hyperplanes for the optimal decision surface $\overline{w}^* \bullet \overline{x} = b^*$ [see equations (6.11) and (6.12) with $k = 1$]. That means that the training set point $(\overline{x}_j, y_j)$ with a nonzero Lagrangian multiplier $\alpha_j^* > 0$ lies on one of the two supporting hyperplanes, depending on its label y_j. This point represents a constraint on the margin in that the supporting hyperplanes cannot be moved beyond it. We call points with nonzero Lagrangian multipliers *support vectors*, and a close inspection of equations (7.42) and (7.47) reveals that only support vectors contribute to the solution of the dual maximum-margin optimization. Now let $\alpha_j^* = 0$ for some point $(\overline{x}_j, y_j) \in D$. That is, the point $\overline{x}_j$ is a point that does not lie in the vicinity of the class boundary because we have $y_j(\overline{w}^* \bullet \overline{x}_j - b^*) - 1 > 0$, or

$$\overline{w}^* \bullet \overline{x}_j > b^* + 1 \quad \text{if } y_j = +1, \tag{7.54}$$

$$\overline{w}^* \bullet \overline{x}_j < b^* - 1 \quad \text{if } y_j = -1. \tag{7.55}$$

This implies that points with zero-valued Lagrangian multipliers do not constrain the size of the margin.

We can relate this to our primal maximum-margin algorithm. Recall that the primal maximum-margin optimization problem finds the respective supporting hyperplanes that are farthest apart, that is, that create the maximum margin between them. Also recall that the points in the training set that limit the size of the margin were called support vectors. We can now make the following statement:

> The primal maximum-margin optimization computes the supporting hyperplanes whose margin is limited by support vectors. The dual maximum-margin optimization computes the support vectors that limit the size of the margin of the supporting hyperplanes.

This is illustrated in Figure 6.3. Here the primal optimization computes the two supporting hyperplanes that are limited by the support vectors, and the dual optimization computes the support vectors that limit the margin of the supporting hyperplanes.

The insight that only support vectors contribute to our dual solution allows us to express the value for b^* in a more elegant way. Rather than searching for the points from each class that lie closest to the decision surface as we did above, we already know which training set points constitute the constraints on the supporting hyperplanes: the points with nonzero Lagrangian multipliers. If we pick a support vector from our training set, say $(\overline{x}_{sv^+}, y_{sv^+})$ with $y_{sv^+} = +1$, then according to (7.52) we can compute b^* as

$$b^* = \overline{w}^* \bullet \overline{x}_{sv^+} - 1 = \sum_{i=1}^{l} \alpha_i^* y_i \overline{x}_i \bullet \overline{x}_{sv^+} - 1, \tag{7.56}$$

where the second identity is due to the expansion of $\overline{w}^*$ using (7.42).

7.2.1 The Dual Decision Function

Recall that decision functions in linear classifiers are based on linear decision surfaces, and the decision function itself returns a $+1$ label for a point that lies above the decision surface and a -1 label for a point that lies below the decision surface. Let $\overline{\alpha}^*$, $\overline{w}^*$, and b^* be a solution to our Lagrangian optimization; then the optimal decision surface is defined as

$$\overline{w}^* \bullet \overline{x} = b^*. \qquad (7.57)$$

This gives us the following maximum-margin decision function:

$$\hat{f}(\overline{x}) = \text{sgn}(\overline{w}^* \bullet \overline{x} - b^*). \qquad (7.58)$$

If we expand $\overline{w}^*$ and b^* using equations (7.42) and (7.56), respectively, our decision function becomes

$$\hat{f}(\overline{x}) = \text{sgn}\left(\sum_{i=1}^{l} \alpha_i^* y_i \overline{x}_i \bullet \overline{x} - \sum_{i=1}^{l} \alpha_i^* y_i \overline{x}_i \bullet \overline{x}_{sv^+} + 1 \right). \qquad (7.59)$$

That is, the dual maximum-margin classifier is determined completely by the support vectors, or given our discussion above, the dual maximum-margin classifier is determined completely by the points that are the constraints on the margin of the supporting hyperplanes. Because of this characteristic, we also call the decision function of a dual maximum-margin classifier a *support vector machine*. Furthermore, it is considered a linear support vector machine since it is based on a linear decision surface.

7.3 LINEAR SUPPORT VECTOR MACHINES

To see what we have accomplished up to this point, let us set the stage by restating our classification problem from Chapter 1 and then put support vector machines into this context. Given:

- A dot product space $\mathbb{R}^n$ as our data universe with points $\overline{x} \in \mathbb{R}^n$
- Some target function $f : \mathbb{R}^n \to \{+1, -1\}$
- A labeled, linearly separable training set

$$D = \{(\overline{x}_1, y_1), (\overline{x}_2, y_2), \ldots, (\overline{x}_l, y_l)\} \subseteq \mathbb{R}^n \times \{+1, -1\},$$

where $y_i = f(\overline{x}_i)$

compute a model $\hat{f} : \mathbb{R}^n \to \{+1, -1\}$ using D such that

$$\hat{f}(\overline{x}) \cong f(\overline{x}) \qquad (7.60)$$

for all $\overline{x} \in \mathbb{R}^n$. Here we take as our model the linear support vector machine from equation (7.59),

$$\hat{f}(\overline{x}) = \mathrm{sgn}\left(\sum_{i=1}^{l} \alpha_i^* y_i \overline{x}_i \bullet \overline{x} - \sum_{i=1}^{l} \alpha_i^* y_i \overline{x}_i \bullet \overline{x}_{sv^+} + 1\right), \qquad (7.61)$$

where points $(\overline{x}_i, y_i) \in D$ are support vectors if their corresponding Lagrangian multipliers are nonzero, $\alpha_i^* > 0$. We pick one support vector from the set of available support vectors,

$$(\overline{x}_{sv^+}, +1) \in \{(\overline{x}_i, +1) \mid (\overline{x}_i, +1) \in D \text{ and } \alpha_i^* > 0\}, \qquad (7.62)$$

in order to calculate the dual offset term. We train our support vector models with the Lagrangian dual optimization for maximum-margin classifiers given in Proposition 7.1,

$$\overline{\alpha}^* = \underset{\overline{\alpha}}{\mathrm{argmax}} \left(\sum_{i=1}^{l} \alpha_i - \frac{1}{2} \sum_{i=1}^{l} \sum_{j=1}^{l} \alpha_i \alpha_j y_i y_j \overline{x}_i \bullet \overline{x}_j\right), \qquad (7.63)$$

subject to the constraints

$$\sum_{i=1}^{l} \alpha_i y_i = 0, \qquad (7.64)$$

$$\alpha_i \geq 0, \qquad (7.65)$$

where $i = 1, \ldots, l$. This means that we can solve our classification problem using linear support vector machines as long as the training data are linearly separable.

7.4 NONLINEAR SUPPORT VECTOR MACHINES

Very few data sets in the real world are linearly separable. What makes support vector machines so remarkable is that the basic linear framework is easily extended to the case where the data set is not linearly separable. The fundamental idea behind this extension is to transform the input space where the data set is not linearly separable into a higher-dimensional space called a *feature space*, where the data are linearly separable. Remarkably, if we choose these transformations carefully, all the computations associated with the feature space can be performed in the input space. That is, even though we are transforming our input space so that the data become linearly separable, we do not have to pay the computational cost for these transformations. The functions associated with these transformations are called *kernel functions*, and the process of using these functions to move from a linear to a nonlinear support vector machine is called the *kernel trick*.

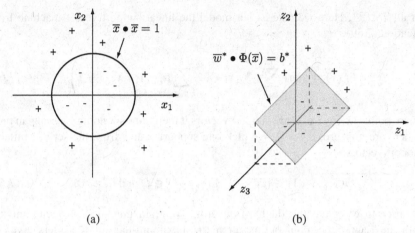

(a)   (b)

FIGURE 7.3 Mapping a nonlinear data set (a) with $\overline{x} = (x_1, x_2) \in \mathbb{R}^2$ into a feature space (b) with $\overline{z} = (z_1, z_2, z_3) \in \mathbb{R}^3$, using the transform $\Phi : \mathbb{R}^2 \to \mathbb{R}^3$ defined in the text.

Consider the following example. Here our data set in Figure 7.3a is embedded in the two-dimensional dot product space $\mathbb{R}^2$. Clearly, there is no linear decision surface of the form

$$\overline{w} \bullet \overline{x} = b \tag{7.66}$$

that would separate the two classes without any errors. In contrast, the nonlinear decision surface

$$\overline{x} \bullet \overline{x} = 1 \tag{7.67}$$

with $\overline{x} \in \mathbb{R}^2$ does separate the data set, as shown in Figure 7.3a. Now, instead of constructing a decision function that relies on a decision surface in the input space, consider a decision function that first maps our points $\overline{x} \in \mathbb{R}^2$ into some higher-dimensional dot product space, say $\mathbb{R}^3$, and then uses a decision surface in this higher-dimensional space to compute the labels,

$$\hat{f}(\overline{x}) = \text{sgn}(\overline{w} \bullet \Phi(\overline{x}) - b), \tag{7.68}$$

where the mapping from input space to feature space $\Phi : \mathbb{R}^2 \to \mathbb{R}^3$ is defined as

$$\Phi(\overline{x}) = \Phi(x_1, x_2) = (x_1^2, x_2^2, \sqrt{2}x_1x_2) = (z_1, z_2, z_3) = \overline{z}, \tag{7.69}$$

with $\overline{x} \in \mathbb{R}^2$ and $\overline{z} \in \mathbb{R}^3$. Notice that Φ maps points from a two-dimensional space into a three-dimensional space. With this mapping any point on the nonlinear decision surface (7.67) in input space is mapped onto a plane in feature space of the form

$$\overline{w}^* \bullet \Phi(\overline{x}) = b^*, \tag{7.70}$$

with $\overline{w}^* = (w_1^*, w_2^*, w_3^*) = (1, 1, 0)$ and $b^* = 1$. Consider the point $\overline{q} = (1, 0)$ in input space. The point clearly lies on the nonlinear decision surface (7.67), $\overline{q} \bullet \overline{q} = (1, 0) \bullet (1, 0) = 1^2 + 0^2 = 1$. We now show that this point also lies on the plane in feature space:

$$
\begin{aligned}
\overline{w}^* \bullet \Phi(\overline{q}) &= (1, 1, 0) \bullet (1^2, 0^2, \sqrt{2} \times 1 \times 0) \\
&= (1, 1, 0) \bullet (1, 0, 0) \\
&= 1^2 + 1 \times 0 + 0 \times 0 \\
&= 1 \\
&= b^*.
\end{aligned}
$$

In addition, any points in the input space labeled $+1$ will be mapped to points above this plane in feature space, and any points labeled -1 in input space will be mapped to points below the plane. The fact that the plane (7.70) separates the classes in feature space implies that the plane is a linear decision surface. This is illustrated in Figure 7.3b. This means that the mapping Φ transforms our nonlinear decision problem in the input space into a linear decision problem in the feature space.[1]

Given our decision surface (7.70) in feature space, we can construct our decision function as

$$\hat{f}(\overline{x}) = \text{sgn}\left(\overline{w}^* \bullet \Phi(\overline{x}) - b^*\right). \tag{7.71}$$

As desired, given any point in our input space $\overline{x} \in \mathbb{R}^2$, this decision function first maps this to a point in feature space $\overline{z} = \Phi(\overline{x}) \in \mathbb{R}^3$ and then uses the linear decision surface in feature space to compute the label.

It is revealing to study the structure of this decision function in more detail. We do this by expanding the function using the identities in equation (7.69):

$$
\begin{aligned}
\hat{f}(\overline{x}) &= \text{sgn}\left(\overline{w}^* \bullet \Phi(\overline{x}) - b^*\right) \\
&= \text{sgn}\left(w_1^* x_1^2 + w_2^* x_2^2 + w_3^* \sqrt{2} x_1 x_2 - b^*\right) \\
&= \text{sgn}\left(\overline{w}^* \bullet \overline{z} - b^*\right) \\
&= \text{sgn}\left(\sum_{i=1}^{3} w_i^* z_i - b^*\right). \tag{7.72}
\end{aligned}
$$

---

[1]Astute readers might discover that at this level of discussion the third dimension is strictly not necessary. However, it is necessary from a more technical point of view because to construct kernels you must have the third dimension.

This shows that the complexity of the decision function is directly related to the number of dimensions in the feature space. As we consider more complex nonlinear decision surfaces in the input space, we would expect that we need higher-and higher-dimensional feature spaces to be able to continue to construct linear decision surfaces. As a consequence, the expression for the corresponding decision functions,

$$\hat{f}(\overline{x}) = \text{sgn}\left(\sum_{i=1}^{d} w_i z_i - b\right),\tag{7.73}$$

will increase in complexity proportional to the number of dimensions d in the feature space.

7.4.1 The Kernel Trick

Now, consider using the dual representation of the normal vector $\overline{w}^*$ of our decision function in (7.71),

$$\overline{w}^* = \sum_{i=1}^{l} \alpha_i^* y_i \Phi(\overline{x}_i)\tag{7.74}$$

with $\Phi : \mathbb{R}^2 \to \mathbb{R}^3$ as defined in (7.69) and where l denotes the number of training points in our input space. We assume that the values α_i^* represent the appropriate Lagrangian multipliers for this dual representation. Notice that the transformation of the training points $\Phi(\overline{x}_i)$ is necessary since $\overline{w}^*$ is a normal vector in the feature space. Plugging this dual representation into our decision function gives us

$$\hat{f}(\overline{x}) = \text{sgn}\left(\overline{w}^* \bullet \Phi(\overline{x}) - b^*\right)$$
$$= \text{sgn}\left(\sum_{i=1}^{l} \alpha_i^* y_i \Phi(\overline{x}_i) \bullet \Phi(\overline{x}) - b^*\right).\tag{7.75}$$

Now something remarkable happens. If we simplify equation (7.75), we would expect to see something complex, akin to equation (7.72); however, what we obtain using the calculations in Table 7.1 is

$$\hat{f}(\overline{x}) = \text{sgn}\left(\sum_{i=1}^{l} \alpha_i^* y_i \Phi(\overline{x}_i) \bullet \Phi(\overline{x}) - b^*\right)$$
$$= \text{sgn}\left(\sum_{i=1}^{l} \alpha_i^* y_i (\overline{x}_i \bullet \overline{x})^2 - b^*\right).\tag{7.76}$$

That is, instead of obtaining a function whose complexity is proportional to the dimensions of the feature space, we obtain an expression whose complexity is proportional to the number of support vectors. Furthermore, we have an expression that computes

TABLE 7.1   Calculation of the Dot Product

Given the mapping $\Phi : \mathbb{R}^2 \to \mathbb{R}^3$ defined as $\Phi(\overline{x}) = (x_1^2, x_2^2, \sqrt{2}\,x_1 x_2)$, the value of the dot product $\Phi(\overline{x}) \bullet \Phi(\overline{y})$ with $\overline{x}, \overline{y} \in \mathbb{R}^2$ can be computed in the input space $\mathbb{R}^2$:

$$
\begin{aligned}
\Phi(\overline{x}) \bullet \Phi(\overline{y}) &= (x_1^2, x_2^2, \sqrt{2}x_1 x_2) \bullet (y_1^2, y_2^2, \sqrt{2}y_1 y_2) \\
&= x_1^2 y_1^2 + x_2^2 y_2^2 + 2 x_1 x_2 y_1 y_2 \\
&= (x_1 y_1 + x_2 y_2)(x_1 y_1 + x_2 y_2) \\
&= (\overline{x} \bullet \overline{y})(\overline{x} \bullet \overline{y}) \\
&= (\overline{x} \bullet \overline{y})^2.
\end{aligned}
$$

the value of the feature space dot product in the input space, making it unnecessary to fully evaluate the transformation Φ. This is possible precisely because we happened to pick the transform Φ in a very clever way.[2]

Let us take a closer look at these transforms. Given an appropriate mapping $\Phi : \mathbb{R}^n \to \mathbb{R}^m$ with $m \geq n$, functions of the form

$$
k(\overline{x}, \overline{y}) = \Phi(\overline{x}) \bullet \Phi(\overline{y}), \tag{7.77}
$$

where $\overline{x}, \overline{y} \in \mathbb{R}^n$, are called *kernels* or *kernel functions*. Kernel functions evaluate a dot product in feature space, and the defining characteristic of a kernel is that the value of this dot product is computed in the input space.

We can now rewrite our decision function given in equation (7.75) in terms of kernel functions,

$$
\hat{f}(\overline{x}) = \text{sgn}\left(\sum_{i=1}^{n} \alpha_i^* y_i k(\overline{x}_i, \overline{x}) - b^* \right). \tag{7.78}
$$

This is known as the *kernel trick*; that is, using any appropriate kernel function we can take advantage of mappings into feature spaces without having to pay the price of actually having to compute the explicit mappings, since the computations in the feature space always simplify to computations in the input space. By selecting the kernel function judiciously, we can control the complexity of this model. The trick lies in finding the appropriate kernel in order to construct a model for a particular data set.

We have already encountered two kernels. For the first kernel let $\Phi : \mathbb{R}^n \to \mathbb{R}^n$ be the identity function on $\mathbb{R}^n$; then

$$
k(\overline{x}, \overline{y}) = \Phi(\overline{x}) \bullet \Phi(\overline{y}) = \overline{x} \bullet \overline{y}, \tag{7.79}
$$

where $\overline{x}, \overline{y} \in \mathbb{R}^n$. This is called the *linear kernel*, and here the feature space is simply the same as the input space. You might wonder why this is useful, but we will see

---

[2]The astute reader might now see why the third dimension in Φ was necessary.

TABLE 7.2   Standard Kernels with Their Free Parameters

Kernel Name	Kernel Function[a]	Free Parameters
Linear kernel	$k(\bar{x}, \bar{y}) = \bar{x} \bullet \bar{y}$	none
Homogeneous polynomial kernel	$k(\bar{x}, \bar{y}) = (\bar{x} \bullet \bar{y})^d$	$d \geq 2$
Nonhomogeneous polynomial kernel	$k(\bar{x}, \bar{y}) = (\bar{x} \bullet \bar{y} + c)^d$	$d \geq 2, c > 0$
Gaussian kernel	$k(\bar{x}, \bar{y}) = e^{-(|\bar{x}-\bar{y}|^2/2\sigma^2)}$	$\sigma > 0$

[a] $\bar{x}, \bar{y} \in \mathbb{R}^n$.

later that this kernel is useful for high-dimensional data sets in conjunction with soft-margin classifiers.

The other kernel, of course, is based on our mapping $\Phi : \mathbb{R}^2 \to \mathbb{R}^3$ such that $\Phi(x_1, x_2) = (x_1^2, x_2^2, \sqrt{2}\,x_1 x_2)$, where

$$k(\bar{x}, \bar{y}) = \Phi(\bar{x}) \bullet \Phi(\bar{y}) = (\bar{x} \bullet \bar{y})^2. \qquad (7.80)$$

Here $\bar{x}, \bar{y} \in \mathbb{R}^2$. Called a *homogeneous polynomial kernel of degree 2*, this can easily be extended to input spaces with arbitrary dimensions where $\bar{x}, \bar{y} \in \mathbb{R}^n$. Table 7.2 provides a list of other popular kernel functions.

In our preceding discussions we have focused solely on the dual representation of the normal vector $\bar{w}^*$ of the decision surface. The dual structure of the offset term b^* can also be represented with a kernel,

$$b^* = \bar{w}^* \bullet \Phi(\bar{x}_{sv+}) - 1$$

$$= \sum_{i=1}^{l} \alpha_i^* y_i \Phi(\bar{x}_i) \bullet \Phi(\bar{x}_{sv+}) - 1$$

$$= \sum_{i=1}^{l} \alpha_i^* y_i k(\bar{x}_i, \bar{x}_{sv+}) - 1,$$

and therefore all the aforementioned observations hold for the offset term of the decision surface in feature space as well.

To actually find the support vectors in feature space, we must also apply the kernel trick to our training algorithm for support vector machine models:

$$\bar{\alpha}^* = \underset{\bar{\alpha}}{\operatorname{argmax}} \left(\sum_{i=1}^{l} \alpha_i - \frac{1}{2} \sum_{i=1}^{l} \sum_{j=1}^{l} \alpha_i \alpha_j y_i y_j k(\bar{x}_i, \bar{x}_j) \right), \qquad (7.81)$$

subject to the constraints

$$\sum_{i=1}^{l} \alpha_i y_i = 0, \qquad (7.82)$$

$$\alpha_i \geq 0, \quad i = 1, \ldots, l. \qquad (7.83)$$

To find our optimal Lagrangian multipliers $\overline{\alpha}^*$, we can now replace the expression $k(\overline{x}_i, \overline{x}_j)$ with any appropriate kernel. Of course, for this to make sense, the kernel used in the training algorithm and the kernel used in the model must be the same. Note that the constraints $\sum_{i=1}^{n} y_i \alpha_i = 0$ and $\alpha_i \geq 0$ for $i = 1, \ldots, l$ are not affected by the kernel trick. These constraints simply have to hold in whatever feature space we are working.

7.4.2 Feature Search

In Section 7.4.1 we saw that we can rewrite our support vector machine model in terms of a kernel function $k(\overline{x}, \overline{y}) = \Phi(\overline{x}) \bullet \Phi(\overline{y})$ with $\overline{x}, \overline{y} \in \mathbb{R}^n$:

$$\hat{f}(\overline{x}) = \text{sgn}\left(\sum_{i=1}^{l} \alpha_i^* y_i k(\overline{x}_i, \overline{x}) - b^* \right). \tag{7.84}$$

Similarly, we can write our training algorithm in terms of a kernel function

$$\overline{\alpha}^* = \underset{\overline{\alpha}}{\text{argmax}} \left(\sum_{i=1}^{l} \alpha_i - \frac{1}{2} \sum_{i=1}^{l} \sum_{j=1}^{l} \alpha_i \alpha_j y_i y_j k(\overline{x}_i, \overline{x}_j) \right), \tag{7.85}$$

subject to the appropriate constraints. We also saw that we are free to change kernels according to the requirements of the classification problem. For example, if our classification problem involves a linearly separable training set, we might consider the linear kernel $k(\overline{x}, \overline{y}) = \overline{x} \bullet \overline{y}$ because a support vector machine algorithm with a linear kernel induces a linear decision surface in input space. We also saw that if our classification problem involves quadratic decision surfaces in input space, we are free to chose a polynomial kernel of degree 2, $k(\overline{x}, \overline{y}) = (\overline{x} \bullet \overline{y})^2$, since it maps quadratic decision surfaces in the input space to linear decision surfaces in the feature space. For more complex decision surfaces in the input space, we might try polynomial kernels of higher degrees or even more complex kernels, such as the Gaussian kernel, to induce linear decision surfaces in some appropriate feature space. The process of selecting a kernel and the associated values of its free parameters, such as the degree d for the polynomial kernel, is called a *feature search*. A feature search is, in general, not trivial and requires some trade-offs in model complexity and model accuracy. Many packages provide tools that automate some aspects of the feature search, and this search is often referred to as a *grid search*. Most support vector machine packages include a set of fairly standard kernels from which to choose. Table 7.2 lists some kernels that appear frequently in support vector machine packages.

7.4.3 A Closer Look at Kernels

In the case of the homogeneous polynomial kernel of degree 2, we saw that if we are clever, we can define a mapping and a feature space so that the identity $\Phi(\overline{x}) \bullet \Phi(\overline{y}) = (\overline{x} \bullet \overline{y})^2$ holds. That is, because we picked Φ in a particular way, we were able to evaluate the feature space dot product in the input space. But what about the more complex kernels such as the Gaussian kernel function? What are the mappings and the feature spaces associated with these types of kernels? Here we show that every kernel has an associated canonical or standard mapping and feature space. The existence of these canonical structures is guaranteed by a set of assumptions on the kernel. One interesting corollary of this is that the mappings and feature spaces associated with kernels are not unique. But this is of no consequence to us, since due to the kernels, we never need explicitly to evaluate the mappings.

The following property for kernels is important because it guarantees that the dot product is defined in feature space. This also characterizes the class of kernels at the core of support vector machines.

Definition 7.1 (Positive-Definite Kernel)   *A function $k : \mathbb{R}^n \times \mathbb{R}^n \to \mathbb{R}$ such that*

$$\sum_{i=1}^{l} \sum_{j=1}^{l} \theta_i \theta_j k(\overline{x}_i, \overline{x}_j) \geq 0 \qquad (7.86)$$

*holds is called a **positive-definite kernel**. Here, $\theta_i, \theta_j \in \mathbb{R}$ and $\overline{x}_1, \ldots, \overline{x}_l$ is a set of points in $\mathbb{R}^n$.*

We need another property of kernels in order to construct our canonical feature spaces. For this we define some new notation: Let $k : \mathbb{R}^n \times \mathbb{R}^n \to \mathbb{R}$ be a kernel; then $k(\cdot, \overline{x})$ is a partially evaluated kernel with $\overline{x} \in \mathbb{R}^n$ and represents a function $\mathbb{R}^n \to \mathbb{R}$.

Theorem 7.1 (Reproducing Kernel Property)   *Let $k : \mathbb{R}^n \times \mathbb{R}^n \to \mathbb{R}^n$ be a positive-definite kernel; then the following property holds:*

$$k(\overline{x}, \overline{y}) = k(\overline{x}, \cdot) \bullet k(\cdot, \overline{y}), \qquad (7.87)$$

with $\overline{x}, \overline{y} \in \mathbb{R}^n$.

In other words, a kernel can be evaluated at points $\overline{x}$ and $\overline{y}$ by taking the dot product of the two partially evaluated kernels at these points. Finally, we need one more identity which will help us in the investigation of the structure of our canonical feature spaces.

Theorem 7.2 (Cauchy–Schwarz Inequality)   *Let $\overline{x}, \overline{y} \in \mathbb{R}^n$; then the Cauchy–Schwarz inequality states that*

$$(\overline{x} \bullet \overline{y})^2 \leq (\overline{x} \bullet \overline{x})(\overline{y} \bullet \overline{y}). \qquad (7.88)$$

We can now show that for every kernel there exists a canonical feature space. That is, for every positive-definite kernel $k : \mathbb{R}^n \times \mathbb{R}^n \to \mathbb{R}$ we can construct a canonical feature space Z with an associated mapping $\Phi : \mathbb{R}^n \to Z$ such that the condition

$$k(\overline{x}, \overline{y}) = \Phi(\overline{x}) \bullet \Phi(\overline{y}) \qquad (7.89)$$

for all $\overline{x}, \overline{y} \in \mathbb{R}^n$ holds. At a very high level we construct our canonical feature space as follows:

- Define a feature space and construct the mapping Φ.
- Turn our feature space into a vector space.
- Define the dot product in this vector space.
- Show that the dot product satisfies the condition in equation (7.89).

Assume that we are given a positive-definite kernel $k : \mathbb{R}^n \times \mathbb{R}^n \to \mathbb{R}$ and a set of points in input space $\overline{x}_1, \ldots, \overline{x}_l \in \mathbb{R}^n$. Then we define our feature space Z as the set of all functions mapping points in input space $\mathbb{R}^n$ to the real numbers,

$$Z = \{\mathbb{R}^n \to \mathbb{R}\}. \qquad (7.90)$$

Notice that our feature space consists of functions rather than vectors. We define the mapping from the input space to the feature space $\Phi : \mathbb{R}^n \to Z$ as

$$\Phi(\overline{x}) = k(\cdot, \overline{x}) \qquad (7.91)$$

for all $\overline{x} \in \mathbb{R}^n$. Notice that Φ takes a point $\overline{x}$ to the partially evaluated kernel $k(\cdot, \overline{x}) : \mathbb{R}^n \to \mathbb{R}$; that is, Φ takes a point $\overline{x} \in \mathbb{R}^n$ to the function $k(\cdot, \overline{x}) \in Z$.

Now we need to turn our feature space into a vector space. We do this by allowing arbitrary functions to be represented by linear combinations of our partially evaluated kernels over the given set of points. That is, some function $h : \mathbb{R}^n \to \mathbb{R}$ can be represented as

$$h = \sum_{i=1}^{l} \theta_i k(\cdot, \overline{x}_i), \qquad (7.92)$$

where $\theta_i \in \mathbb{R}$. Another way to think about this is that the partially evaluated kernels on the given set of points in input space represent the "dimensions" of our feature space,[3] and just as in any other vector space where we are able to construct new vectors from linear combinations of the basis vectors, here we construct new functions from linear combinations of the functions due to the partially evaluated kernels.

We continue by defining the dot product in our vector space. For this we let $g = \sum_{j=1}^{l} \gamma_j k(\cdot, \overline{x}_j)$, where $\gamma_j \in \mathbb{R}$, be another function in our feature space. Then

---

[3]We put "dimensions" in quotations for if these were true dimensions, we would have to prove linear independence.

we define the dot product as

$$h \bullet g = \sum_{i=1}^{l} \sum_{j=1}^{l} \theta_i \gamma_j k(\cdot, \overline{x}_i) \bullet k(\cdot, \overline{x}_j) = \sum_{i=1}^{l} \sum_{j=1}^{l} \theta_i \gamma_j k(\overline{x}_i, \overline{x}_j). \tag{7.93}$$

We need to show that for any functions $f, g, h \in Z$ and constants $p, q \in \mathbb{R}$, the following identities hold (see Table 3.4):

1. $f \bullet g = g \bullet f$.
2. $(pf + qg) \bullet h = pf \bullet h + qg \bullet h$.
3. $f \bullet f \geq 0$.
4. $f \bullet f = 0$ if and only if $f = 0$.

Identity (1) follows directly from the symmetry of kernel k [see (7.93)]. We now show identity (2) and let $h = \sum_{i=1}^{l} \theta_i k(\cdot, \overline{x}_i)$ as before. Then

$$(pf + qg) \bullet h = (pf + qg) \bullet \sum_{i=1}^{l} \theta_i k(\cdot, \overline{x}_i)$$

$$= \sum_{i=1}^{l} \theta_i (pf + qg) \bullet k(\cdot, \overline{x}_i)$$

$$= \sum_{i=1}^{l} \theta_i (pf \bullet k(\cdot, \overline{x}_i) + qg \bullet k(\cdot, \overline{x}_i))$$

$$= \sum_{i=1}^{l} \theta_i pf \bullet k(\cdot, \overline{x}_i) + \sum_{i=1}^{l} \theta_i qg \bullet k(\cdot, \overline{x}_i)$$

$$= pf \bullet \sum_{i=1}^{l} \theta_i k(\cdot, \overline{x}_i) + qg \bullet \sum_{i=1}^{l} \theta_i k(\cdot, \overline{x}_i)$$

$$= pf \bullet h + qg \bullet h.$$

To show identities (3) and (4), assume that $f = \sum_{i=1}^{l} \theta_i k(\cdot, \overline{x}_i)$. Identity (3) follows directly from the positive definiteness (7.86) of the kernel k:

$$f \bullet f = \sum_{i=1}^{l} \sum_{j=1}^{l} \theta_i \theta_j k(\overline{x}_i, \overline{x}_j) \geq 0. \tag{7.94}$$

In identity (4), if $f = 0$, then $f \bullet f = 0$ is straightforward. To show the converse, we use

$$f(\overline{x}) = \sum_{i=1}^{l} \theta_i k(\overline{x}, \overline{x}_i) = \sum_{i=1}^{l} \theta_i k(\cdot, \overline{x}) \bullet k(\cdot, \overline{x}_i) = k(\cdot, \overline{x}) \bullet f, \tag{7.95}$$

which is a direct consequence of the reproducing kernel property (Theorem 7.1). Now, combining the Cauchy–Schwarz inequality and this identity,

$$(k(\cdot, \overline{x}) \bullet f)^2 \leq (k(\cdot, \overline{x}) \bullet k(\cdot, \overline{x}))(f \bullet f), \tag{7.96}$$

gives us

$$(f(\overline{x}))^2 \leq k(\overline{x}, \overline{x})(f \bullet f) \tag{7.97}$$

for all $\overline{x} \in \mathbb{R}^n$. It follows that $f \bullet f = 0$ implies that $f = 0$. This shows that our dot product is well defined.

Finally, we need to show that our construction preserves the kernel condition (7.89). From the definition of our feature space mapping and the reproducing kernel property, we see that

$$\Phi(\overline{x}) \bullet \Phi(\overline{y}) = k(\cdot, \overline{x}) \bullet k(\cdot, \overline{y}) = k(\overline{x}, \overline{y}). \tag{7.98}$$

Therefore, our construction does preserve the kernel conditions.

A direct consequence of our construction is that feature spaces for kernels are not unique. We illustrate this using our homogeneous polynomial kernel to the power of 2; that is, $k(\overline{x}, \overline{y}) = (\overline{x} \bullet \overline{y})^2$ with $\overline{x}, \overline{y} \in \mathbb{R}^2$. Let $\Phi : \mathbb{R}^2 \to \mathbb{R}^3$ and $\Psi : \mathbb{R}^2 \to \{\mathbb{R}^2 \to \mathbb{R}\}$ be two mappings from our input space to two different feature spaces such that

$$\Phi(\overline{x}) = \Phi(x_1, x_2) = (x_1^2, x_2^2, \sqrt{2}\, x_1^2 x_2^2) \tag{7.99}$$

and

$$\Psi(\overline{x}) = k(\cdot, \overline{x}) = ((\cdot) \bullet \overline{x})^2. \tag{7.100}$$

Then

$$\begin{aligned}
\Phi(\overline{x}) \bullet \Phi(\overline{y}) &= (\overline{x}_1^2, \overline{x}_2^2, \sqrt{2}\, \overline{x}_1^2 \overline{x}_2^2) \bullet (\overline{y}_1^2, \overline{y}_2^2, \sqrt{2}\, \overline{y}_1^2 \overline{y}_2^2) \\
&= (\overline{x} \bullet \overline{y})^2 \\
&= k(\overline{x}, \overline{y}) \\
&= k(\cdot, \overline{x}) \bullet k(\cdot, \overline{y}) \\
&= ((\cdot) \bullet \overline{x})^2 \bullet ((\cdot) \bullet \overline{y})^2 \\
&= \Psi(\overline{x}) \bullet \Psi(\overline{y}).
\end{aligned}$$

This shows that feature spaces are not unique, but the dot product values they compute are unique in the sense that given a pair of input space elements, the dot products in the various spaces will evaluate to the same value for this pair.

7.5 SOFT-MARGIN CLASSIFIERS

Real-world training data are not perfect and usually contain noise due to measurement or data entry errors. Here we generalize our maximum-margin classifiers to deal with noisy training data by allowing the classifiers to make mistakes. By essentially allowing the training algorithm to ignore certain training points which are thought to be due to noise gives rise to much simpler decision surfaces in noisy data than would otherwise be possible. This is desirable because simpler decision surfaces tend to generalize better.

Recall that our maximum-margin classifiers are models of the form

$$\hat{f}(\overline{x}) = \text{sgn}(\overline{w} \bullet \overline{x} - b), \tag{7.101}$$

where the normal vector $\overline{w}$ and the offset term b of the decision surface are computed via the primal optimization problem,

$$\min \phi(\overline{w}, b) = \min \frac{1}{2} \overline{w} \bullet \overline{w}, \tag{7.102}$$

subject to the constraints

$$y_i(\overline{w} \bullet \overline{x}_i - b) - 1 \geq 0, \tag{7.103}$$

with $i = 1, \ldots, l$, given the training set $(\overline{x}_1, y_1), \ldots, (\overline{x}_l, y_l) \in \mathbb{R}^n \times \{+1, -1\}$.

The optimization constructs a maximum-margin classifier by positioning the supporting hyperplanes as far away from the decision surface as possible so that they just touch their respective class boundaries. This construction is only partially successful in the case of noisy training data where the size of the margin is limited by a few noisy training points. However, we can reduce the impact that these points have on the size of the margin by allowing them to lie on the "wrong" side of their respective supporting hyperplanes with the introduction of *slack variables*, error terms that measure how far a particular point lies on the wrong side of its respective supporting hyperplane. That is, a slack variable measures how much of an error is committed by allowing the supporting hyperplane to be unconstrained by that point. Figure 7.4 illustrates this. In part (a) we see a maximum-margin classifier with its margin limited by the (perhaps noisy) point $(\overline{x}_j, +1)$. In part (b) the supporting hyperplane $\overline{w} \bullet \overline{x} = b + 1$ is unconstrained by the training point $(\overline{x}_j, +1)$. Here the training point is allowed to lie on the wrong side of the supporting hyperplane and the amount of the error is measured by the corresponding slack variable ξ_j.

Notice that in this case the constraint $\overline{w} \bullet \overline{x}_j - b - 1 \geq 0$ of our optimization problem is violated. However, we can recover a sensible constraint by taking the slack variable into account, $\overline{w} \bullet \overline{x}_j - b + \xi_j - 1 \geq 0$. That is, the slack variable ξ_j of the point $(\overline{x}_j, +1)$ creates the illusion that the point appears to be located right on the supporting hyperplane and therefore appears to satisfy the original constraint. Note that $\xi_j \geq 0$; that is, the error is always measured as a positive quantity. Now, if we introduce a slack variable for each training point $(\overline{x}_i, y_i)$, the corresponding modified

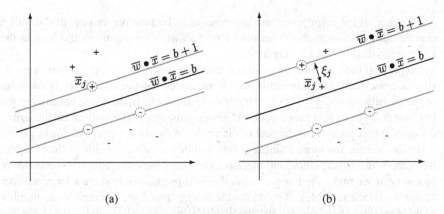

(a)   (b)

FIGURE 7.4   Soft-margin classifier: (a) the margin is constrained by the point $(\overline{x}_j, +1)$; (b) the supporting hyperplane $\overline{w} \bullet \overline{x} = b + 1$ is unconstrained by the training point $(\overline{x}_j, +1)$, and the resulting error is measured by the corresponding slack variable ξ_j.

constraints are

$$y_i(\overline{w} \bullet \overline{x}_i - b) + \xi_i - 1 \geq 0, \qquad\qquad (7.104)$$

with $\xi_i \geq 0$. It is straightforward to see that if some point $\overline{x}_i$ does not represent a constraint on its respective supporting hyperplane, the corresponding slack variable $\xi_i = 0$ since there is nothing to correct. In this case we obtain our original constraint for that point, $y_i(\overline{w} \bullet \overline{x}_i - b) - 1 \geq 0$. If, on the other hand, the point $\overline{x}_i$ lies on the wrong side of its respective supporting hyperplane, equation (7.104) represents a new constraint with $\xi_i > 0$.

Putting all this together, we can rewrite our maximum-margin objective function that takes slack variables into account as in the following proposition.

Proposition 7.2 (Soft-Margin Optimization)   *Given a training set*

$$D = \{(\overline{x}_1, y_1), (\overline{x}_2, y_2), \dots, (\overline{x}_l, y_l)\} \subseteq \mathbb{R}^n \times \{+1, -1\},$$

we can compute a soft-margin decision surface $\overline{w}^* \bullet \overline{x} = b^*$ with an optimization

$$\min_{\overline{w}, \overline{\xi}, b} \phi(\overline{w}, \overline{\xi}, b) = \min_{\overline{w}, \overline{\xi}, b} \left(\frac{1}{2} \overline{w} \bullet \overline{w} + C \sum_{i=1}^{l} \xi_i \right), \qquad (7.105)$$

subject to the constraints

$$y_i(\overline{w} \bullet \overline{x}_i - b) + \xi_i - 1 \geq 0, \qquad\qquad (7.106)$$

$$\xi_i \geq 0, \qquad\qquad (7.107)$$

with $i = 1, \dots, l$, $\overline{\xi} = (\xi_1, \dots, \xi_l)$, and $C > 0$.

Because all the error terms are constrained to be positive values, this is still a convex optimization problem: an important fact when we continue and look at the Lagrangian dual of this optimization.

To prevent the construction of trivial solutions where all training points are considered noise during margin optimization, we added the slack variables in the form of the penalty term $C \sum_{i=1}^{l} \xi_i$ to the objective function. In this way, optimizing the function $\phi(\overline{w}, \overline{\xi}, b)$ becomes a trade-off between the size of the margin and the size of the error, where the error is the sum of the values of the slack variables. The larger we make the margin, the more training points will be on the wrong side of their respective supporting hyperplanes, and therefore the larger the error, and vice versa. More precisely, if we make the margin large, this will probably introduce a large number of nonzero slack variables. If we make the margin small, we can reduce the number of nonzero slack variables, but we are also back to where we started in the sense that noisy points will dictate the position of the decision surface. The constant C, called the *cost*, allows us to control the trade-off between margin size and error. Notice that C is positive and cannot be zero; that is, we cannot simply ignore the slack variables by setting $C = 0$. With a large value for C, the optimization will try to find a solution with as small a number of nonzero slack variables as possible because errors are costly, due to the large C. More precisely, a large value for C forces the optimization to consider solutions with small margins. If we specify a small value for C, the introduction of nonzero slack variables is much more forgiving and we can find solutions with a larger margin, ignoring some of the noisier points near the decision surface. This gives us the following relation between the cost and margin size:

$$\text{large } C \sim \text{small margin,}$$
$$\text{small } C \sim \text{large margin.}$$

(7.108)

In concrete terms, a solution $\overline{w}^*$, $\overline{\xi}^*$, and b^* to the optimization problem

$$\min_{\overline{w}, \overline{\xi}, b} \phi(\overline{w}, \overline{\xi}, b) = \frac{1}{2}\overline{w}^* \bullet \overline{w}^* + C \sum_{i=1}^{l} \xi_i^* = m^*$$

is then a trade-off between the size of the margin m^* and the size of the error, $\sum_{i=1}^{l} \xi_i^*$, for a given cost C.

Since the slack variables only appear as part of the training algorithm, our maximum-margin classifier model itself remains unchanged:

$$\hat{f}(\overline{x}) = \text{sgn}(\overline{w}^* \bullet \overline{x} - b^*).$$

(7.109)

The only difference here between the model in a hard-margin setting and in a soft-margin setting is that we now allow our model to make a certain number of classification errors governed by the cost constant C. To quantify these possible misclassification errors, we examine a bit closer the error terms due to slack variables. If a particular point $(\overline{x}_j, y_j)$ has a slack variable with value less than 1, $\xi_j \leq 1$, that point will be classified correctly by the decision function even though the point lies in the margin. If, on the other hand, the point has a slack variable such that $\xi_j > 1$, this point will be misclassified by the decision function. To see this, recall that the difference in terms of offset between a supporting hyperplane and the decision surface is 1, and as long as the error of ignoring the point $\overline{x}_j$ as a constraint is less or equal to 1, the point $\overline{x}_j$ will be on the correct side of or directly on the decision surface and will be classified correctly. However, as soon as the error term is larger than 1, the point $\overline{x}_j$ will be on the wrong side of the decision surface and will be misclassified. More precisely, if we assume the point to be $(\overline{x}_j, +1)$ and we rewrite the constraint (7.106) accordingly as

$$\overline{w} \bullet \overline{x}_j = b + (1 - \xi_j), \tag{7.110}$$

the point $\overline{x}_j$ lies above the decision surface $\overline{w} \bullet \overline{x} = b$ as long as the quantity $1 - \xi_j \geq 0$, which implies that the point lies above or on the decision surface if $\xi_j \leq 1$. Otherwise, the point $\overline{x}_j$ lies below the decision surface. Figure 7.5 illustrates this. In part (a) we have an error term $\xi_j \leq 1$ and we can see that the point $(\overline{x}_j, +1)$ will still be classified according to its label. In part (b), however, we see that an error term $\xi_j > 1$ leads to a misclassification of the point $\overline{x}_j$. Instead of assigning a $+1$ label to this point, the decision function will assign a label -1 to this point. This means that the introduction of slack variables can introduce misclassification errors into our support vector model. However, since we assume that the points that violate the constraints are due to noise and therefore unreliable, misclassifying such a point does not do as much damage to our model as perhaps assumed.

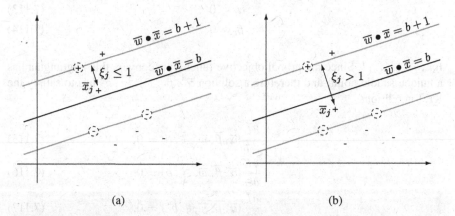

(a)   (b)

FIGURE 7.5 Soft-margin misclassifications: (a) a point $(\overline{x}_j, +1)$ with an error term $\xi_j \leq 1$ lies above the decision surface; (b) the error term $\xi_j > 1$ leads to a misclassification of the point $(\overline{x}_j, +1)$ since it now lies below the decision surface.

7.5.1 The Dual Setting for Soft-Margin Classifiers

We know from our previous work that the primal setting for maximum-margin classifiers is limited, since it does not allow us to apply the kernel trick in order to extend linear classifiers to the nonlinear case. Therefore, to generalize the soft-margin classifier to the nonlinear case, we develop its Lagrangian dual here. We start with the primal objective function (7.105) together with the constraints (7.106) and (7.107) and rewrite it as the Lagrangian using (7.3):

$$L(\overline{\alpha}, \overline{\beta}, \overline{w}, \overline{\xi}, b) = \frac{1}{2}\overline{w} \bullet \overline{w} + C \sum_{i=1}^{l} \xi_i$$

$$- \sum_{i=1}^{l} \alpha_i (y_i(\overline{w} \bullet \overline{x}_i - b) + \xi_i - 1)$$

$$- \sum_{i=1}^{l} \beta_i \xi_i. \tag{7.111}$$

This Lagrangian has an additional primal variable $\overline{\xi}$ due to the slack variables and an additional dual variable $\overline{\beta} = (\beta_1, \ldots, \beta_l)$ which constitutes the Lagrangian multipliers for the constraints $\xi_i \geq 0$. The Lagrangian optimization problem is then

$$\max_{\overline{\alpha},\overline{\beta}} \min_{\overline{w},\overline{\xi},b} L(\overline{\alpha}, \overline{\beta}, \overline{w}, \overline{\xi}, b), \tag{7.112}$$

subject to the constraints,

$$\alpha_i \geq 0, \tag{7.113}$$

$$\beta_i \geq 0 \tag{7.114}$$

for $i = 1, \ldots, l$. Since the primal objective function is convex, this Lagrangian has a unique saddle point, and therefore a solution $\overline{\alpha}^*, \overline{\beta}^*, \overline{w}^*, \overline{\xi}^*, b^*$ has to satisfy the KKT conditions

$$\frac{\partial L}{\partial \overline{w}}(\overline{\alpha}, \overline{\beta}, \overline{w}^*, \overline{\xi}, b) = 0, \tag{7.115}$$

$$\frac{\partial L}{\partial \xi_i}(\overline{\alpha}, \overline{\beta}, \overline{w}, \xi_i^*, b) = 0, \tag{7.116}$$

$$\frac{\partial L}{\partial b}(\overline{\alpha}, \overline{\beta}, \overline{w}, \overline{\xi}, b^*) = 0, \tag{7.117}$$

$$\alpha_i^*(y_i(\overline{w}^* \bullet \overline{x}_i - b^*) + \xi_i^* - 1) = 0, \tag{7.118}$$

$$\beta_i^* \xi_i^* = 0, \tag{7.119}$$

$$y_i(\overline{w}^* \bullet \overline{x}_i - b^*) + \xi_i^* - 1 \geq 0, \tag{7.120}$$

$$\alpha_i^* \geq 0, \tag{7.121}$$

$$\beta_i^* \geq 0, \tag{7.122}$$

$$\xi_i^* \geq 0 \tag{7.123}$$

for $i = 1, \ldots, l$. The first three conditions ensure that the solutions to the primal variables lie on the saddle point of the Lagrangian. Equations (7.118) and (7.119) are the complementarity conditions. In particular, equation (7.119) represents the complementarity condition due to the new constraints $\xi_i \geq 0$. The last four conditions are the constraints of the respective primal and Lagrangian optimization problems. Since all these conditions will be satisfied by any solution to the Lagrangian optimization problem, it follows that

$$\max_{\overline{\alpha}, \overline{\beta}} \min_{\overline{w}, \overline{\xi}, b} L(\overline{\alpha}, \overline{\beta}, \overline{w}, \overline{\xi}, b) = L(\overline{\alpha}^*, \overline{\beta}^*, \overline{w}^*, \overline{\xi}^*, b^*)$$

$$= \frac{1}{2}\overline{w}^* \bullet \overline{w}^* + C \sum_{i=1}^{l} \xi_i^*.$$

That is, we can use Lagrangian optimization to solve our primal optimization problem.

As in the hard-margin case, we can solve this optimization problem much more readily by computing the Lagrangian dual. To accomplish this we apply the KKT conditions and differentiate the Lagrangian with respect to the primal variables and then evaluate the derivatives at the saddle point. Differentiating the Lagrangian with respect to $\overline{w}$ and evaluating the derivative at $\overline{w}^*$,

$$\frac{\partial L}{\partial \overline{w}}(\overline{\alpha}, \overline{\beta}, \overline{w}^*, \overline{\xi}, b) = \overline{w}^* - \sum_{i=1}^{l} \alpha_i y_i \overline{x}_i = \overline{0}, \tag{7.124}$$

gives us

$$\overline{w}^* = \sum_{i=1}^{l} \alpha_i y_i \overline{x}_i. \tag{7.125}$$

Not unexpectedly, the optimal normal vector of the decision surface for soft-margin classifiers is a linear combination of the training points. Now, differentiating the Lagrangian with respect to b and evaluating the derivative at the point b^*,

$$\frac{\partial L}{\partial b}(\overline{\alpha}, \overline{\beta}, \overline{w}, \overline{\xi}, b^*) = \sum_{i=1}^{l} \alpha_i y_i = 0, \tag{7.126}$$

gives us the same constraint as in the hard-margin case:

$$\sum_{i=1}^{l} \alpha_i y_i = 0. \tag{7.127}$$

Finally, differentiating the Lagrangian with respect to each of the slack variables ξ_i and evaluating the derivatives at ξ_i^*,

$$\frac{\partial L}{\partial \xi_i}(\overline{\alpha}, \overline{\beta}, \overline{w}, \xi_i^*, b) = C - \alpha_i - \beta_i = 0, \tag{7.128}$$

gives us the new constraints

$$\alpha_i = C - \beta_i \tag{7.129}$$

for $i = 1, \ldots, l$. Plugging the terms obtained from the partial differentiations back into the Lagrangian and applying the constraints, we obtain our Lagrangian dual,

$$\phi'(\overline{\alpha}) = \sum_{i=1}^{l} \alpha_i - \frac{1}{2} \sum_{i=1}^{l} \sum_{j=1}^{l} \alpha_i \alpha_j y_i y_j \overline{x}_i \bullet \overline{x}_j. \tag{7.130}$$

Interestingly, this objective function has the same structure as the dual objective function of the hard-margin classifier given in (7.49). Therefore, the basic nature of the optimization problem has not changed—what has changed are the constraints. We have picked up the additional constraints (7.129) due to the additional primal variable $\overline{\xi}$. We can write these constraints in a more convenient way by considering that the Lagrangian multipliers α_i and β_i for some point $\overline{x}_i$ cannot be negative, $\alpha_i \geq 0$ and $\beta_i \geq 0$. This implies that we can rewrite the constraints (7.129) as

$$0 \leq \alpha_i \leq C \tag{7.131}$$

and

$$0 \leq \beta_i \leq C. \tag{7.132}$$

This gives us the following Lagrangian dual optimization for soft-margin classifiers.

Proposition 7.3 (Soft-Margin Lagrangian Dual) *Given a soft-margin optimization as in Proposition 7.2, the Lagrangian dual optimization for a soft-margin* *classifier is*

$$\max_{\overline{\alpha}} \phi'(\overline{\alpha}) = \max_{\overline{\alpha}} \left(\sum_{i=1}^{l} \alpha_i - \frac{1}{2} \sum_{i=1}^{l} \sum_{j=1}^{l} \alpha_i \alpha_j y_i y_j \overline{x}_i \bullet \overline{x}_j \right), \tag{7.133}$$

subject to the constraints

$$\sum_{i=1}^{l} \alpha_i y_i = 0, \tag{7.134}$$

$$C \geq \alpha_i \geq 0, \tag{7.135}$$

with $i = 1, \ldots, l$. Here C is the cost constant.

It is remarkable that the only difference between the maximum-margin optimization problem given in Proposition 7.1 and the soft-margin optimization problem given here is that for the soft-margin classifier the value of the Lagrangian multipliers is limited by the cost constant C.

To interpret this result we can go back to the complementarity condition (7.119) and the constraints (7.129). The complementarity condition asserts that if we are given a point $\overline{x}_i$ with a nonzero slack variable $\xi_i > 0$, the associated Lagrangian multiplier has to be zero, $\beta_i = 0$. From the constraint (7.129) it follows that $\alpha_i = C$. That is, for any point that lies on the wrong side of its respective supporting hyperplane, the corresponding Lagrangian multiplier is bound to the value C. This means that, the influence of this point on the decision surface is limited by the cost constant C. If, on the other hand, the point $\overline{x}_i$ is associated with a zero-valued slack variable, $\xi_i = 0$, β_i can assume any value such that $0 < \beta_i \leq C$. The value of β_i cannot be greater than C, since this would violate our constraints (7.129). It follows from (7.129) that for points with zero-valued slack variables, the range of the corresponding Lagrangian multipliers α_i is $0 \leq \alpha_i < C$. This means that for points $\overline{x}_i$ with zero-valued slack variables that are support vectors, the range of the corresponding Lagrangian multipliers is $0 < \alpha_i < C$.

It is clear that the larger we make the value of C, the larger the influence of the points on the wrong side of their respective supporting hyperplanes on the position of the decision surface, and vice versa. It is nice to see that both the primal and dual forms of the optimization problem agree on the the behavior of the constant C: Large values of C constrain the decision surface; small values of C allow a much more liberal positioning of the decision surface.

We have to be cautious when computing the optimal offset term b^* for a soft-margin classifier. In the hard-margin case we were free to pick an arbitrary support vector and use it to compute the offset term. In the soft-margin case we can still pick a support vector for our computation, but we need to avoid support vectors whose Lagrangian multiplier is equal to the cost constant C, since this indicates that this support vector is associated with a nonzero slack variable and therefore lies on the wrong side of its respective supporting hyperplane, giving us an incorrect value for b^*. This means that we can pick a training set point $(\overline{x}_{sv^+}, +1)$ with a zero-valued slack variable $\xi_{sv^+}^* = 0$ whose corresponding Lagrangian multiplier $\alpha_{sv^+}^*$ therefore lies in the range $0 < \alpha_{sv^+}^* < C$. From the complementarity condition (7.118) we have

$$\sum_{i=1}^{l} \alpha_i^* y_i \overline{x}_i \bullet \overline{x}_{sv^+} - b^* - 1 = 0. \tag{7.136}$$

That is, the point $\overline{x}_{sv^+}$ lies on the supporting hyperplane because its corresponding Lagrangian multiplier is larger than zero but less than the cost constant and $\xi_{sv^+}^* = 0$. Solving for b^* gives us

$$b^* = \sum_{i=1}^{l} \alpha_i^* y_i \overline{x}_j \bullet \overline{x}_{sv^+} - 1. \tag{7.137}$$

If we select our support vector carefully, the calculation for b^* is identical to the case of the hard-margin classifiers [see (7.56)].

The actual model is not affected by the introduction of slack variables and is the same as the model for hard-margin classifiers [see (7.59)]. From the perspective of the model, the introduction of slack variables simply means that certain Lagrangian multipliers α_i^* are limited by the cost constant C but has no other effect on the structure of the model itself. This also means that the only difference between support vector machines that represent hard-margin classifiers and those that represent soft-margin classifiers is that the latter has an additional free parameter during training: the user-defined cost constant C.

Finally, notice that both the training algorithm for soft-margin classifiers given as the Lagrangian dual in Proposition 7.3 and the model given in (7.59) are expressed in terms of a dot product of points in the input space $\mathbb{R}^n$. This means that we can apply the kernel trick to the dual soft-margin classifier and obtain nonlinear soft-margin classifiers. It is perhaps interesting to note that certain data sets which are not linearly separable can be separated by a linear soft-margin classifier where the points that make the data nonlinear are considered noise.

7.6 TOOL SUPPORT

We have developed support vector machines to a point where we can take a look at actual implementations. Support vector machines that encode soft-margin classifiers are often called *C-classification support vector machines*, due to the additional free parameter, and are available in many tool sets. In particular, C-classification support vector machines are available in both WEKA and R. Here we illustrate these implementations through examples using the linearly separable biomedical data set given in Exercise 4.3 and the nonlinear data set given in Table 7.3. Before working through the next sections, be sure to create CSV files for the two data sets so that you can load

TABLE 7.3 Simple Data Set That Is Not Linearly Separable

x_1	x_2	y
0	0.7	One
0.7	0	One
0	−0.7	One
−0.7	0	One
0.5	0.5	One
−0.5	0.5	One
−0.5	−0.5	One
0.5	−0.5	One
0	2.8	Two
−2.8	0	Two
0	−2.8	Two
2.8	0	Two
2.0	2.0	Two
−2.0	2.0	Two
−2.0	−2.0	Two
2.0	−2.0	Two

them conveniently into WEKA and R. Also, before proceeding, it might be a good idea to visualize these data sets in order to get a feel for the structure of the data.

7.6.1 WEKA

Let us start with the linearly separable biomedical data set. Load this data set into WEKA using the explorer interface. You should see a window as in Figure 7.6 once the data are loaded. The data set consists of nine instances labeled either *Angina* or *Myocardial Infarction* (MI). Now we want to build support vector machines. To do this you will need to open the *Classify* tab. Use the *Choose* button to navigate to the support vector machine models called *SMO* in WEKA after the particular implementation strategy used:

weka → classifiers → functions → SMO.

Clicking on the resulting SMO box brings up a parameter dialog box. There are many parameters which allow the user to tune the training algorithm. At this point we should be able to recognize a fair number of parameters from our support vector machine development above. For example, there is the cost constant C (in WEKA it is a lowercase 'c'). There is also the *exponent* parameter, which represents the degree d for a homogeneous polynomial kernel. Finally, the *useRBF* parameter together with the *gamma* parameter enables Gaussian kernels (Gaussian kernels are sometimes also called *radial basis functions*—therefore the parameter name). This means that WEKA supports three kernels, the homogeneous polynomial kernel together with the linear kernel, by setting the polynomial exponent to 1, and the Gaussian kernel.

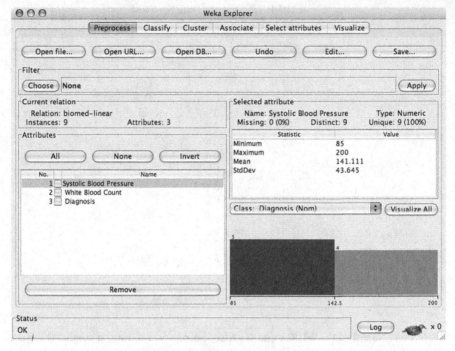

FIGURE 7.6   Loaded biomedical data set from Exercise 4.3 in WEKA.

Linear Support Vector Machines   For our first experiment we will use a linear kernel (a polynomial kernel with exponent 1.0). We leave the cost constant at 1.0 for now. Make sure that that the *useRBF* parameter is set to *false* and that the *filterType* parameter is set to *No normalization or standardization*. We want to evaluate our support vector machine on the training data; therefore, we will need to set the *Test options* to the value *Use training set*. Once we have set the parameters and test options we are ready to build a model by pressing the *Start* button. When the training has completed you should see a window as shown in Figure 7.7. Notice that in the *Classifier output* panel we have a summary where the number of correctly classified instances is reported as nine, with zero instances incorrectly classified. This means that a support vector machine with a linear kernel and a default cost of $C = 1.0$ is an appropriate model for this training set.

In our discussion on soft-margin classifiers we stated that large values for the cost constant C implies small margins and, conversely, that small values for C imply large margins [see (7.108)]. Let us test this theory by making our cost constant in WEKA smaller. We would expect the margin to grow and with it the possibility of misclassification of training points. For our next experiment we leave all the parameters as they were from the previous experiment with the exception of C, which we set to the value 1.0×10^{-6}. Now we build a new model by pressing the *Start* button. Notice that this model no longer classifies correctly all instances in the training set. The margin has grown to such an extent that one of the training instances is now located on the wrong

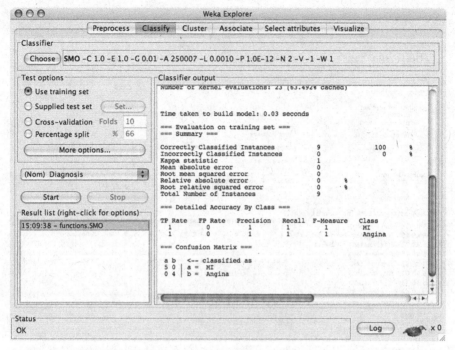

FIGURE 7.7   WEKA report for a linear support vector machine.

side of the decision surface of the soft-margin classifier and therefore is misclassified by the support vector machine. Figure 7.8 shows the window after the support vector machine has been trained. If we make the cost even smaller, say 1.0×10^{-9}, we see that the resulting support vector machine will commit even more errors; that is, the margin is even larger.

On the other hand, increasing the value of C beyond the default of 1.0 has no visible effect on our model. This is easily explained by again referring to equation (7.108): A large value for C results in a small margin. Since the classifier with a margin at $C = 1.0$ already separates the data perfectly, certainly any classifier with a smaller margin will separate the data equally well. However, increasing the cost C to a value beyond the default 1.0 can have a negative impact on the generalizability of the model. The decision surface of a classifier with an artificially small margin can be very close to one of the class boundaries introducing possible classification errors for unseen data points (refer to Figure 6.2).

Nonlinear Support Vector Machines   We now turn our attention to data sets that are not linearly separable. For the next set of experiments we use the data set given in Table 7.3. Go back to the *Preprocess* tab in the WEKA explorer window and load the CSV file for this data set. Now return to the *Classify* tab. Let us first try to build a linear support vector machine model and see if we can fit it to the data by

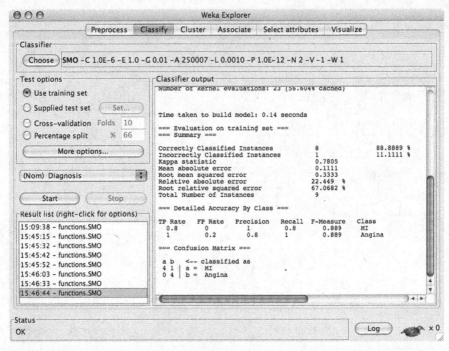

FIGURE 7.8 WEKA report for a linear support vector machine with a small value for the cost constant C.

selecting C in a clever way. Set $C = 1.0$ and make sure that the *filterType* parameter is set to *No normalization or standardization* and that the *useRBF* parameter is set to *false*. Again we use the training set in the test options. After building the model, we see in the classifier summary that the model commits a large number of errors, in this case 50%. It does not matter how large or small we make C; that is, it does not matter how much we change the size of the margin—the model continues to commit large numbers of misclassification errors. This implies that the linear kernel is not the appropriate kernel to construct a model for this data set. Let us try a homogeneous polynomial kernel of degree 2. To select this kernel we set the *exponent* parameter to the value 2.0. We also need to reset the value of the cost constant, $C = 1.0$. When we build the model now, the model summary shows that a support vector machine with a homogeneous polynomial kernel of degree 2 and the default margin size separates the data set perfectly. We have just performed a simple feature search to determine a kernel that will allow the support vector machine to classify all the instances correctly.

7.6.2 R

Let us take a look at a set of similar model construction experiments in R. To perform the following set of experiments, make sure that you have installed and loaded the e1071 package using R's package installer and loader.

Linear Support Vector Machines   Assume that the biomedical data are stored in a file called "biomed.csv"; then the following code loads the data set, builds a linear support vector model, and evaluates the model against the training set:

```
> biomed.df <- read.csv("biomed.csv")
> svm.model <- svm(Diagnosis~.,
                   data=biomed.df,
                   type="C-classification",
                   cost=1.0,
                   kernel="linear")
> svm.model

Parameters:
   SVM-Type:  C-classification
 SVM-Kernel:  linear
       cost:  1

Number of Support Vectors:  2

> pred <- fitted(svm.model)
> pred == biomed.df$Diagnosis
[1] TRUE TRUE TRUE TRUE TRUE TRUE TRUE TRUE TRUE
```

With a cost of 1.0, the model classifies all training points correctly.

If we experiment with the value of the cost constant, we can observe that the cost C has the same effect on the model as it did in WEKA: A small C (large margin) entails many classification errors; conversely, a large C (small margin) entails no classification errors. R allows us to visualize the decision surface. We can plot the linear support vector machine that we constructed above with $C = 1.0$ using the command

```
> plot(svm.model,biomed.df,grid=100)
```

Part (a) of Figure 7.9 shows this plot. Notice that the decision surface is equidistant from the two classes. Also notice that we have two support vectors, one for each class (data points represented as crosses). Part (b) shows a support vector model for the same data set with $C = 0.045$. That is, the model shown is a model with a large margin. Here all data points are support vectors; that is, all data points are either on or in the margin. Also notice that this model misclassifies one of the angina data points.

Nonlinear Support Vector Machines   Let us turn to data sets that are not linearly separable. Here we assume that the data set from Table 7.3 is stored in the file "simple-non-linear.csv". The following R code loads the data set, builds a support vector

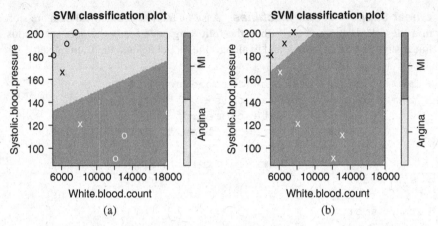

FIGURE 7.9 Visualization of the linear decision surface of the support vector machine constructed for the biomedical data set: (a) $C = 1.0$; (b) $C = 0.045$.

machine with a homogeneous polynomial kernel of degree 2, evaluates the accuracy of the model, and then plots the decision surface:

```
> non.linear.df <- read.csv("simple-non-linear.csv")
> svm.model <- svm(y~.,
                 data=non.linear.df,
                 type="C-classification",
                 cost=1,
                 kernel="polynomial",
                 degree=2,
                 coef0=0)
> pred <- fitted(svm.model)
> pred == non.linear.df$y
 [1] TRUE TRUE TRUE TRUE TRUE TRUE TRUE TRUE
        TRUE TRUE TRUE TRUE TRUE TRUE TRUE TRUE
> plot(svm.model,non.linear.df,grid=100)
```

The decision surface for this model can be seen in Figure 7.10. As expected, the decision surface is nonlinear and it classifies all training points correctly.

7.7 DISCUSSION

By considering the Lagrangian dual of maximum-margin classifiers we were able to extend the classification algorithms from the linear case to the case where the training data are not linearly separable. The key insight here is that in the Lagrangian dual all data points in the input space appear in the context of dot products. By taking advantage of the kernel trick we are able to replace these dot products with appropriate

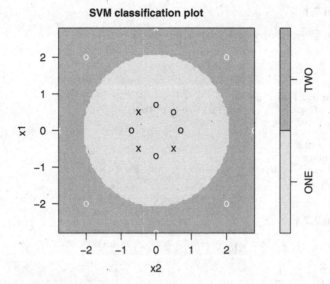

FIGURE 7.10 Visualization of the nonlinear decision surface of a support vector machine constructed for the data set in Table 7.3.

kernel functions with implicit mappings into higher-dimensional feature spaces where decision surfaces that appear to be nonlinear in the input space are again linear.

One of the interesting implications of kernel functions is that the kernel trick can be applied to any linear classification algorithm whose data points appear in dot products. This means that any linear classification algorithm with dot products can be extended to the nonlinear case using the kernel trick. Consider, for example, the dual perceptron learning algorithm depicted in Algorithm 5.2. Notice that all training data points appear only in the dot product $\overline{x}_j \bullet \overline{x}_i$. Applying our kernel trick would make this dot product appear as $k(\overline{x}_j, \overline{x}_i)$, where k is some appropriate kernel (see Table 7.2). The only difficulty that remains before we can consider this algorithm a training algorithm for a nonlinear classifier is the radius r. In Algorithm 5.2 it is computed as the maximum size of all training point vectors, $|\overline{x}_i|$. However, when we apply the kernel trick, this should be computed as $|\Phi(\overline{x}_i)|$, where Φ is the implicit transformation due to the kernel function. This is a problem because in general we don't know exactly what Φ is. Here we compromise with respect to the original dual perceptron algorithm and let $r = 1$. We also let the learning rate η be a user-defined constant with a larger range than the original learning rate in order to compensate for the fact that $r = 1$. The resulting kernel-perceptron algorithm is shown in Algorithm 7.1. A variant of the kernel-perceptron algorithm is shown in Algorithm 7.2. Here the offset term computation has been eliminated, $b = 0$, which means that decision surfaces in feature space will have to go through the origin of the feature space.

It is assumed that we can always find kernel functions that have sufficiently complex implicit transformations to allow decision surfaces in feature space to go through the origin. It turns out that in many cases such a kernel can be found, and therefore

Algorithm 7.1

let $D = \{(\overline{x}_1, y_1), (\overline{x}_2, y_2), \ldots, (\overline{x}_l, y_l)\} \subset \mathbb{R}^n \times \{+1, -1\}$
let $\eta > 0$
$\overline{\alpha} \leftarrow \overline{0}$
$b \leftarrow 0$
repeat
   for $i = 1$ to l do
      if $\text{sgn}(\sum_{j=1}^{l} \alpha_j y_j k(\overline{x}_j, \overline{x}_i) - b) \neq y_i$ then
        $\alpha_i \leftarrow \alpha_i + 1$
        $b \leftarrow b - \eta y_i$
      end if
   end for
until $\text{sgn}(\sum_{j=1}^{l} \alpha_j y_j k(\overline{x}_j, \overline{x}_k) - b) = y_k$ with $k = 1, \ldots, k$
return $(\overline{\alpha}, b)$

Algorithm 7.2

let $D = \{(\overline{x}_1, y_1), (\overline{x}_2, y_2), \ldots, (\overline{x}_l, y_l)\} \subset \mathbb{R}^n \times \{+1, -1\}$
let $b = 0$
$\overline{\alpha} \leftarrow \overline{0}$
repeat
   for $i = 1$ to l do
      if $\text{sgn} \sum_{j=1}^{l} \alpha_j y_j k(\overline{x}_j, \overline{x}_i) \neq y_i$ then
        $\alpha_i \leftarrow \alpha_i + 1$
      end if
   end for
until $\text{sgn} \sum_{j=1}^{l} \alpha_j y_j k(\overline{x}_j, \overline{x}_k) = y_k$ with $k = 1, \ldots, k$
return $(\overline{\alpha}, b)$

this restriction does not pose a serious limitation on our ability to find appropriate models. Furthermore, just because the decision surface goes through the origin of the feature space does not necessarily imply that the decision surface goes through the origin of the input space. Note that even though these perceptron training algorithms will find decision surfaces in nonlinear data, the algorithms do not guarantee to find optimal decision surfaces, since they will stop iterating as soon as they find a surface that separates the training data.

EXERCISES

7.1 Given the objective function $\phi(x) = x^2 - x$ and the constraint $g(x) = x - 3 \geq 0$, solve the optimization min $\phi(x)$ subject to the constraint $g(x) \geq 0$ using the Lagrangian dual.

7.2 Show that given the Lagrangian

$$L(\overline{\alpha}, \overline{w}, b) = \phi(\overline{w}, b) - \sum_{i=1}^{l} \alpha_i g_i(\overline{w}, b),$$

then

$$\max_{\overline{\alpha}} \min_{\overline{w},b} L(\overline{\alpha}, \overline{w}, b) = L(\overline{\alpha}^*, \overline{w}^*, b^*) = \phi(\overline{w}^*, b^*)$$

if the KKT conditions are satisfied.

7.3 Compute the derivatives given in equations (7.41) and (7.43).

7.4 Express the offset term b^* given in equation (7.47) only in terms of the dual variable $\overline{\alpha}^*$.

7.5 Formally derive the dual given in equation (7.48).

7.6 Construct an offset term b^* similar to equation (7.56), but instead of using a support vector from the $+1$ class, use a support vector from the -1 class.

7.7 Prove that in Figure 7.3 every point on the decision surface $\overline{x} \bullet \overline{x} = 1$ in input space lies on the decision surface $\overline{w}^* \bullet \overline{z} = b^*$ in feature space with $\overline{w}^* = (1, 1, 0)$ and $b^* = 1$. Use the transformation Φ defined in equation (7.69).

7.8 Compute the derivatives given in equations (7.124), (7.126), and (7.128).

7.9 Justify that the constraint (7.129) can be rewritten as equations (7.131) and (7.132).

7.10 Derive the Lagrangian dual in (7.130).

7.11 [*challenging*] Construct a formula for the offset term b^* for soft-margin dual classifiers similar to equation (7.137). But instead of considering only a single support vector in the calculation, compute b^* as the average of all offset terms due to support vectors with Lagrangian multipliers in the range $0 < \alpha_i^* < C$.

7.12 Find a data set that represents a binary classification problem and construct a C-classification support vector machine using either the WEKA or R implementation. Which kernel did you use to achieve reasonable accuracy? What value of the cost constant C did you use? What were the effects of changing the value of C?

7.13 [*challenging*] Implement the kernel-perceptron algorithm given in Algorithm 7.1 in R and then train your perceptron with the training set given in Table 7.3 using a kernel from Table 7.2. Does the kernel-perceptron construct a decision surface that separates the two classes?

BIBLIOGRAPHIC NOTES

Joseph Lagrange created the Lagrangian multipliers to deal with constrained optimization problems in the late eighteenth century. Karush in the 1930s [41] and later, Kuhn and Tucker [49] extended this theory to inequality constraints. A nice tutorial on

Lagrangian functionals and multipliers is [45]. Boyd and Vandenberghe [14] discuss the Lagrangian dual in some detail.

Kernel methods were first introduced to the machine learning community by Aizermann et al. in 1964 [3]. However, these methods were not truly appreciated until the seminal paper published by Boser et al. in 1992 [12]. Support vector machines themselves in the formulation given here were introduced by Cortes and Vapnik in 1995 [22]. Our construction of canonical feature spaces follows closely a proof given in [65]. Cortes and Vapnik introduced soft-margin classifiers in the context of support vector machines in [22]. A nice overview of support vector machines with a more geometric slant is [6]. This geometric interpretation is discussed even further in [5].

Kernel-perceptrons are discussed by Freund and Schapire [32] and Herbrich [38]. General kernel methods in the area of pattern recognition are discussed in [67].

CHAPTER 8

IMPLEMENTATION

In this chapter we discuss implementation of support vector machines. When we refer to the implementation of support vector machines, we usually mean the implementation of the training algorithm that produces the necessary values for the Lagrangian multipliers and the offset term for a support vector machine model. This is due to the fact that beyond the values of the Lagrangian multipliers and the offset term, the structure of the support vector machine model itself is otherwise fixed, with the exception that the kernel function is a free parameter for both the model and the training algorithm.

We start our implementation discussion by taking a look at a simple gradient ascent optimization algorithm, also known as the *kernel-adatron algorithm*. This straightforward optimization technique solves the Lagrangian dual optimization problem for support vector machines with some simplifying assumptions. We then take a look at the use of quadratic programming solvers. The fact that data matrices associated with a quadratic program for support vector machines grow quadratically with the size of the training data limits the straightforward use of quadratic programming solvers in many knowledge discovery projects. However, a technique called *chunking* which takes advantage of the sparseness of the optimization problem associated with support vector machines (only a few training instances are actual support vectors) remedies this situation and allows us to apply quadratic programming solvers to fairly large knowledge discovery projects. We conclude the chapter with a discussion of sequential minimal optimization which has become the defacto standard implementation technique of the Lagrangian dual optimization associated with support vector machines.

Knowledge Discovery with Support Vector Machines, by Lutz Hamel
Copyright © 2009 John Wiley & Sons, Inc.

8.1 GRADIENT ASCENT

Assume that we are given the training set

$$D = \{(\bar{x}_1, y_1), (\bar{x}_2, y_2), \ldots, (\bar{x}_l, y_l)\} \subseteq \mathbb{R}^n \times \{+1, -1\}. \tag{8.1}$$

We are interested in computing a classifier in the form of a support vector machine model,

$$\hat{f}(\bar{x}) = \text{sgn}\left(\sum_{i=1}^{l} y_i \alpha_i^* k(\bar{x}_i, \bar{x}) - b^*\right), \tag{8.2}$$

using a training algorithm based on the Lagrangian dual

$$\bar{\alpha}^* = \underset{\bar{\alpha}}{\text{argmax}} \, \phi'(\bar{\alpha}) = \underset{\bar{\alpha}}{\text{argmax}} \left(\sum_{i=1}^{l} \alpha_i - \frac{1}{2} \sum_{i=1}^{l} \sum_{j=1}^{l} y_i y_j \alpha_i \alpha_j k(\bar{x}_i, \bar{x}_j)\right), \tag{8.3}$$

subject to the constraints,

$$\sum_{i=1}^{l} y_i \alpha_i = 0, \tag{8.4}$$

$$C \geq \alpha_i \geq 0, \tag{8.5}$$

with $i = 1, \ldots, l$. The values C and k are free parameters and represent the cost and the kernel function, respectively. The values $\bar{\alpha}^*$ and b^* in the model are the optima computed by the training algorithm. Even though the offset term b^* does not appear in the training algorithm directly, it can be computed from the support vectors according to equation (7.137). We constrain the Lagrangian multipliers by the cost constant C; this implies that the models we are interested in are soft-margin classifiers (see Proposition 7.3).

Perhaps the most straightforward implementation of the Lagrangian dual optimization problem (8.3) is by *gradient ascent*. The gradient of a differentiable function is a vector composed of the partial derivatives of that function with respect to the dimensions of the underlying vector space. Formally, let $h(\bar{x})$ be a differentiable function with $\bar{x} \in \mathbb{R}^n$; then the *gradient* of h is defined as

$$\nabla h = \left(\frac{\partial h}{\partial x_1}, \ldots, \frac{\partial h}{\partial x_n}\right). \tag{8.6}$$

We often write

$$\nabla_i h = \frac{\partial h}{\partial x_i} \tag{8.7}$$

for the ith component of ∇h with $i = 1, \ldots, n$. When we evaluate the gradient at some point $\overline{y} \in \mathbb{R}^n$, we obtain a vector in $\mathbb{R}^n$ that points in the direction of the largest increase in the function at that point. The length of the vector represents the increase of the function at that point. Formally, we have

$$\nabla h(\overline{y}) = \left(\frac{\partial h}{\partial x_1}, \ldots, \frac{\partial h}{\partial x_n} \right)(\overline{y}) = \left(\frac{\partial h}{\partial x_1}(\overline{y}), \ldots, \frac{\partial h}{\partial x_n}(\overline{y}) \right). \tag{8.8}$$

We can also write this definition in our gradient component notation as

$$\nabla h(\overline{y}) = (\nabla_1 h, \ldots, \nabla_n h)(\overline{y}) = (\nabla_1 h(\overline{y}), \ldots, \nabla_n h(\overline{y})). \tag{8.9}$$

The gradient is evaluated componentwise at the point $\overline{y}$ where each component is computed as $\nabla_i h(\overline{y})$.

In gradient ascent we take advantage of the gradient and use it to point the way toward the maximum value of the function. Should the gradient become zero at a particular point, we know that we are at a maximum because there is no further increase in the value of the function at that point. To use gradient ascent as an optimization procedure for some objective function, we pick a random starting point on the surface of the objective function and then iteratively move along the surface of the function in the direction of the gradient until the gradient evaluated at some point becomes zero. Following is a sketch of the gradient ascent algorithm for our Lagrangian optimization problem:

> **let** $\eta > 0$
> $\overline{\alpha} \leftarrow \overline{0}$
> **repeat**
> $\quad \overline{\alpha}_{\text{old}} \leftarrow \overline{\alpha}$
> $\quad$ **for** $i = 1$ **to** l **do**
> $\quad\quad \alpha_i \leftarrow \alpha_i + \eta \nabla_i \phi'(\overline{\alpha})$
> $\quad$ **end for**
> **until** $\overline{\alpha} - \overline{\alpha}_{\text{old}} \approx \overline{0}$
> **return** $\overline{\alpha}$

We start our optimization with a vector $\overline{\alpha}$ whose components have been set to zero, $\alpha_i = 0$. That is, we initially assume that none of the training points are support vectors. We then iterate over the training points, and at each iteration we update the Lagrangian multipliers proportional to the gradient of the Lagrangian dual ϕ' evaluated at the current point $\overline{\alpha}$,

$$\alpha_i \leftarrow \alpha_i + \eta \nabla_i \phi'(\overline{\alpha}). \tag{8.10}$$

Here η is the learning rate and $\nabla_i \phi'(\overline{\alpha})$ computes the ith component of the gradient $\nabla \phi'$ evaluated at point $\overline{\alpha}$. The algorithm continues to iterate until we have converged on the maximum value. The maximum value is reached when the gradient is zero, or in our case, the difference between the new and old values of $\overline{\alpha}$ is approximately zero. Because the Lagrangian dual ϕ' has a unique maximum (see Section 7.1) we are guaranteed to find a solution for $\bar{\alpha}$ provided that we pick the learning rate η small enough.[1] Typical values for η are in the interval $[0, 1]$. The version of gradient ascent described here is called *stochastic gradient ascent*, since we use the components of the gradient as soon as they become available during the iteration over the training points.

Algorithm 8.1

> **let** $D = \{(\bar{x}_1, y_1), (\bar{x}_2, y_2), \ldots, (\bar{x}_l, y_l)\} \subset \mathbb{R}^n \times \{+1, -1\}$
> **let** $\eta > 0$
> **let** $C > 0$
> **let** $b = 0$
> $\bar{\alpha} \leftarrow \bar{0}$
> **repeat**
> $\bar{\alpha}_{\text{old}} \leftarrow \bar{\alpha}$
>   **for** $i = 1$ **to** l **do**
> $\alpha_i \leftarrow \min\left\{C, \max\left\{0, \alpha_i + \eta - \eta y_i \sum_{j=1}^{l} y_j \alpha_j k(\bar{x}_j, \bar{x}_i)\right\}\right\}$
>   **end for**
> **until** $\bar{\alpha} - \bar{\alpha}_{\text{old}} \approx \bar{0}$
> **return** $(\bar{\alpha}, b)$

8.1.1 The Kernel-Adatron Algorithm

There are two problems with the simple gradient ascent algorithm sketched above. One is that we have treated our optimization problem as an unconstrained optimization. That is, we ignored the constraints given in (8.4) and (8.5). The second is that we have not addressed the computation of the optimal offset term b^*. By addressing these two problems in the simple gradient ascent algorithm above, we obtain the *kernel-adatron algorithm*.

Recall that the constraint (8.4) is due to optimization of the offset term [see equation (7.126)]. This constraint restricts the values of the components of $\bar{\alpha}$ in such a way that their linear combination has to be equal to zero. This constraint is impossible to satisfy at each optimization step in an algorithm that updates only one Lagrangian multiplier at a time. Consider that initially this constraint is satisfied trivially in our algorithm by the fact that $\alpha_i = 0$ for $i = 1, \ldots, l$. However, as soon as we modify the first Lagrangian multiplier, this constraint is no longer satisfied. In fact, to maintain constraint satisfaction at each step of the algorithm, we would need to modify at least two Lagrangian multipliers simultaneously at each update. This insight is the cornerstone of the sequential minimal optimization algorithm discussed below. Here we take a different approach; rather than trying to optimize the offset term, we set it to zero (i.e., we let $b^* = 0$). Once we fix the value for the offset term the constraint (8.4) disappears, since the offset term no longer needs to be optimized. This takes care of the constraint (8.4) and the offset term.

---

[1] Specific theoretical bounds on η that guarantee convergence have been established (see [18]). Here we treat η as a free parameter that needs to be set by the user.

We are now left with the constraints (8.5), which limit the values of the Lagrangian multipliers to values between zero and the cost constant C. These constraints are easily implemented, however. We simply do not let the values of the components α_i fall below zero or grow larger than the constant C. We accomplish this by rewriting our update rule for the gradient ascent (8.10) as follows:

$$\alpha_i \leftarrow \min\{C, \max\{0, \alpha_i + \eta\nabla_i\phi'(\overline{\alpha})\}\}. \tag{8.11}$$

Here the max operator only admits values that are greater than or equal to zero, and the min operator only admits values less than or equal to the constant C.

Now, to make our update rule more concrete, we differentiate the Lagrangian dual ϕ' with respect to α_i, which gives us the following:

$$\nabla_i\phi'(\overline{\alpha}) = \frac{\partial\phi'}{\partial\alpha_i}(\overline{\alpha}) = 1 - y_i \sum_{j=1}^{l} y_j\alpha_j k(\overline{x}_j, \overline{x}_i). \tag{8.12}$$

Plugging (8.12) into (8.11) gives us our rule:

$$\alpha_i \leftarrow \min\left\{C, \max\left\{0, \alpha_i + \eta - \eta y_i \sum_{j=1}^{l} y_j\alpha_j k(\overline{x}_j, \overline{x}_i)\right\}\right\}. \tag{8.13}$$

The complete kernel-adatron training algorithm for a soft-margin classifier is given in Algorithm 8.1. As expected, the algorithm is virtually identical to the original gradient ascent algorithm, with the difference that the update rule clips the values of the Lagrangian multipliers, and the algorithm returns a pair of values representing the optimal values $\overline{\alpha}^*$ and b^*, with $b^* = 0$ always.

It is interesting to note the similarities between the kernel-perceptron algorithm given in Algorithm 7.2 and the kernel-adatron algorithm here. Both algorithms iterate over the training data and use an incremental approach to update the component values of the vector $\overline{\alpha}$. The big difference is that the kernel-perceptron algorithm stops iterating as soon as it has found *some* decision surface, whereas the kernel-adatron algorithm terminates when it has found the *optimal* decision surface.

Algorithm 8.2

> **let** $D = \{(\overline{x}_1, y_1), (\overline{x}_2, y_2), \ldots, (\overline{x}_l, y_l)\} \subset \mathbb{R}^n \times \{+1, -1\}$
> **let** $C > 0$
> **let** $\mathbf{Q}$ be a $l \times l$ matrix with components $Q_{ij} = y_i y_j k(\overline{x}_i, \overline{x}_j)$
> **let** $\mathbf{Y}$ be a $1 \times l$ matrix with components $Y_{1j} = y_j$
> **let** $\overline{q}$ be a constant vector with $q_i = 1$
> **let** $\overline{u}$ be a constant vector with $u_i = 0$
> **let** $\overline{v}$ be a constant vector with $v_i = C$
> $\overline{\alpha} \leftarrow \text{solve}(\mathbf{Q}, \overline{q}, \mathbf{Y}, \overline{u}, \overline{v})$
> $b \leftarrow$ compute according to equation (7.137)
> **return** $(\overline{\alpha}, b)$

8.2 QUADRATIC PROGRAMMING

Off-the-shelf optimization packages that handle quadratic optimization problems can be used to implement support vector machines. In most cases these packages represent optimization problems in the generalized form

$$\overline{\alpha}^* = \operatorname*{argmin}_{\overline{\alpha}} \left(\tfrac{1}{2} \overline{\alpha}^{\mathrm{T}} \mathbf{Q} \overline{\alpha} - \overline{q} \bullet \overline{\alpha} \right), \tag{8.14}$$

subject to the constraints

$$\mathbf{Y} \overline{\alpha} = 0, \tag{8.15}$$

$$\overline{u} \leq \overline{\alpha} \leq \overline{v}. \tag{8.16}$$

This generalized form of quadratic programming problems is very similar to the form we considered in Section 6.4 for the solution of primal maximum-margin classifiers. However, for the implementation of support vector machines it is important that the optimization package supports both the equality constraints (8.15) and inequality constraints (8.16).

The shape of the generalized objective function optimization (8.14) is very close to the form we need to implement our Lagrangian dual optimization (8.3). The biggest difference is that the generalized form is expressed as a minimization, whereas the optimization of the Lagrangian dual is a maximization. However, applying identity (6.4) to optimization of the Lagrangian dual (8.3) gives us our Lagrangian dual optimization in the necessary minimization format,

$$\operatorname*{argmax}_{\overline{\alpha}} \phi'(\overline{\alpha}) = \operatorname*{argmin}_{\overline{\alpha}} \left(-\phi'(\overline{\alpha}) \right)$$

$$= \operatorname*{argmin}_{\overline{\alpha}} \left(\frac{1}{2} \sum_{i=1}^{l} \sum_{j=1}^{l} y_i y_j \alpha_i \alpha_j k(\overline{x}_i, \overline{x}_j) - \sum_{i=1}^{l} \alpha_i \right). \tag{8.17}$$

If we assume that we have a training set with l observations as in (8.1), it is easy to show that

$$\frac{1}{2} \overline{\alpha}^{\mathrm{T}} \mathbf{Q} \overline{\alpha} - \overline{q} \bullet \overline{\alpha} = \frac{1}{2} \sum_{i=1}^{l} \sum_{j=1}^{l} y_i y_j \alpha_i \alpha_j k(\overline{x}_i, \overline{x}_j) - \sum_{i=1}^{l} \alpha_i, \tag{8.18}$$

where the matrix $\mathbf{Q}$ is an $l \times l$ matrix with components

$$Q_{ij} = y_i y_j k(\overline{x}_i, \overline{x}_j) \tag{8.19}$$

and the vector $\overline{q}$ has l components initialized to 1:

$$\overline{q} = \overline{1}. \tag{8.20}$$

We often refer to the matrix $\mathbf{Q}$ as the *kernel matrix* since it consists of all possible kernel values for a training set with l observations. Furthermore, if we let $\mathbf{Y}$ be a $1 \times l$ matrix with components

$$Y_{1i} = y_i, \tag{8.21}$$

where $(\overline{x}_i, y_i) \in D$, we can show that the generalized constraint (8.15) is equal to the equality constraint (8.4) of our:

$$\mathbf{Y}\overline{\alpha} = \sum_{i=1}^{l} y_i \alpha_i. \tag{8.22}$$

Recall that by default vectors are represented as a single column matrix. Finally, if we let $\overline{u} = \overline{0}$ and let vector $\overline{v}$ be a constant vector with $v_i = C$, the generalized inequality constraint (8.16) is equal to the inequality constraint (8.5),

$$u_i \leq \alpha_i \leq v_i, \tag{8.23}$$

with $i = 1, \ldots, l$. This shows that the generalized optimization problem can be instantiated as our Lagrangian dual optimization problem.

We summarize this construction in Algorithm 8.2. Here the function `solve` is assumed to be a quadratic programming solver that operates on the generalized representation of an optimization problem according to (8.14), (8.15), and (8.16). Because the solver satisfies the equality constraint, we can use the vector $\overline{\alpha}$ to determine the offset term [see equation (7.137)].

8.2.1 Chunking

The size of the kernel matrix $\mathbf{Q}$ above is a problem for the straightforward application of quadratic programming solvers to the implementation of support vector models. This matrix grows quadratically with the size of the training set. This poses problems even for moderately sized knowledge discovery projects. Consider a training set with 50,000 instances. To implement a training algorithm for a support vector model using a quadratic programming solver we would have to construct a kernel matrix with 2.5 billion elements. Not only will the memory requirements for a matrix of this size exceed the capabilities of many machines, but the size of this kernel matrix also implies that solution of the optimization problem will be very slow.

We can take advantage of the sparseness of the support vector model to reduce the memory requirements of the kernel matrix. That is, we can take advantage of the fact that typically very few instances in a training set are support vectors that constrain the position of the decision surface. This sparseness allows us to view the overall Lagrangian dual optimization problem as a succession of smaller optimization problems, each tailored to find support vectors in a *chunk* of training data. The key to this approach is that the position of the decision surface is determined completely

Algorithm 8.3

> **let** $D = \{(\overline{x}_1, y_1), (\overline{x}_2, y_2), \ldots, (\overline{x}_l, y_l)\} \subset \mathbb{R}^n \times \{+1, -1\}$
> **let** $k > 0$
> $\overline{a} \leftarrow \overline{0}$
> Select a subset W of size k from D.
> **repeat forever**
>   Solve the Lagrangian dual for W (update $\overline{a}$ accordingly).
>   Delete observations from W that are not support vectors.
> $b \leftarrow$ compute according to equation (7.137)
>   **if** all $d \in D$ satisfy the KKT conditions [see equation (8.29)] **then**
>   **return** $(\overline{a}, b)$
>   **end if**
> $D_k \leftarrow$ the k worst offenders in D of the KKT conditions
> $W \leftarrow W \cup D_k$
> **end repeat**

by the support vectors, and all other observations in the training set can be removed without changing this. We will see that the chunking algorithm makes repeated use of this property.

The training algorithm based on chunking is shown in Algorithm 8.3. Here, the constant k is the *chunk size* and the set W is often referred to as the *working set*. The algorithm iterates over a succession of smaller optimization problems characterized by the training observations in W. At each iteration the solution to the Lagrangian dual optimization of W is used to estimate how far the overall optimization has progressed. To accomplish this we discard points that are not support vectors in W, and the remaining support vectors are used to construct a model. This model is then applied to all observations in the training set. The algorithm terminates when the support vectors in W define a model such that the KKT conditions are fulfilled for all training observations. That is, we have converged on a global solution if all observations in the training set satisfy the KKT conditions. Otherwise, the model is used to find the training observations in D that violate the KKT conditions. As can be seen in the algorithm, in the last step of the loop we identify the k worst offenders of the KKT conditions. This is done by measuring how far away each training observation is from satisfying the KKT conditions. This allows us to sort the offenders and extract the k top offenders from this list. These top offenders are then added to the working set W, which now constitutes a new optimization problem for the next iteration.

The algorithm monitors the two complementarity conditions (7.118) and (7.119) for soft-margin classifiers in order to detect global convergence. Rewriting these constraints slightly gives us

$$\alpha_i \left(y_i \left(\sum_{j=1}^{l} y_j \alpha_j k(\overline{x}_j, \overline{x}_i) - b \right) - 1 + \xi_i \right) = 0 \qquad (8.24)$$

and

$$(C - \alpha_i)\xi_i = 0 \qquad (8.25)$$

for all $(\overline{x}_i, y_i) \in D$ with $i = 1, \ldots, l$. We don't have direct access to the values of the slack variables ξ_i in order to monitor the conditions as given. However, through a case analysis of the Lagrangian multipliers α_i for each training observation $(\overline{x}_i, y_i)$, we can derive a set of rules that are implied by these conditions and that we can use directly as convergence criteria.

1. Let $\alpha_i = 0$; then by (8.25) we have $\xi_i = 0$. From condition (8.24) we then obtain

$$y_i \left(\sum_{j=1}^{l} y_j \alpha_j k(\overline{x}_j, \overline{x}_i) - b \right) \geq 1. \tag{8.26}$$

That is, since $\alpha_i = 0$ and $\xi_i = 0$, the condition (8.24) is fulfilled as long as the observation $(\overline{x}_i, y_i)$ lies on or above its corresponding supporting hyperplane.

2. Let $0 < \alpha_i < C$. Again, condition (8.25) implies that $\xi_i = 0$. By condition (8.24) we have

$$y_i \left(\sum_{j=1}^{l} y_j \alpha_j k(\overline{x}_j, \overline{x}_i) - b \right) = 1. \tag{8.27}$$

Since $\alpha_i \neq 0$ and $\alpha_i \neq C$ as well as $\xi_i = 0$, the observation $(\overline{x}_i, y_i)$ is a support vector positioned directly on its corresponding supporting hyperplane.

3. Let $\alpha_i = C$. Constraint (8.25) then implies that $\xi_i > 0$. Using equation (8.24) gives us the following condition for bound support vectors:

$$y_i \left(\sum_{j=1}^{l} y_j \alpha_j k(\overline{x}_j, \overline{x}_i) - b \right) \leq 1. \tag{8.28}$$

Since $\alpha_i = C$ and $\xi_i > 0$, the instance $(\overline{x}_i, y_i)$ is a support vector below its corresponding supporting hyperplane.

Putting this all together gives us the following conditions that we need to monitor in Algorithm 8.3 to detect global convergence:

$$y_i \left(\sum_{j=1}^{l} y_j \alpha_j k(\overline{x}_j, \overline{x}_i) - b \right) \begin{cases} \geq 1 \text{ if } \alpha_i = 0 \\ = 1 \text{ if } 0 < \alpha_i < C \\ \leq 1 \text{ if } \alpha_i = C \end{cases} \tag{8.29}$$

for all $(\overline{x}_i, y_i) \in D$ with $i = 1, \ldots, l$. One way to view these conditions is as a consistency test: If the values of the Lagrangian multipliers are consistent with the locations of the corresponding training points vis-à-vis a decision surface, we have found a global solution.

Algorithm 8.4

> let $D = \{(\overline{x}_1, y_1), (\overline{x}_2, y_2), \ldots, (\overline{x}_l, y_l)\} \subset \mathbb{R}^n \times \{+1, -1\}$
> $\overline{\alpha} \leftarrow \overline{0}$
> **repeat**
>   1. Pick two points, $\overline{x}_j$ and $\overline{x}_k$ in D together with their respective Lagrangian multipliers, α_j and α_k, where $j \neq k$.
>   2. Optimize the subproblem max $\phi'(\alpha_j, \alpha_k)$ (keeping the other Lagrangian multipliers constant).
>   3. Compute b.
> **until** the KKT conditions hold for all $d \in D$
> **return** $(\overline{\alpha}, b)$

To see that chunking reduces the size of sparse optimization problems, consider that the algorithm breaks the overall problem into successive smaller optimization problems based on the working set W of size k. If we pick k large enough, the size of W will stay roughly constant,

$$|W \cup D_k| \approx k. \tag{8.30}$$

That is, the size of W after removing all the training observations that are not support vectors is negligible compared to the value of k. A typical value for k is 500, which implies that each optimization subproblem uses a kernel matrix on the order of 250,000 elements. This is significantly smaller than the 2.5 billion elements in our knowledge discovery project with 50,000 training observations from the beginning of this section. It is interesting to observe that if our sparseness assumption does not hold, that is, almost all training points are considered to be support vectors, the algorithm degenerates into the original overall optimization problem. This is due to the fact that for a solution that is not sparse, very few nonsupport vectors can be removed from W at each iteration, and therefore

$$|W \cup D_k| \gg k. \tag{8.31}$$

This means that the working set W will grow to the size of D after a sufficient number of iterations. However, most real-world data sets give rise to sparse solutions, and therefore the latter is not of great concern. Furthermore, the chunking algorithm has been shown to converge in a robust fashion in real-world situations.

8.3 SEQUENTIAL MINIMAL OPTIMIZATION

Sequential minimal optimization (SMO) is a fast and elegant optimization algorithm that computes a solution to the Lagrangian dual optimization problem in (8.3) with constraints (8.4) and (8.5). This algorithm works similar to the chunking algorithm of Section 8.2 in that it breaks the global optimization problem down into several smaller optimization problems, taking advantage of the fact that the smallest possible working set for the Lagrangian dual optimization problem is a set of two training points. As mentioned before, updating a single Lagrangian multiplier does not work since it is not guaranteed that the constraint (8.4) is satisfied at every step.

Algorithm 8.4 outlines the optimization. As can be seen from the algorithm sketch, the computation first picks two training points, optimizes this working set of two points, and then checks if the KKT conditions given in (8.29) hold for all training points. If so, the algorithm terminates. Otherwise, it will continue to iterate. During the computation, if possible, the first training point is always picked such that it does satisfy the KKT conditions, and the second point is always picked in such a way that it is the most serious violator of the KKT conditions at that point of the optimization. That is, a viable Lagrangian multiplier is always optimized against a nonviable Lagrangian multiplier. With this it can be shown that the algorithm is guaranteed to converge.

What is remarkable and sets this algorithm apart from previous implementations is the fact that the optimization subproblem over the two training instances can be solved analytically, and therefore a call to a computationally expensive optimization library is not necessary. Consider the subproblem of our Lagrangian dual optimization using the Lagrangian multipliers α_j and α_k:

$$\max_{\alpha_j, \alpha_k} \phi'(\alpha_j, \alpha_k), \tag{8.32}$$

subject to the constraints:

$$y_j \alpha_j + y_k \alpha_k = \delta, \tag{8.33}$$

$$C \geq \alpha_j, \alpha_k \geq 0, \tag{8.34}$$

with $j, k = 1, \ldots, l$ and $j \neq k$. We can compute the constant δ of the equality constraint as

$$\delta = - \sum_{i=1, i \neq j, i \neq k}^{l} y_i \alpha_i. \tag{8.35}$$

That is, the values of α_j and α_k are constrained by all the other Lagrangian multipliers of the global optimization problem. We can simplify this optimization problem even further by rewriting constraint (8.33) as,[2]

$$\alpha_k = y_k(\delta - y_j \alpha_j). \tag{8.36}$$

Plugging equation (8.36) into equation (8.32) results in

$$\max_{\alpha_j, \alpha_k} \phi'(\alpha_j, \alpha_k) = \max_{\alpha_j} \phi'\left(\alpha_j, y_k(\delta - y_j \alpha_j)\right) = \max_{\alpha_j} \psi(\alpha_j). \tag{8.37}$$

---

[2] $1/y_j = y_j$ for $y_j \in \{+1, -1\}$.

That is, our two-variable optimization problem becomes an optimization problem over the single variable α_j. We represent the objective function of this single-variable optimization problem as $\psi(\alpha_j)$. Furthermore, $\phi'(\alpha_j, \alpha_k)$ is a function with a unique global maximum where α_i and α_k lie on the unique saddle point of the original Lagrangian optimization problem. This means that $\psi(\alpha_j)$ also has a unique maximum and we can find it by differentiating ψ with respect to α_j,

$$\frac{d\psi}{d\alpha_j} = 0, \tag{8.38}$$

and solving for α_j. Once we have a value α_j we can use equation (8.36) to find a value for α_k. Some care needs to be taken that this optimization respects the inequality constraints (8.34). There are many more details to this algorithm that make it as efficient and effective as it is, but these details are beyond the scope of the discussion here. Refer to the bibliographic notes for pointers to the relevant literature.

8.4   DISCUSSION

We have discussed three increasingly difficult implementation strategies for support vector machine training algorithms. All three strategies share the characteristic that they represent incremental improvements of the global optimization problem until the global maximum is reached. Of the three strategies discussed, the quadratic programming solution lends itself to a straightforward implementation of support vector machines, and SMO is the most popular. SMO is the foundation of many support vector machine packages available on the Web. It is also the foundation of the support vector machine implementation in WEKA and in the R package that we use. Today, the implementation of support vector machines remains an active area of research. With respect to SMO, much of the research concentrates on the selection of appropriate Lagrangian multipliers to optimize.

Algorithm 8.5

> **let** $\eta > 0$
> $\overline{x} \leftarrow \overline{0}$
> **repeat**
> $\overline{x}_{old} \leftarrow \overline{x}$
> $\overline{x} \leftarrow \overline{x} + \eta \nabla h(\overline{x})$
> **until** $\overline{x} - \overline{x}_{old} \approx \overline{0}$
> **return** $\overline{x}$

EXERCISES

8.1   Let the function $h(\overline{x}) = 6 - (x_1 - 2)^2 - (x_2 + 1)^2$ with $\overline{x} = (x_1, x_2) \in \mathbb{R}^2$ be the objective function in the unconstrained optimization problem

$$\overline{x}^* = \operatorname*{argmax}_{\overline{x}} h(\overline{x}).$$

(a) Compute the gradient ∇h.

(b) Compute the value $\nabla h(\overline{0})$.

(c) Implement the gradient ascent algorithm given in Algorithm 8.5 in R and use it to compute the optimum $\overline{x}^*$.

(d) Convert the gradient ascent algorithm (Algorithm 8.5) into a stochastic gradient ascent algorithm. Implement it in R and compare the results to the simple gradient ascent in part (c).

8.2 Derive equation (8.12).

8.3 Show that equation (8.18) holds for the values of $\mathbf{Q}$ and $\overline{q}$ given in the text.

8.4 Implement Algorithm 8.1 in R. Test the implementation on your favorite data set using an appropriate kernel from Table 7.2.

8.5 Implement Algorithm 8.2 in R using the quadratic programming solver ipop available in the package kernlab. Test the implementation on your favorite data set using an appropriate kernel from Table 7.2.

8.6 [*challenging*] Implement Algorithm 8.3 in R using the quadratic programming solver ipop available in the package kernlab. Test the implementation on a data set that has at least 5000 instances, using an appropriate kernel from Table 7.2.

8.7 [*challenging*] Research and fill out the details for SMO given in Algorithm 8.4. Then implement the algorithm in R.

BIBLIOGRAPHIC NOTES

Any college-level calculus book will have a discussion of the gradient of a function. We based our discussion here on a book by Kreyszig [48]. Gradient ascent optimization methods are discussed in [14] and [69]. Again, any introductory book on mathematical optimization will have a discussion on gradient ascent methods. The kernel-adatron was introduced by Friess et al. in [33]. Here we present a simpler version of this algorithm as given in [67]. Our chunking algorithm was first suggested by Vapnik in [74]. Another, more sophisticated chunking algorithm is given by Osuna et al. in [57]. There are many industrial-strength optimization packages available that can be used to solve the convex optimization problem due to support vector machines. Two packages that have been used routinely in this context are LOQO (http://www.princeton.edu/~rvdb/loqo) and MINOS (http://www.sbsi-sol-optimize.com/asp/sol_product_minos.htm). Platt proposed his sequential minimal optimization algorithm in [58]. There is a lot of information with respect to SMO on his Website (http://research.microsoft.com/~jplatt/smo.html). Our own presentation of SMO was inspired by the machine learning class notes of Andrew Ng at Stanford (http://www.stanford.edu/class/cs229) and Mak's thesis [50]. LIBSVM [20] is a very popular C++ implementation of the SMO algorithm. More recently, advanced selection heuristics for the Lagrangian multipliers have been proposed for SMO (e.g., [30]). A nice summary of different implementations of support vector machines in R is a paper by Karatzoglou et al. [40]. A recent collection of papers dealing with support vector machine implementations for very large knowledge discovery projects is [13].

CHAPTER 9

EVALUATING WHAT HAS BEEN LEARNED

The data universes associated with most knowledge discovery projects are too large to be considered as training sets for support vector machines. It is therefore necessary to use subsets of the data universes as training sets. As soon as we use only a subset of a data universe as a training set, we are faced with the question: How does our model perform on instances of the data universe that are not part of the training set? In this chapter we introduce techniques that will allow us to quantify the performance of our models in the context of this uncertainty.

We begin this chapter with an introduction to simple performance metrics for classification models. We then introduce the confusion matrix, which gives us a more detailed insight into model performance. In particular, the confusion matrix characterizes the types of errors that models make. Based on the confusion matrix, we define some additional performance metrics that are commonly used when evaluating classification models.

With these metrics and tools in hand, we discuss formal model evaluation. In particular, we discuss the difference between training and test error. We show that we can use test error as a way to estimate model parameters which promise the best model performance on instances of the data universe that are not part of the training set. The testing techniques we discuss include the hold-out method and N-fold cross-validation. Model evaluation is not complete without a discussion of the uncertainty of the estimated model performance. We show how to construct confidence intervals that characterize this performance uncertainty using the bootstrap. Confidence intervals also allow us to draw conclusions with respect to the statistical significance of performance differences between models. We conclude the chapter with a discussion of these techniques applied to models within WEKA and R.

Knowledge Discovery with Support Vector Machines, by Lutz Hamel
Copyright © 2009 John Wiley & Sons, Inc.

9.1 PERFORMANCE METRICS

Given a model and an appropriate labeled data set, perhaps the most intuitive metric for model performance is the *error* of a model. The error is defined as the number of mistakes that the model makes on the data set divided by the number of observations in the data set:

$$\text{err} = \frac{\text{number of mistakes}}{\text{total number of observations}}. \tag{9.1}$$

To define the model error formally, we introduce the *0–1 loss function*. This function compares the output of a model for a particular observation with the label of this observation. If the model commits a prediction error on this observation, the loss function returns a 1; otherwise, it returns a 0. Formally, let $(x, y) \in D$ be an observation where $D \subseteq \mathbb{R}^n \times \{+1, -1\}$ and let $\hat{f} : \mathbb{R}^n \to \{+1, -1\}$ be a model. Then we define the 0–1 loss function $\mathcal{L} : \{+1, -1\} \times \{+1, -1\} \to \{0, 1\}$ as

$$\mathcal{L}\left(y, \hat{f}(\overline{x})\right) = \begin{cases} 0 & \text{if } y = \hat{f}(\overline{x}), \\ 1 & \text{if } y \neq \hat{f}(\overline{x}). \end{cases} \tag{9.2}$$

The loss function accepts a pair of labels and returns 0 if the labels agree and 1 if the labels are not the same. With this we can rewrite the expression of the model error in a formal fashion. Let $D = \{(\overline{x}_1, y_1), \ldots, (\overline{x}_l, y_l)\} \subset \mathbb{R}^n \times \{+1, -1\}$, and let the model $\hat{f}$ and the loss function $\mathcal{L}$ be as defined above. Then the model error is

$$\text{err}_D[\hat{f}] = \frac{1}{l} \sum_{i=1}^{l} \mathcal{L}\left(y_i, \hat{f}(\overline{x}_i)\right), \tag{9.3}$$

where $(\overline{x}_i, y_i) \in D$. The model error is computed by summing the number of errors committed by the model on the data set D and dividing by the size of the data set D. In other words, the model error is the average loss over the data set D. Notice that here we are more specific with naming the model error. The subscript D indicates that we use the data set D to compute the error. We have also parameterized the error with respect to the model. The notation $\text{err}_D[\hat{f}]$ reads as "the error of model $\hat{f}$ computed on data set D."

We can also characterize the performance of a model in terms of its *accuracy*,

$$\text{acc} = \frac{\text{number of correct predictions}}{\text{total number of observations}}. \tag{9.4}$$

Again, we can use the 0–1 loss function to define this metric more concisely,

$$\text{acc}_D[\hat{f}] = \frac{1}{l} \left(l - \sum_{i=1}^{l} \mathcal{L}\left(y_i, \hat{f}(\overline{x}_i)\right) \right)$$

$$= 1 - \frac{1}{l} \sum_{i=1}^{l} \mathcal{L}\left(y_i, \hat{f}(\overline{x}_i)\right)$$

$$= 1 - \mathrm{err}_D[\hat{f}]. \tag{9.5}$$

Since the accuracy and the error of a model are related by the simple identity above, we can always compute one from the other given either the model accuracy or the model error.

As an example of the metrics above, consider a model $\hat{g}$ that commits five prediction errors when applied to a data set Q of length 100. We can compute the error using (9.3),

$$\mathrm{err}_Q[\hat{g}] = \frac{1}{100}(5) = 0.05.$$

We can compute the accuracy of the model using (9.5),

$$\mathrm{acc}_Q[\hat{g}] = 1 - 0.05 = 0.95.$$

It is customary to express the error and the accuracy as percentages. Therefore, here we have a model error of 5% and an accuracy of 95%, respectively.

9.1.1 The Confusion Matrix

When dealing with a binary classification problem, there are four possible outcomes when a model is applied to an observation. Let $(\overline{x}, y) \in \mathbb{R}^n \times \{+1, -1\}$ be an observation and let $\hat{f} : \mathbb{R}^n \to \{+1, -1\}$ be a model. Then we have the following four possibilities when the model is applied to the observation:

$$\hat{f}(\overline{x}) = \begin{cases} +1 \text{ if } y = +1, \text{ called the } \textit{true positive}, \\ -1 \text{ if } y = +1, \text{ called the } \textit{false negative}, \\ +1 \text{ if } y = -1, \text{ called the } \textit{false positive}, \\ -1 \text{ if } y = -1, \text{ called the } \textit{true negative}. \end{cases} \tag{9.6}$$

If the model output $\hat{f}(\overline{x})$ matches the label y of the observation, we have either a true positive or a true negative outcome. If the model output does not match the label observed, we have either a false positive or a false negative outcome, both of which are error outcomes.

In many situations it is important to distinguish these two error outcomes when evaluating model performance. Consider the following clinical example. Suppose you are developing a model that, given the parameters of a tissue biopsy, will predict whether or not this tissue is cancerous. Now, from the discussion above, your model can commit two types of errors. It can commit a false positive error; that is, it predicts that the tissue sample is cancerous when it is not. It can also commit a false negative

TABLE 9.1   Layout of a Confusion Matrix

Observed (y)	Predicted ($\hat{y}$)	
	+1	−1
+1	True positive (TP)	False negative (FN)
−1	False positive (FP)	True negative (TP)

error. Here the model predicts that the tissue sample is not cancerous when in reality it is. In a clinical setting the latter is a much more serious error than the former since a false negative implies that the patient will remain untreated, whereas a false positive usually results in more tests until the false positive error is detected and the patient is discharged appropriately.

When analyzing model performance in these types of situations we would like to understand the different types of errors that our model commits. Unfortunately, the simple performance metrics that we just discussed, based on the 0–1 loss function, do not allow us to distinguish these errors. However, a representation of model performance called the *confusion matrix* does distinguish between the two types of errors and is therefore the tool of choice when analyzing model performance where one or the other type of error can have serious implications.

A confusion matrix for a binary classification model is a 2×2 table that displays the labels observed against the labels predicted for a data set. One way to visualize the confusion matrix is to consider that applying a model $\hat{f}$ to an observation $(\overline{x}, y)$ will give us two labels. The first label, y, is due to the observation, and the second label, $\hat{y} = \hat{f}(\overline{x})$, is due to the prediction of the model. That is, for each observation we obtain the pair of labels $(y, \hat{y})$. This pair of labels specifies the coordinates of each observation within the confusion matrix: The first label specifies the row of the matrix and the second label specifies the column of the matrix. Therefore, an observation with the label pair $(y, \hat{y})$ will be mapped onto a confusion matrix as given in Table 9.1 as follows:

$$
\begin{aligned}
(+1, +1) &\mapsto \text{TP}, \\
(-1, +1) &\mapsto \text{FP}, \\
(+1, -1) &\mapsto \text{FN}, \\
(-1, -1) &\mapsto \text{TN}.
\end{aligned}
$$

True positive predictions are mapped into the top left corner of the confusion matrix, and true negative predictions are mapped into the bottom right corner of the matrix. False positives and false negatives are mapped into the bottom left and top right corners of the matrix, respectively. For a model that does not commit any errors, we see that all predictions will be mapped onto the top left and bottom right fields. For models that do commit errors, we see that the errors will be mapped into the confusion matrix according to the type of error the model commits.

Table 9.2 shows a confusion matrix of a model applied to a set of 200 observations. On this set of observations the model commits 7 false negative errors and 4 false positive errors in addition to the 95 true positive and 94 true negative predictions.

TABLE 9.2 Typical Confusion Matrix for a Model Applied to a Particular Set of Observations

Observed	Predicted	
	+1	−1
+1	95	7
−1	4	94

If this were a model for the clinical example above, the fact that the model commits almost twice as many false negative errors than false positive errors would be cause for concern. Here it would be advisable to build a new model with more balanced errors. Only the confusion matrix is able to provide this type of insight. The simple model error metric discussed above would give us the overall error the model commits as

$$err = \frac{1}{200}(4+7) = 0.055.$$

A model that commits a 5.5% prediction error seems like a reasonable model. However, in the context where model errors can have serious consequences, we will have to look more closely at the types of errors that a model commits.

Given a confusion matrix of a model as in Table 9.1, we can compute our model error and accuracy directly from the matrix as

$$err = \frac{FP + FN}{TP + TN + FP + FN} \tag{9.7}$$

and

$$acc = \frac{TP + TN}{TP + TN + FP + FN}, \tag{9.8}$$

respectively. In addition to these metrics we have two other metrics that are commonly used to characterize model performance: sensitivity and specificity. The *sensitivity* of a model is defined as the true positive predictions divided by the sum of all positive observations,

$$sensitivity = \frac{TP}{TP + FN}. \tag{9.9}$$

The *specificity* of a model is defined as the true negative predictions divided by the sum of all negative observations,

$$specificity = \frac{TN}{TN + FP}. \tag{9.10}$$

A sensitivity of 1.0 for a model means that the model predicts all positive observations correctly: in other words, the model does not commit any false negative predictions.

A specificity of 1.0 for a model means that the model predicts all negative observations correctly; in other words, the model does not commit any false positive predictions.

Going back to the confusion matrix of our model given in Table 9.2, we can compute the metrics as follows:

$$\text{err} = \frac{4+7}{95+94+4+7} = 0.055,$$

$$\text{acc} = \frac{95+94}{95+94+4+7} = 0.945,$$

$$\text{sensitivity} = \frac{95}{95+7} = 0.93,$$

$$\text{specificity} = \frac{94}{94+4} = 0.96.$$

9.2   MODEL EVALUATION

One way to construct a model is to select the model parameters such that the model classifies as many training set observations correctly as possible. Typically, this process takes several iterations as we refine the parameters in order to obtain the best possible model performance. This iterative model evaluation process stops when we obtain a model with a satisfactory performance. We touched upon this topic briefly in Section 7.4.2 in the context of feature search. To make our discussion more concrete, we assume that

$$D = \{(\overline{x}_1, y_1), \ldots, (\overline{x}_l, y_l)\} \subset \mathbb{R}^n \times \{+1, -1\} \tag{9.11}$$

represents our training set for the remainder of the chapter.

We need to introduce some additional notation to formalize our model evaluation process. Recall that soft-margin support vector machine models have several free parameters that need to be set by the user. These free parameters include the cost constant and the kernel function, with its corresponding parameters (for details on various kernels, see Table 7.2). Therefore, we formally represent a support vector machine model with its free parameters and its training set D as

$$\hat{f}_D[k, \lambda, C](\overline{x}) = \text{sgn}\left(\sum_{i=1}^{l} \alpha_{C,i} y_i k[\lambda](\overline{x}_i, \overline{x}) - b\right), \tag{9.12}$$

where $(\overline{x}_i, y_i) \in D$. The notation $\hat{f}_D[k, \lambda, C]$ denotes a model $\hat{f}$ that is parameterized over the kernel function k with its corresponding parameters λ and the cost constant C. In addition, the subscript D indicates that the model was trained on set D. Notice that this parameterized model still takes an element of the data universe as an argument, $\hat{f}[k, \lambda, C](\overline{x})$, and returns a $+1$ or -1 label. On the right side of the identity (9.12), we see how the free parameters are employed within the model. As expected, we see the kernel function k parameterized over its own parameters λ. The notation $\alpha_{C,i}$ is intended to show that the values of the Lagrangian multipliers are dependent on the precise value of the user-defined cost constant C. Recall that the training algorithm has to obey the constraints $0 \le \alpha_i \le C$. Therefore, the values of the Lagrangian multipliers depend on the cost constant. For convenience we make this dependence explicit with our notation.

With this notation we can formally define the model error as follows: The error of model $\hat{f}_D[k, \lambda, C]$ computed on the training set D according to equation (9.3) is

$$\text{err}_D \left[\hat{f}_D[k, \lambda, C] \right] = \frac{1}{l} \sum_{i=1}^{l} \mathcal{L}\left(y_i, \hat{f}_D[k, \lambda, C](\overline{x}_i) \right), \qquad (9.13)$$

where $(\overline{x}_i, y_i) \in D$. That is, the model error $\text{err}_D[\hat{f}_D[k, \lambda, C]]$ is the average loss of model $\hat{f}_D[k, \lambda, C]$ over the data set D. Since we use the training set D for both the construction of the model $\hat{f}_D[k, \lambda, C]$ and the computation of the model error, we refer to this as the *training error*. As mentioned above, when performing model evaluation we try to find a set of model parameters that minimize the training error. That is, we express the model evaluation process as the optimization

$$\min_{k, \lambda, C} \text{err}_D \left[\hat{f}_D[k, \lambda, C] \right] = \min_{k, \lambda, C} \frac{1}{l} \sum_{i=1}^{l} \mathcal{L}\left(y_i, \hat{f}_D[k, \lambda, C](\overline{x}_i) \right). \qquad (9.14)$$

This equation states that we optimize over the model parameters such that the training error is minimized. Figure 9.1 illustrates the relationship between the training error

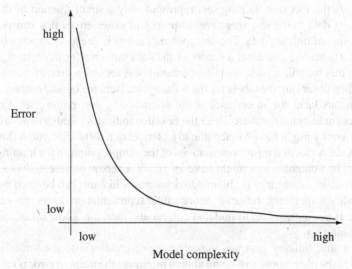

FIGURE 9.1 Typical training error curve for support vector machines.

and the possible models for a typical training set. The horizontal axis represents support vector models governed by the three model parameters k, λ, and C. These three model parameters control the complexity of the models. For example, we consider a model with a linear kernel a low complexity model because of its limited ability to model complex class boundaries. On the other hand, we consider a model with a high-degree polynomial kernel or a model based on a Gaussian kernel to be a complex model because of its ability to model complex class boundaries. Low-complexity models appear on the left side of the horizontal axis; high-complexity models appear on the right. The training error is mapped onto the vertical axis. Notice that the training error decreases with the growing complexity of the models. That is, the more complex a model is, the better it can model individual observations in the training data, and the fewer mistakes it makes. Here the error curve is depicted in an idealized fashion. In real knowledge discovery projects the curve would exhibit many local maxima and minima.

For most training sets it is possible to find optimal model parameters $k^{\bullet}$, $\lambda^{\bullet}$, and $C^{\bullet}$ such that the training error is close to zero:

$$\min_{k,\lambda,C} \mathrm{err}_D\left[\hat{f}_D[k, \lambda, C] \right] = \mathrm{err}_D\left[\hat{f}_D[k^{\bullet}, \lambda^{\bullet}, C^{\bullet}] \right] \approx 0. \qquad (9.15)$$

This would represent an ideal situation if our training set D were a perfect representation of the corresponding data universe. But unfortunately, training data sets are never perfect representations of the corresponding data universes since they typically consist of only a small fraction of a data universe. Therefore, the fact that we can reduce the training error to zero is meaningless since it does not allow us to draw any conclusions with respect to the performance of the model over the remaining data universe.

Besides the fact that training sets represent only a small fraction of the overall underlying data universes, there are a number of other errors that can pollute the construction of training data. The first source of errors is due to a *sampling bias* in the sense that when we construct a subset of the data universe for our training set, it is possible that we will miss some telling examples. A second source of errors is due to noise when observing the labels for the training set. Here the target function produces an erroneous label for an instance while constructing our training set. Consider a customer credit rating database where the field that indicates whether or not a customer is creditworthy might be corrupted due to a clerical or a software error. A third source of errors are accidental misrepresentations of the sample points in the training set. For example, in a database you might have an age of a person represented as a negative number due to a data entry problem. Obvious errors like this can be fixed by diligent data quality inspections; however, more subtle representation errors are much more difficult, if not impossible, to find and correct and therefore show up as noise in the final training set.

Given that training sets are imperfect representations of the underlying data universes, the phenomenon of being able to minimize the training error is called *overfitting*. An overfitted model is a perfect model of the training set; that is, it is a model with a small or zero training error. In an overfitted model, much of the complexity is due to possible sampling biases and noise in the training data. This additional model complexity can lead to classification errors when the model is applied to instances in the data universe that are not part of the training set. This means that overfitted models have a limited generalization capability. In the following sections we look at some testing techniques that allow us to quantify the performance of a model more precisely. Most important, these testing techniques allow us to draw conclusions about the performance of a model with respect to the overall data universe by limiting the effects that training data noise and sampling bias have on the model evaluation process. Furthermore, these techniques allow us to quantify the uncertainty with which a training set acts as a representation of the underlying data universe.

9.2.1 The Hold-Out Method

Perhaps the simplest testing technique that avoids overfitting is the *hold-out method*. Here we assume that the training data *is* the data universe. We then split the training data into two parts: one that we actually use for training and one that we reserve ("hold-out") for additional testing. In this way we still have a training set that is a subset of the data universe but we now also have a set of instances that are reserved for testing purposes only, and we can view these as representatives of the data universe at large. The importance of these reserved test observations is that they allow us to quantify the generalization ability of our model by measuring the model error on these test observations. In other words, by having a separate test set we can measure whether overfitting is limiting a model's generalization abilities. We call the model error computed on the test set the *test error*.

Let us formalize these ideas. We let D be our original training set as defined in (9.11). According to what we said above, we split this data set into two parts: a training set P and a test set Q such that

$$D = P \cup Q \text{ and } P \cap Q = \emptyset. \tag{9.16}$$

The *training error* on P given some model $\hat{f}_P[k, \lambda, C]$ is computed using (9.3) as

$$\text{err}_P\left[\hat{f}_P[k, \lambda, C]\right] = \frac{1}{|P|} \sum_{(\overline{x}_i, y_i) \in P} \mathcal{L}\left(y_i, \hat{f}_P[k, \lambda, C](\overline{x}_i)\right), \tag{9.17}$$

where $|P|$ denotes the size of set P. As before, the training error is the model error computed on the training set of the model, and we indicate this by giving both the model and the error the same subscript, P. The optimal training error is computed as the optimization problem

$$\min_{k, \lambda, C} \text{err}_P\left[\hat{f}_P[k, \lambda, C]\right] = \text{err}_P\left[\hat{f}_P[k^{\bullet}, \lambda^{\bullet}, C^{\bullet}]\right]. \tag{9.18}$$

Here the optimal training error is obtained with the model $\hat{f}_P[k^\bullet, \lambda^\bullet, C^\bullet]$. Conversely, the *test error* on Q given some model $\hat{f}_P[k, \lambda, C]$ is computed using (9.3) as

$$\text{err}_Q\left[\hat{f}_P[k, \lambda, C]\right] = \frac{1}{|Q|} \sum_{(\overline{x}_i, y_i) \in Q} \mathcal{L}\left(y_i, \hat{f}_P[k, \lambda, C](\overline{x}_i)\right). \tag{9.19}$$

The error is indexed by the test set Q and the model is indexed by the training set P. More precisely, to obtain the test error we use a model trained on P to predict the observations in Q and compute the fraction of errors the model commits on Q. The optimal test error is computed as an optimization using Q as the test set,

$$\min_{k, \lambda, C} \text{err}_Q\left[\hat{f}_P[k, \lambda, C]\right] = \text{err}_Q\left[\hat{f}_P[k^*, \lambda^*, C^*]\right]. \tag{9.20}$$

The optimal test error is achieved by some model $\hat{f}_P[k^*, \lambda^*, C^*]$.

As noted above, the model $\hat{f}_P[k^\bullet, \lambda^\bullet, C^\bullet]$ gives the smallest training error, and the model $\hat{f}_P[k^*, \lambda^*, C^*]$ gives the smallest test error. In general, it holds that the parameters $k^\bullet \neq k^*$, $\lambda^\bullet \neq \lambda^*$, and $C^\bullet \neq C^*$. This implies that the model that minimizes the training error is different from the model that minimizes the test error. This can be seen in Figure 9.2, which displays the characteristic error curves associated with the training and test errors. As before, we see that the training error grows smaller with the rising complexity of the models. However, the test error exhibits very different trends. Starting with low-complexity models on the left, the test error will typically first drop with an increase in model complexity and then at a certain point it will start to increase with the complexity of the model. We mark the turnaround

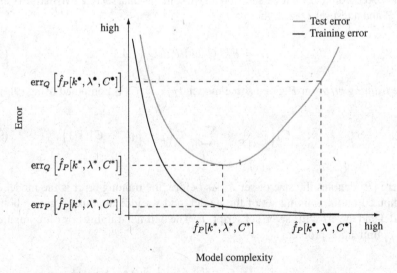

FIGURE 9.2   Error curves typical for support vector machines.

point with the optimal test error model $\hat{f}_P[k^*, \lambda^*, C^*]$ in the graph. This is also precisely the point where the models that minimize the training error start to overfit. That is, models with a complexity greater than the optimal model $\hat{f}_P[k^*, \lambda^*, C^*]$ will do poorly on the test set but will do increasingly better on the training set. Notice that our optimal training error model $\hat{f}_P[k^\bullet, \lambda^\bullet, C^\bullet]$ is far to the right of the test error minimum, indicating that it overfit the training data. This overfitting manifests itself in the poor test error performance of this model. This poor performance is due to the fact that the greater complexity of overfitting models allows them to model structure in the training data that is not present in the test set. This added complexity, however, prevents these models from generalizing well to instances in the test set.

Because the separate test set can be considered a representation of instances in the data universe at large, the performance of the model on the test set allows us to draw conclusions about the model performance on the overall data universe. That is, the test set allows us to quantify the generalization ability of a model in the presence of the error sources discussed in Section 9.1. In summary, rather than trying to minimize the training error when evaluating model performance, we want to minimize the test error. Minimizing the test error gives us a more realistic assessment as to how the model will perform on the underlying data universe.

9.2.2 The Leave-One-Out Method

It is interesting to observe that the quality of the test error estimate err_Q of Section 9.2.1 depends greatly on the random split of the data set D into a training set and a test set. A poorly executed split can introduce biases such as the extreme case where all positive examples are in the training set and all negative examples are in the test set.

One way to mitigate the bias of the random split of D is to perform the split-train test cycle multiple times. A straightforward way to accomplish this is by splitting the data set D of size l into l partitions of size 1 such that

$$D = Q_1 \cup Q_2 \cup \cdots \cup Q_{l-1} \cup Q_l \tag{9.21}$$

and

$$Q_i \cap Q_j = \emptyset, \tag{9.22}$$

where $Q_i = \{(\overline{x}_i, y_i)\}$ and $Q_j = \{(\overline{x}_j, y_j)\}$ for $i, j = 1, \ldots, l$ and $i \neq j$. Each partition Q_i is used systematically for testing exactly once, whereas the remaining partitions are used for training. Let $P_i = D - Q_i$ be the training set with respect to the test partition Q_i with $i = 1, \ldots, l$; then we can compute the error for each test partition as

$$\text{err}_{Q_i}\left[\hat{f}_{P_i}[k, \lambda, C]\right] = \mathcal{L}\left(y_i, \hat{f}_{P_i}[k, \lambda, C](\overline{x}_i)\right), \tag{9.23}$$

where $\hat{f}_{P_i}[k, \lambda, C]$ is the model trained on data set P_i with parameters k, λ, and C. The test error err_{Q_i} is computed as the loss over the single element in the test partition Q_i. As you might have guessed, the leave-one-out method got its name from the fact that we train l models on training sets of size $l - 1$.

Once each of the l partitions has been used for testing, we can compute the *leave-one-out error* (LOOE) as the average error over all partitions,

$$\text{LOOE}_D[k, \lambda, C] = \frac{1}{l} \sum_{i=1}^{l} \text{err}_{Q_i} \left[\hat{f}_{P_i}[k, \lambda, C] \right]. \tag{9.24}$$

Note that the leave-one-out error, $\text{LOOE}_D[k, \lambda, C]$, is now an error estimate only in terms of the model parameters, not the models themselves, since in general we have $\hat{f}_{P_i}[k, \lambda, C] \neq \hat{f}_{P_j}[k, \lambda, C]$ for any $i, j = 1, \ldots, l$ and $i \neq j$. That is, models with the same parameters but trained on different data sets are rarely the same. However, the set of parameters that minimizes the leave-one-out error over all partitions,

$$(k^*, \lambda^*, C^*) = \operatorname*{argmin}_{k, \lambda, C} \text{LOOE}_D[k, \lambda, C], \tag{9.25}$$

can be considered to be an optimal parameter set giving rise to the optimal model $\hat{f}_D[k^*, \lambda^*, C^*]$. This model is constructed by training it on the entire data set D using the optimal leave-one-out parameter set. It might be surprising that we use the original training data D in order to construct the optimal model. However, we do not use D to compute the model parameters. The model parameters were computed using separate training and test sets, and therefore there is no danger of overfitting.

We have achieved our goal of minimizing the bias of the single split in the hold-out method by splitting the data in all possible ways. This limits the effects of the bias due to any particular split of the data. We also minimized the possibility of a bias by maximizing the amount of training data available at any particular split: We remove only one element at a time for testing. Unfortunately, a closer look at (9.24) reveals that to calculate the leave-one-out error for any particular set of parameters, we will have to construct l models. This means that for real-world data sets containing several thousand to several million observations, we would have to build as many models as there are observations in the data set. Considering that in a typical model evaluation cycle we would evaluate tens to hundreds of different sets of parameters, it is clear that this approach is impractical for all but the smallest knowledge discovery projects.

9.2.3 *N*-Fold Cross-Validation

A good compromise between the potential bias of the hold-out method and the computational complexity of the leave-one-out method is *N-fold cross-validation*. Here we split the data set D into N partitions or *folds* with $N \ll l$ such that

$$D = Q_1 \cup Q_2 \cup \cdots \cup Q_{N-1} \cup Q_N \tag{9.26}$$

and

$$Q_i \cap Q_j = \emptyset, \tag{9.27}$$

with $|Q_i| = |Q_j| = l/N$ for $i, j = 1, \ldots, N$ and $i \neq j$. Similar to the leave-one-out method, we will use each fold for testing exactly once, with the remaining folds used to train the models. Let Q_i be a fold of the data set D; then we can construct our corresponding training set as

$$P_i = D - Q_i \tag{9.28}$$

for $i = 1, \ldots, N$. We can compute the error of some fold Q_i as

$$\text{err}_{Q_i}\left[\hat{f}_{P_i}[k, \lambda, C]\right] = \frac{1}{|Q_i|} \sum_{(\overline{x}_j, y_j) \in Q_i} \mathcal{L}\left(y_j, \hat{f}_{P_i}[k, \lambda, C](\overline{x}_j)\right), \tag{9.29}$$

where $\hat{f}_{P_i}[k, \lambda, C]$ is the model trained on data set P_i with parameters k, λ, and C. In cross-validation each fold has more than one element; therefore, the error is computed as the average loss over this fold.

We compute the *cross-validated error* (CVE) of the parameter set k, λ, and C as the average over the individual fold errors:

$$\text{CVE}_D[k, \lambda, C] = \frac{1}{N} \sum_{i=1}^{N} \text{err}_{Q_i}\left[\hat{f}_{P_i}[k, \lambda, C]\right]. \tag{9.30}$$

Similar to the leave-one-out error, the cross-validated error is computed over the parameter set, and the models themselves are part of the individual fold error computations. We find the optimal parameter set by minimizing the cross-validated error,

$$(k^*, \lambda^*, C^*) = \underset{k, \lambda, C}{\text{argmin}} \, \text{CVE}_D[k, \lambda, C], \tag{9.31}$$

and the optimal model $\hat{f}_D[k^*, \lambda^*, C^*]$ can then be constructed using the full data set D.

Note that in N-fold cross-validation we only need to construct N models for the evaluation of a single parameter set, in contrast to $|D|$ models in the leave-one-out method. This makes this approach computationally tractable even for large data sets. It has been shown that cross-validation with values for N of 3, 5, and 10 factors out biases very effectively.

9.3   ERROR CONFIDENCE INTERVALS

In general, it does not matter how carefully we construct our training set D from the data universe—there will always remain some uncertainty in terms of how effectively D represents the overall data universe. This implies that there will always be some uncertainty in terms of the model error computations based on the data set D. Here we construct *error confidence intervals* that characterize this uncertainty. Given a certain probability or confidence value, confidence intervals provide us with a range of values that our model error can assume with this confidence value.

In more formal terms, let err_D be a model error computed on data set D. Then the error confidence interval is defined as the probability p that our model error err_D lies between some lower bound lb and some upper bound ub:

$$\Pr(\text{lb} \leq \text{err}_D \leq \text{ub}) = p. \tag{9.32}$$

With $p = 95\%$, the interval [lb, ub] is called the 95% *confidence interval*. Paraphrasing equation (9.32) with $p = 95\%$: *We are 95% percent sure that our error err_D is not worse than lb and not better than ub*. For practical confidence interval computations, we typically fix the probability p to a desired value such as 90% or 95% and then solve equation (9.32) for the lower and upper bounds.

A particular effective and computationally straightforward way to estimate the lower and upper bounds of confidence intervals is the *bootstrap*. What is remarkable about the bootstrap is that we use the data set D itself to capture the uncertainty with which it represents the data universe at large. In the bootstrap we create b copies of our data set D using sampling with replacement. In sampling with replacement we use elements of D without deleting them from D in order to construct the copies of D. This means that each copy B_i of D called a *bootstrap sample*, where $i = 1, \ldots, b$, is probably not identical to D, due to the nature of the random sampling. Furthermore, since we don't delete any elements from D during the sampling process, some elements of D might be repeated in certain bootstrap samples. This implies that other elements of D will be missing from these bootstrap samples since each bootstrap sample is the same size as the original data set D. One way to look at this is that each bootstrap sample represents an alternative way of constructing a training set from the data universe, and the variation among the bootstrap samples captures the uncertainty of a single training set appropriately representing the data universe at large. We can use this variation among the bootstrap samples to compute the variation in respective model errors. Figure 9.3 illustrates this process. As the figure shows, we start with our data set D, create a set of bootstrap samples, and then compute the model error on each sample. During this process the model parameter set k, λ, and C is held constant for all bootstrap samples. Usually, this is the optimal parameter set found by one of the testing techniques discussed in Section 9.2. Now, to compute the error confidence interval, we sort the model errors obtained from the bootstrap samples into a list and then extract the lower and upper bounds of the model error from this list according to the percentiles specified by the confidence value. If we are given a confidence value of 90%, we extract the lower bound at the 5th percentile and the upper bound at the

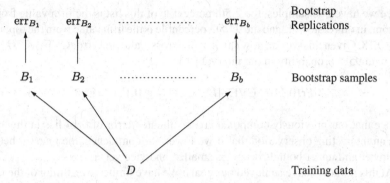

FIGURE 9.3 Computing bootstrap samples and their respective model errors.

95th percentile of the sorted list. If we are given a confidence value of 95%, we extract the lower bound at the 2.5th percentile and the upper bound at the 97.5th percentile of the sorted list.

Let us make this discussion more concrete with an example. Assume that we have a data set D and we computed a cross-validated error for the optimal parameter set k^*, λ^*, and C^* as

$$\text{CVE}_D[k^*, \lambda^*, C^*] = 0.14.$$

That is, the model $\hat{f}_D[k^*, \lambda^*, C^*]$ is expected to have an error rate of 14% when applied to the data universe at large. At this point we would like to compute the 95% confidence interval of our cross-validated error in order to quantify the effect of the uncertainty that D has on the error rate. Assume that we generate 200 bootstrap samples B_i from D with $i = 1, \ldots, 200$. For each bootstrap sample B_i we can compute a cross-validated error,

$$\text{CVE}_{B_i}[k^*, \lambda^*, C^*].$$

We proceed by sorting the values of the cross-validated errors. This gives us a vector of 200 numbers sorted from the best performance to the worst: say,

$$(0.07, 0.08, 0.09, 0.11, 0.11, 0.12, \ldots, 0.17, 0.18, 0.19, 0.21, 0.21, 0.22).$$

Algorithm 9.1

```
given data set D
for i = 1 to 200 do
    B[i] ← sample D with replacement, note |B[i]| = |D|.
    err[i] ← compute model error using parameter set (k*, λ*, C*) and B[i].
end for
Sort err in ascending fashion.
ub ← err[195]
lb ← err[5]
return (lb, ub)
```

Since we have 200 samples, the 2.5th percentile of this list is the fifth value from the bottom, in this case 0.11, and the 97.5th percentile is the fifth value from the top, in this case 0.18. Given this we can now say that our cross-validated error $CVE_D[k^*, \lambda^*, C^*]$ lies with 95% probability in the interval $[0.11, 0.18]$, or

$$\Pr\left(0.11 \leq CVE_D[k^*, \lambda^*, C^*] \leq 0.18\right) \approx 95\%. \tag{9.33}$$

Notice that our previously computed cross-validated error of 0.14 lies in this range. It is an interesting observation that if we lower our confidence, the interval between the lower and upper bounds becomes smaller, and vice versa.

At this point we have achieved our goals: We have limited overfitting of the model by using the cross-validated error, and we have a characterization of the uncertainty of the model error due to the data set D.

In this example we have shown the calculations involved in the computation of the bootstrapped confidence interval for the cross-validated error. However, the bootstrap can be used to compute the confidence interval for any model error computation, including the hold-out method and the leave-one-out method. Algorithm 9.1 shows the outline of an algorithm computing the upper and lower bounds of the 95% confidence interval for some model error using 200 bootstrap samples. The algorithm first generates the bootstrap samples and computes the model error on each sample. Once the model errors for all the samples have been computed, the array holding the error values is sorted in ascending fashion. Given that we are using 200 bootstrap samples, the extraction of the upper and lower bounds is trivial with the appropriate indices.

Here we have consistently used 200 bootstrap samples as a convenient number in order to easily extract the upper and lower bounds. As a general rule, the larger the number of bootstrap samples, the more accurate the approximation of the true confidence interval. That is, a large number of bootstrap samples would bring the approximation in (9.33) closer to a true identity. The actual number of bootstrap samples that we construct depends on available computer power and on how critical an exact estimate of the confidence interval is.

9.3.1 Comparison of Models

In practice, it is often the case that we have two or more reasonable models for a particular knowledge discovery project, and we are faced with selecting one of them to deploy. We might have a choice between a less complex model with a larger model error and a more complex model with a smaller model error. This is often a nontrivial decision because less complex models are often more attractive. The question we might ask is: Are the two model performances significantly different? We can use confidence intervals to answer this question. Suppose that we construct the 95% error confidence interval for both models. If the confidence intervals do not overlap, the model performances are considered to be significantly different, and the best performing model should be used. If, on the other hand, the two confidence intervals do overlap, the model performances are considered *not* significantly different and other criteria, such as model complexity, can be taken into consideration when selecting a model. In general, when comparing or reporting model performances it is always a good idea to state the model performances together with a confidence interval. Most often, the 95% confidence interval is used for these purposes.

As an example, consider the model $\hat{f}_D[k^*, \lambda^*, C^*]$ with a cross-validated error,

$$\mathrm{CVE}_D[k^*, \lambda^*, C^*] = 0.1,$$

and a 95% confidence interval $[0.08, 0.12]$. Consider another model $\hat{f}_D[k^\bullet, \lambda^\bullet, C^\bullet]$ with a cross-validated error,

$$\mathrm{CVE}_D[k^\bullet, \lambda^\bullet, C^\bullet] = 0.05,$$

and a 95% confidence interval $[0.01, 0.09]$. Even though the model performance of the second model seems superior, a look at the confidence intervals reveals that in fact the model performances are not significantly different because the intervals overlap and we need to use other criteria to decide which of the models to deploy.

9.4 MODEL EVALUATION IN PRACTICE

Let us put these techniques into practice by investigating how they work in WEKA and R. For this purpose we use the Wisconsin Diagnostic Breast Cancer data set.[1] This data set consists of about 600 observations, where each observation describes the physical aspects of a tumor. The 31 independent real-valued attributes include characteristics such as radius, texture, and smoothness. The dependent attribute classifies each observation as either a malignant (M) or a benign (B) tumor. Once you download the data from the UCI Web site, you will have to transform the data into a CSV file so that you can load it into WEKA and R. You can accomplish this easily with your favorite text editor. Below we assume that the data set is stored in the file "wdbc.csv".

9.4.1 WEKA

Let us begin with WEKA. We first look at the model performance metrics as reported by WEKA. We then perform model evaluation using the training and cross-validated errors. To perform these experiments you will have to start WEKA and load the "wdbc.csv" file using the *Preprocess* tab. Once the data are loaded, make sure that the *Class* field is set to 'Diagnosis'. In the following we assume that you have the WEKA system running and that the data set is loaded.

---

[1]This data set is available from the UCI Machine Learning Repository: http://archive.ics.uci.edu/ml.

Performance Metrics   To look at performance metrics as they are reported by WEKA, we will first have to build a model and then test the model. We construct a support vector model by selecting the SMO classifier with the *Choose* button in the *Classify* tab:

$$\text{weka} \rightarrow \text{classifiers} \rightarrow \text{functions} \rightarrow \text{SMO}.$$

The SMO default parameters specify a linear kernel with a cost constant of 1, which is fine for our purposes here. For testing we will use the training set; that is, we use the training error as our model error estimate. To do this, select the *Use training set* radio button in the *Test option* panel. We are now ready to build our model. A quick check that the appropriate dependent attribute 'Diagnosis' is selected is probably prudent at this point. We now hit the *Start* button; WEKA responds with the model construction output in the *Classifier output* panel. There is quite a bit of information on the model and the model construction process in this text panel. If you scroll down, you will see the test information under the heading

```
=== Evaluation on training set ===
```

The first set of numbers we see reported are

```
Correctly Classified Instances      559        98.2425 %
Incorrectly Classified Instances     10         1.7575 %
```

The first number corresponds to our accuracy; that is, the model we just constructed has an accuracy of 98.24%. Conversely, the second number is the error the model committed on the data set. Since the data set we tested with is the training set, this number is the training error reported as 1.76%. Following these numbers we have a number of other error metrics. For the time being, we ignore these since in a classification setting they are not often used. At the bottom of the generated output, WEKA reports the confusion matrix for this model:

```
   a    b   <-- classified as
 203    9 |   a = M
   1  356 |   b = B
```

If we let the malignant tumors (M) be represented by the $+1$ label and the benign tumors (B) by the -1 label, the top left corner of the confusion matrix represents the true positive predictions, and the bottom right, the true negative predictions. The top right corner displays the false negative predictions, and the bottom left corner displays the false positives. With this definition of the labels, a false negative prediction means that a cancerous tumor was wrongly predicted to be benign, and a false positive prediction means that a noncancerous tumor was predicted to be cancerous. In this case our model commits nine times more false negative errors than false positive errors. This is also reflected in the sensitivity and specificity

TABLE 9.3 Support Vector Model Complexity and the Associated Training and Cross-Validated Errors[a]

ID	Kernel	Cost Constant	Training Error (%)	Cross-Validated Error (%)
1	Linear	0.01	11.95	12.65
2	Linear	0.10	3.87	4.39
3	Linear	1.00	1.76	2.28
4	Linear	10.00	1.76	2.28
5	Linear	100.00	1.05	3.16
6	Linear	1000.00	0.88	3.34
7	Polynomial, degree = 3	10.00	0.70	3.16
8	Polynomial, degree = 3	100.00	0.00	5.45

[a]As reported by WEKA on the Wisconsin Diagnostic Breast Cancer data set.

of the model:

$$\text{sensitivity} = \frac{203}{203 + 9} = 0.958,$$

$$\text{specificity} = \frac{356}{356 + 1} = 0.997.$$

Model Evaluation Table 9.3 lists eight models of the Wisconsin Diagnostic Breast Cancer data set in increasing complexity, together with their training error and their cross-validated error as computed by WEKA. Let us first investigate the relationship between training error and model complexity. The first entry in the table with ID 1 is a model with a linear kernel and a cost constant of 0.01. WEKA reports a training error of 11.95% for this model. The next model that is shown with ID 2 is a linear model with cost constant 0.1. Recall that an increase in the cost constant implies a decrease in the size of the margin. We consider a support vector machine with a small margin more complex than a support vector machine with a large margin because a model with a small margin can fit data more readily than a model with a large margin. We have more to say about this in Chapter 10. In this case, making the model more complex by increasing the cost constant drops the training error to 3.87%. As we go down the table the complexity of the models increases, and we can observe that the training error decreases steadily until it reaches zero. The last two entries in the table are models with polynomial kernels of degree 3 and are therefore clearly more complex than linear models. In addition, we consider model 8 more complex than model 7 because it has a smaller margin.

The dark curve in Figure 9.4 displays the relationship between training error and model complexity. Here the models are plotted along the horizontal axis by their IDs from lowest complexity to highest complexity, and we can observe that the training error decreases and eventually drops to zero with increasing complexity.

Let us turn our attention to the cross-validated error. The cross-validated error for a set of parameters is obtained in WEKA by selecting the *Cross-validation* option in the

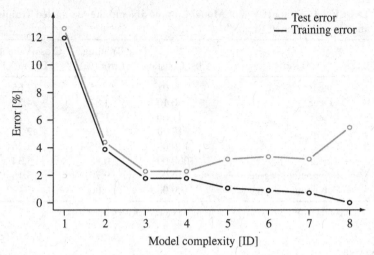

FIGURE 9.4 Training and cross-validated errors for the models given in Table 9.3.

Test options panel. The default is 10-fold cross-validation. Going back to Table 9.3, we see that the cross-validated error for the eight model parameter sets behaves differently from the training error. We can observe that for the first couple of parameter sets the cross-validated error drops rapidly with increasing complexity. Then for sets 3 and 4 it stays constant at 2.28%. For the remaining model parameters it then grows with increasing model complexity. The light gray curve in Figure 9.4 displays the cross-validated error against model complexity. As discussed in Section 9.2.1, we see the typical test error curve, where initially the test error falls with increasing model complexity and then after a certain point in model complexity it starts to grow. From this graph it is clear that parameter sets 3 and 4 specify the interesting models because they minimize the test error.

We now have two models to choose from, and since they both have the same cross-validated error we need to use some other performance metric to make our final choice. In this case we can use the confusion matrix of the cross-validated error. For model 3 with a linear kernel and cost constant 1.0, WEKA reports the following cross-validated confusion matrix:

```
  a    b    <-- classified as
201   11  |   a = M
  2  355  |   b = B
```

This model commits 11 false negatives and two false positives. For model 4 with a linear kernel and a cost constant of 10.0, WEKA reports the cross-validated confusion matrix:

```
  a    b    <-- classified as
202   10  |   a = M
  3  354  |   b = B
```

This model commits 10 false negatives and three false positives. Even though both models report the same cross-validated error, a look at their confusion matrices reveals that model 4 is slightly more balanced and in a clinical setting is perhaps the preferred model.

9.4.2 R

Let us perform similar computations in R. As in Section 9.4.1, we will be using the "wdbc.csv" file. Recall that to use support vector machine models in R, you will have to load the e1071 package.

Performance Metrics   The following R script loads the data set, computes a support vector machine model, and prints out the confusion matrix.

```
> library(e1071)
> wdbc.df <- read.csv("wdbc.csv")
> svm.model <- svm(Diagnosis ~ .,
                   data=wdbc.df,
                   type="C-classification",
                   kernel="linear",
                   cost=1)
> predict <- fitted(svm.model)
> cm <- table(wdbc.df$Diagnosis,predict)
> cm
   predict
      B   M
  B 355   2
  M   5 207
> err <- (cm[1,2] + cm[2,1])/length(predict) * 100
> err
[1] 1.230228
```

The argument C-classification to the function that builds the support vector model specifies that models be used that include the cost constant C. The function fitted reports the labels as predicted by the model on the training set. We can plot the confusion matrix by comparing the wdbc.df$Diagnosis labels observed in the original data set with the labels computed by the model and stored in the vector predict. The function table does just that in the usual confusion table format. When interpreting this table we have to be a bit careful, in that R reports the labels in the reverse order from WEKA. If we let malignant tumors (M) represent the +1 class and benign tumors (B) represent the −1 class, the bottom right field of the table represents the true positive classifications and the bottom left field represents the false negatives. The top left represents the true negatives and the top right represents the false positives. Therefore, this model commits two false positive errors and five false negative errors. From the confusion matrix we can immediately compute the training error as given in the last two lines in the script above. The training error reported

TABLE 9.4   Support Vector Model Complexity and the Associated Training and Cross-Validated Errors[a]

ID	Kernel	Cost Constant	Training Error (%)	Cross-Validated Error (%)
1	Linear	0.01	2.46	3.51
2	Linear	0.10	1.41	2.46
3	Linear	1.00	1.23	2.81
4	Linear	10.00	0.88	3.34
5	Linear	100.00	0.35	3.34
6	Linear	1000.00	0.35	3.87
7	Polynomial, degree = 3	10.00	2.81	4.39
8	Polynomial, degree = 3	100.00	0.53	3.34
9	Polynomial, degree = 3	1000.00	0.00	5.45

[a]As reported by R on the Wisconsin Diagnostic Breast Cancer data set.

here is 1.23%. We leave computing the sensitivity and specificity of this model as an exercise for the reader.

Model Evaluation   Table 9.4 lists nine models of the Wisconsin Diagnostic Breast Cancer data set in increasing complexity together with their training and cross-validated errors. We see the by-now familiar relation between training error and model complexity: With a complex enough model the training error becomes zero. We have one anomaly here, in that model 7 reports a large training error even though it is on the more complex side. However, the overall trend is clear. The dark curve in Figure 9.5 displays this relationship graphically. See above for the R code that computes the training error for a model.

In R the function that computes the support vector model can also perform cross-validation. Following is an example of how one would compute the cross-validated accuracy for a set of parameters.

```
> svm.model <- svm(Diagnosis ~ .,
                 data=wdbc.df,
                 type="C-classification",
                 kernel="polynomial",
                 degree=3,
                 cost=1000,
                 cross=10)
> summary(svm.model)

10-fold cross-validation on training data:

Total Accuracy: 94.55185
Single Accuracies:
 91.07143 94.73684 98.24561 96.49123 100
 87.7193 94.73684 94.73684 94.73684 92.98246
```

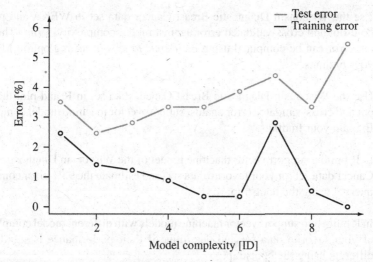

FIGURE 9.5 Training and cross-validated errors for the models given in Table 9.4.

Here we compute the cross-validated accuracy of a model with a polynomial kernel of degree 3 and a cost constant of 1000. The last argument to the svm function specifies that we want to perform 10-fold cross-validation. The accuracies reported are given in percent, and we can easily convert them to cross-validated errors by subtracting the given accuracies from 100%. This is what we report in the last column of Table 9.4 for the nine model parameter sets. Again, we see the by now familiar trend that the test error first drops with increasing model complexity and then grows after a certain complexity level. The light gray curve in Figure 9.5 shows this graphically. In this case there is only a single parameter set that minimizes the cross-validated error: namely, the linear kernel with a cost constant of 0.1. It is also clear from Figure 9.5 that the error curves are not always as clean as depicted in the idealized setting in Figure 9.2. However, the overall trends of the errors are clearly preserved.

EXERCISES

9.1 Given the confusion matrix compute the following performance metrics:

	Predicted	
Observed	+1	−1
+1	275	31
−1	28	310

(a) Model error

(b) Model accuracy

(c) Sensitivity

(d) Specificity

9.2   Use the Wisconsin Diagnostic Breast Cancer data set in WEKA and plot the hold-out and cross-validated error against model complexity. (*Hint:* The hold-out error can be computed using the *Percentage split* testing option.) Explain your findings.

9.3   Use the Wisconsin Diagnostic Breast Cancer data set in R and plot the hold-out and cross-validated error against support vector machine model complexity. Explain your findings.

9.4   In R build a support vector machine model of the Wisconsin Diagnostic Breast Cancer data set (or your favorite data set) and estimate the 95% error confidence interval using the bootstrap.

9.5   In R build two support vector machine models with different model complexities of your favorite data set and determine if their performance is significantly different using the bootstrap.

BIBLIOGRAPHIC NOTES

Any book on classification theory or data mining will have definitions and explanations of the most common model performance metrics (e.g., [8, 26, 36]). Kohavi discusses and compares the hold-out, leave-one-out, and cross-validation methods in [46]. The bootstrap was introduced by Efron in his seminal paper [27] and was developed further in [29]. A readable introduction to computational statistics is the paper by Efron and Tibshirani in *Science* [28]. A more recent treatment of computational statistics is a book by Gentle [34]. A practical tutorial for the bootstrap based on the SAS scripting language is [52].

CHAPTER 10

ELEMENTS OF STATISTICAL LEARNING THEORY

Up to this point we have developed support vector machines based almost exclusively on computational considerations. The key concept we used was the intuitive notion that a linear decision surface with the largest possible margin gives rise to an optimal decision function. By *optimal decision function* we mean a function that generalizes well beyond the training data or, in terms of model evaluation, a function that minimizes the test error. In this chapter we formalize the notion of maximum-margin classifier in the context of statistical learning theory and show that a linear decision surface with the largest possible margin does indeed represent the optimal classifier.

We begin the chapter by defining model complexity in terms of the VC-dimension. We will see that decision surfaces with small margins have a high VC-dimension and therefore are considered more complex than decision surfaces with large margins that possess a low VC-dimension. We continue the chapter by defining the theoretical setting for machine learning in terms of expected risk minimization over some appropriate data universe. However, since the probability distributions for the data universes of interest are generally unknown, we have to rely on empirical risk minimization, which is the risk minimization over a subset of the data universe. We will see that, similar to minimizing the training error, minimizing the empirical risk is overly optimistic in the sense that we can always construct a model that will reduce the empirical risk to zero. A key contribution of statistical learning theory is that the VC-confidence captures the generalization error of a model. The key insight is that the sum of the empirical risk and the VC-confidence denotes an upper bound on the expected risk for a model.

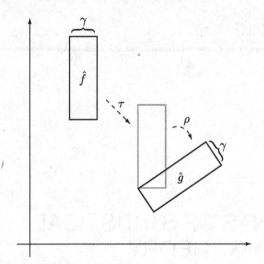

FIGURE 10.1 Model $\hat{f}$ can be mapped into model $\hat{g}$ with an appropriate translation τ followed by an appropriate rotation ρ.

10.1 THE VC-DIMENSION AND MODEL COMPLEXITY

Informally, the VC-dimension is a measure of the complexity of a classifier. By that we mean that it is a measure of how well a binary classifier can model the boundary between the two classes: The larger the VC-dimension, the more complex the classifier and the better it can separate the observations belonging to their respective classes. This is in line with our findings in Chapter 9, where we found that complex classifiers can model complicated class boundaries better than can less complex models. More precisely, we found that the more complex a model, the better it can separate the observations in a training set.

Let us formalize the VC-dimension as a way to measure model complexity. Consider a class of linear classifiers all with a margin of the same size γ. We let $\hat{F}[\gamma]$ denote that class. We also assume that the model class $\hat{F}[\gamma]$ is closed under rotation and translation; that is, it contains all possible models with margin γ. Formally, for all models $\hat{f} \in \hat{F}[\gamma]$, all rotations ρ, and all translations τ, we have $\rho(\hat{f}) \in \hat{F}[\gamma]$ and $\tau(\hat{f}) \in \hat{F}[\gamma]$. Figure 10.1 demonstrates this in $\mathbb{R}^2$ for some model class $\hat{F}[\gamma]$. For any two models, $\hat{f}, \hat{g} \in \hat{F}[\gamma]$, we can always construct a translation τ and a rotation ρ such that $\rho(\tau(\hat{f})) = \hat{g}$. Here, a linear decision surface with its supporting hyperplanes and margin of size γ is stylized as a rectangle with width γ. One could also imagine a line bisecting the rectangle lengthwise that represents the actual decision surface.

With the notion of a model class with a fixed margin width, we can define the VC-dimension more rigorously. Consider a data set D; then the VC-dimension of the classifiers in a model class is the number of instances in D that can be separated by the classifiers in this model class for *all possible binary label assignments* to the instances in D. If all instances in D can be separated for all possible label assignments,

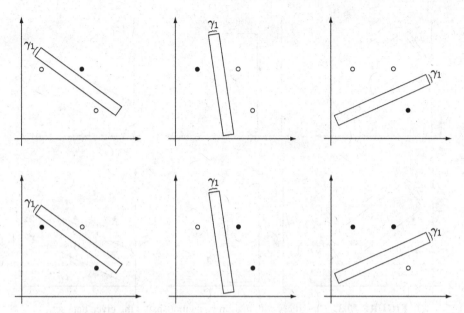

FIGURE 10.2   VC-dimension of a class of classifiers with margin γ_1.

we say that the model class *shatters* the data set D. This gives rise to the following definition of the VC-dimension:

Definition 10.1   *The **VC-dimension** of a model class $\hat{F}[\gamma]$ defined over some data set D is the size of the largest finite subset of D shattered by $\hat{F}[\gamma]$.*

As an example let us consider a data set with three instances in two-dimensional real space (i.e., $D \subset \mathbb{R}^2$ and $|D| = 3$). Let the class of classifiers $\hat{F}[\gamma_1]$ be defined over D. We also pick the margin γ_1 in such a way that we can separate all three instances for all possible binary label assignments. In this case we say that the VC-dimension of $\hat{F}[\gamma_1]$ is 3 and we write $h_1 = 3$. Since the VC-dimension is equal to the size of the data set, $h_1 = |D|$, we say that $\hat{F}[\gamma_1]$ shatters D. This is shown in Figure 10.2. The full and empty balls denote the different binary label assignments to the instances in D. We have not shown the trivial assignments where all points are labeled with the same label, since there is nothing to separate.

Let us consider a second class of classifiers $\hat{F}[\gamma_2]$ over the same data set with $\gamma_2 > \gamma_1$. In particular, the size of γ_2 is such that the classifiers in $\hat{F}[\gamma_2]$ cannot separate all instances perfectly, as seen in Figure 10.3. However, if we delete one of the instances in D, the classifiers in $\hat{F}[\gamma_2]$ can shatter this subset of D. This is demonstrated in Figure 10.4. Here the light gray point represents the deleted instance. The graphs in the leftmost column now represent trivial separations because the remaining instances in D are labeled with the same label. Since $\hat{F}[\gamma_2]$ can separate the subset of D with two elements, we say that for the model class $\hat{F}[\gamma_2]$ the VC-dimension is 2; $h_2 = 2$.

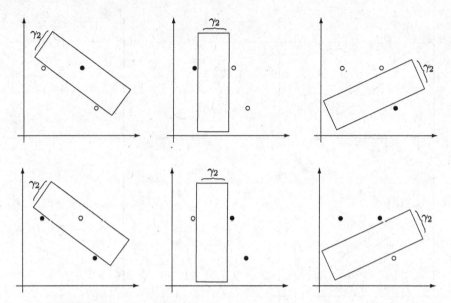

FIGURE 10.3   Classifiers with margin γ_2 cannot shatter the given data set.

Large VC-dimensions represent classes of models with high complexity, and vice versa. In our case, since $h_1 > h_2$ we say that the classifiers in $\hat{F}[\gamma_1]$ are more complex than the classifiers in $\hat{F}[\gamma_2]$ and we write $\hat{F}[\gamma_1] \supset \hat{F}[\gamma_2]$. Since $\gamma_1 < \gamma_2$, this implies that classifiers with small margins are more complex than classifiers with

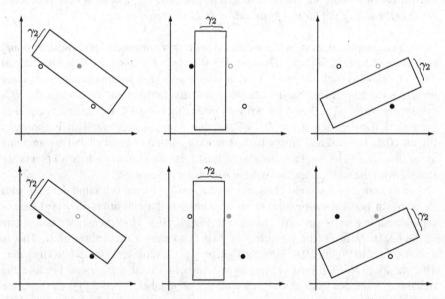

FIGURE 10.4   Classifiers with margin γ_2 can shatter a subset of the data set. Here the light gray point represents the deleted instance.

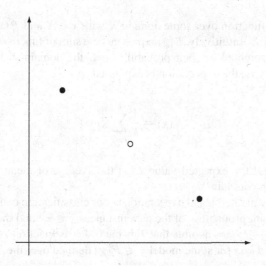

FIGURE 10.5   Data set that cannot be shattered by the classifiers of any model class regardless of how small we make the margin.

large margins. Furthermore, the examples demonstrated that complex models can fit data better than can less complex models, corroborating the results of Chapter 9. The set notation $\hat{F}[\gamma_1] \supset \hat{F}[\gamma_2]$ is suggestive of the fact that anything that can be modeled with less complex classifiers can also be modeled with more complex classifiers. The VC-dimension of a model class is data dependent. Figure 10.5 illustrates an arrangement of the instances in D that cannot be shattered by the classifiers of any model class regardless of how small we make the margin of the model class.

In our theoretical development here, we have assumed that all classifiers use the linear kernel and are considered hard-margin classifiers. It is straightforward to extend the constructions above to include classifiers with polynomial and Gaussian kernels as well as soft margins. This would imply that the instances in some data set would be shattered by nonlinear decision surfaces rather than the linear decision surfaces we showed above. This implies that the complexity of the individual model classes is governed not only by the size of the margin but also by the cost constant and by the type of kernel being used in the models of the individual model classes.

10.2   A THEORETICAL SETTING FOR MACHINE LEARNING

Central to our theoretical setting of machine learning is the notion of *mathematical expectation*, defined as

$$E[g] = \int g(x)\, dP(x), \tag{10.1}$$

where $g(x)$ is a function over some domain X with $x \in X$ and $P(x)$ is a probability distribution over X. Intuitively, $E[g]$ represents the sum of function evaluations over the domain X weighted by their probabilities. If the domain X is discrete with k elements $x_1, \ldots, x_k$, the expectation is expressed as

$$E[g] = \frac{1}{k} \sum_{i=1}^{k} g(x_i). \tag{10.2}$$

Typically, we call the expected value $E[g]$ the average or mean over all function evaluations on the domain X.

We now apply mathematical expectation to our classification context. Assume that $P(\overline{x}, y)$ is the joint probability of the data instances $\overline{x} \in \mathbb{R}^n$ and their corresponding labels $y \in \{+1, -1\}$; also assume that L is the 0–1 loss function as defined in (9.2); then the *expected loss* for some model $\hat{f} \in \hat{F}[\gamma]$ defined over the data universe is

$$E[L(y, \hat{f}(\overline{x}))] = \int L(y, \hat{f}(\overline{x})) \, dP(\overline{x}, y). \tag{10.3}$$

In other words, the expected loss is the expected number of mistakes a model will commit over the underlying data universe. We often write

$$R[\hat{f}] = E[L(y, \hat{f}(\overline{x}))], \tag{10.4}$$

where $R[\hat{f}]$ is called the *expected risk*. With this we can define machine learning as the minimization of the expected risk,

$$\hat{f}^* = \operatorname*{argmin}_{\hat{f} \in \hat{F}} R[\hat{f}], \tag{10.5}$$

where $\hat{F}$ represents the class of all model classes such that $\hat{F}[\gamma] \subset \hat{F}$ for all margins γ. During optimization we draw our models $\hat{f}$ from this class in order to find the optimal model $\hat{f}^* \in \hat{F}[\gamma^*]$ that minimizes the expected risk.

10.3 EMPIRICAL RISK MINIMIZATION

Unfortunately, machine learning in the formulation given in (10.5) is impossible because we do not know the joint probability distribution $P(\overline{x}, y)$. If we did, there would be nothing to learn. However, we do have some information on the joint probability distribution in the form of the observations in our training data D,

$$D = \{(\overline{x}_1, y_1), \ldots, (\overline{x}_l, y_l)\} \subset \mathbb{R}^n \times \{+1, -1\}. \tag{10.6}$$

We can use these observations to estimate the risk. We call this the *empirical risk* $R_{\text{emp}}[\hat{f}]$ of some model $\hat{f}$ and define it as

$$R_{\text{emp}}[\hat{f}] = E[L(y, \hat{f}(\overline{x}))] = \frac{1}{l} \sum_{i=1}^{l} L(y_i, \hat{f}(\overline{x}_i)), \tag{10.7}$$

where $(\overline{x}_i, y_i) \in D$. Here we apply our discrete definition of mathematical expectation (10.2) since training sets are usually finite and contain discrete instances. Analogous to the expected risk, we find our best model by minimizing the empirical risk:

$$\hat{f}^* = \underset{\hat{f} \in \hat{F}}{\text{argmin}} \, R_{\text{emp}}[\hat{f}] \tag{10.8}$$

$$= \underset{\hat{f} \in \hat{F}}{\text{argmin}} \left(\frac{1}{l} \sum_{i=1}^{l} L(y_i, \hat{f}(\overline{x}_i)) \right). \tag{10.9}$$

Now, since we are allowed to pick a model from the class of all possible models $\hat{F}$ in order to minimize the empirical risk, it is clear that we can always find a model that reduces the empirical risk to zero or close to zero. That is, minimizing the empirical risk is likely to be overly optimistic. This can also be seen by comparing equation (10.9) to equation (9.14), which is the minimization of the training error. These two equations are virtually identical. This again implies that minimizing the empirical risk is overly optimistic.

10.4 VC-CONFIDENCE

From a theoretical point of view, this leaves us in a bind. We cannot use the expected risk to find the optimal model for a data universe because the joint probability distribution is unknown. We cannot use the empirical risk to find an optimal model, because minimizing it is too optimistic. Vapnik suggested a way out of this conundrum by introducing a measure of the generalization error of a model based on its VC-dimension. This measure is called the *VC-confidence*,

$$\upsilon(l, h, \eta) = \sqrt{\frac{h(\log(2l/h) + 1) - \log(\eta/4)}{l}}, \tag{10.10}$$

where l is the size of the training data, h is the VC-dimension of the model class under consideration, and η is some small number such that $0 < \eta < 1$. Notice that the VC-confidence υ is directly proportional to the VC-dimension h. The intuition is that a large VC-dimension implies a complex model, and this in turn implies a large generalization error. Recall that overly complex models tend to overfit their training data and therefore do not generalize well. This is precisely what the VC-confidence tries to capture. Also notice that the VC-confidence is inversely

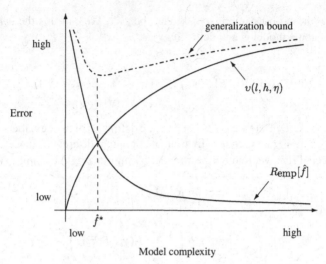

FIGURE 10.6 Relationship between the empirical risk $R_{emp}[\hat{f}]$ and the VC-confidence $\upsilon(l, h, \eta)$. The sum of the two gives rise to the generalization bound.

proportional to the size l of the data set. This means that the larger the training data, the more we know about the data universe, and therefore the smaller the generalization error.

The fundamental insight is that together with the empirical risk, the VC-confidence can be considered an upper bound on the expected risk for some model $\hat{f}$,

$$R[\hat{f}] \leq R_{emp}[\hat{f}] + \upsilon(l, h_{\hat{f}}, \eta), \tag{10.11}$$

where $h_{\hat{f}}$ is the VC-dimension of $\hat{f}$ and l the size of the training data. That is, given the empirical risk and the VC-confidence of a model, we can estimate an upper bound on the expected loss of the model over the entire underlying data universe. Vapnik has shown that this upper bound holds with a probability of $1 - \eta$.

Figure 10.6 illustrates the relationship between the empirical risk $R_{emp}[\hat{f}]$ and the VC-confidence $\upsilon(l, h_{\hat{f}}, \eta)$. Observe that as the complexity of the models increases, the empirical risk decreases. That is, complex models allow us to model the training data well. On the other hand, as model complexity increases, so does the VC-confidence. Here, complex models will commit more errors on data not contained in the training data than will less complex models. The sum of the empirical risk and the VC-confidence represents an envelope of these two curves. This envelope is often referred to as the *generalization bound*. The shape of this generalization bound looks very similar to the curve of the idealized test error in Figure 9.2, and just as minimizing the test error gives us our optimal model, minimizing the generalization bound is equivalent to making just the right trade-off between model complexity and generalization error and will also give us our optimal model. This gives us the following optimization problem for finding the optimal model $\hat{f}^*$:

$$\hat{f}^* = \underset{\hat{f} \in \hat{F}}{\operatorname{argmin}} \left(R_{\operatorname{emp}}[\hat{f}] + \upsilon(l, h_{\hat{f}}, \eta) \right), \tag{10.12}$$

where $\hat{F}$ is the superclass of all model classes. Visually we can see the solution to this optimization problem in Figure 10.6 as the model that gives rise to the minimum of the generalization bound.

10.5 STRUCTURAL RISK MINIMIZATION

Given an appropriate data set, equation (10.12) allows us to find a model in $\hat{F}$ that makes just the right trade-off between complexity and generalization error. The question remains: How exactly do we find this model given the stated optimization problem? Typically, the model class $\hat{F}$ is infinite and traversing it blindly without additional guidance to find the optimal model $\hat{f}^*$ is probably not a fruitful endeavor. Vapnik suggested that instead of traversing the model class $\hat{F}$ blindly, the VC-dimensions of the individual model subclasses of $\hat{F}$ can serve as a guide to finding the optimal model. Vapnik called this procedure *structural risk minimization*.

More precisely, suppose that we have a class of linear models $\hat{F}$ with

$$\hat{F}[\gamma_1], \dots, \hat{F}[\gamma_k] \subset \hat{F}, \tag{10.13}$$

where

$$\hat{F}[\gamma_1] \subset \hat{F}[\gamma_2] \subset \cdots \subset \hat{F}[\gamma_k] \text{ if } h_1 < h_2 < \cdots < h_k, \tag{10.14}$$

where h_i is the VC-dimension of model class $\hat{F}[\gamma_i]$. Given that we assume linear models, equation (10.14) implies that the margins of the various model classes are also partially ordered,

$$\gamma_k < \cdots < \gamma_2 < \gamma_1. \tag{10.15}$$

We now have an effective procedure to find the optimal model. We start with the least complex model class $\hat{F}[\gamma_1]$ and minimize the generalization bound according to equation (10.12). One way to think of this is as picking an arbitrary model $\hat{f}_1 \in \hat{F}[\gamma_1]$ and then computing an appropriate rotation ρ and translation τ such that

$$\hat{f}_1^* = \rho(\tau(\hat{f}_1)) = \underset{\hat{f} \in \hat{F}[\gamma_1]}{\operatorname{argmin}} \left(R_{\operatorname{emp}}[\hat{f}] + \upsilon(l, h_{\hat{f}}, \eta) \right). \tag{10.16}$$

We then move on to the next model class, in this case $\hat{F}[\gamma_2]$, and compute the optimal model $\hat{f}_2^*$ in a similar fashion. We terminate our search if we find that the generalization bound of some model $\hat{f}_{i+1}^* \in \hat{F}[\gamma_{i+1}]$ is larger than the generalization bound

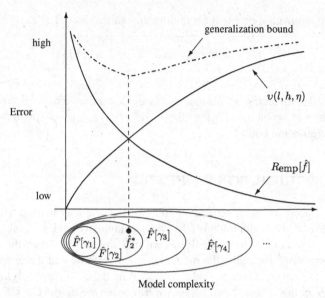

FIGURE 10.7 Using structural risk minimization to find the optimal model f_2^*.

of the model $\hat{f}_i^* \in \hat{F}[\gamma_i]$. In this case, $\hat{f}_i^*$ is the optimal model according to (10.12). Furthermore, the margin γ_i is the maximum margin that guarantees optimal model performance over the data universe at large. We call this process structural risk minimization because we use the structure of the model classes to guide our search. Figure 10.7 shows this structural risk minimization. Here we show four increasingly complex model classes $\hat{F}[\gamma_1] \subset \cdots \subset \hat{F}[\gamma_4]$ and we see that model $\hat{f}_2^* \in \hat{F}[\gamma_2]$ minimizes the generalization bound and is therefore considered the optimal model.

10.6 DISCUSSION

The theory of structural risk minimization provides the mathematical underpinnings for two important concepts that we have encountered a number of times previously. First, structural risk minimization shows that there is a trade-off between complexity and generalization error. We can paraphrase this as: *The least complex model that fits the data well will also generalize well.* Second, structural risk minimization formalizes our idea of maximum-margin classifiers. Our search procedure above finds the model class with the largest margin that generalizes well.

EXERCISES

10.1 Given the data set in Figure 10.8, what is the maximum possible VC-dimension for any linear model class? Justify your answer.

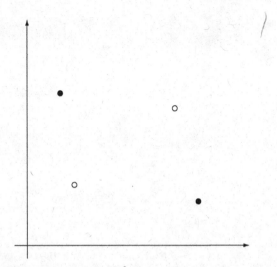

FIGURE 10.8 Data set in $\mathbb{R}^2$ with a particular binary labeling.

10.2 Given the data set D and the model class $\hat{F}[\gamma_2]$ in Figure 10.3, show that it does not matter which point we remove from D—$\hat{F}[\gamma_2]$ will always shatter the resulting subset.

10.3 Assume that some model $\hat{f}$ has a training error of 0.17 on a data set with 1000 observations. Also assume that this model has a VC-dimension $h_{\hat{f}} = 925$. Compute the generalization bound of this model with 0.9 probability.

10.4 [*challenging*] Assume that a linear model class can shatter a data set $D \subset \mathbb{R}^n$. Show that the VC-dimension $h \geq n + 1$ for this model class for all n (*Hint*: Use the n unit basis vectors as part of your data set.)

BIBLIOGRAPHIC NOTES

A discussion on mathematical expectation may be found in any elementary statistics text (e.g., [78]). Vapnik and Chervonenkis formalized the notion of VC-dimension in the early 1970s [75]. Here we only touched on the major points of the learning theory developed by Vapnik and his collaborators. A full account of the theory is given in [71]. An account of the theory that is slightly less mathematically demanding may be found in [73]. A paper by Vapnik provides a high-level overview of statistical learning [72]. A nice description of support vector machines that deals with some of the theoretical underpinnings is a tutorial by Burges [17]. Another mathematical treatment of learning along lines similar to those of Vapnik is [59].

PART III

CHAPTER 11

MULTICLASS CLASSIFICATION

The standard theory of support vector machines supports only binary classification problems. However, many real-world problems deal with classifying objects into more than two classes. Here we show how we can use binary support vector machines to classify objects into an arbitrary number of classes.

We start the chapter with a discussion of the one-versus-the-rest classification scheme that requires the construction of as many support vector machines as there are classes in the classification problem. We continue our discussion with a pairwise classification scheme where we construct a binary classifier for each possible pair of classes. We close the chapter by mentioning alternative methods such as the error-correcting-output-codes scheme and the direct support of multiple classes within the objective function for support vector machines.

11.1 ONE-VERSUS-THE-REST CLASSIFICATION

By far the most popular technique for multiclass classification using binary support vector machines is called *one-versus-the-rest classification*. Consider the training set

$$D = \{(\overline{x}_1, y_1), (\overline{x}_2, y_2), \ldots, (\overline{x}_l, y_l)\} \subset \mathbb{R}^n \times \{1, 2, \ldots, M\}, \qquad (11.1)$$

where the label y_i for each observation can take on any value in $\{1, 2, \ldots, M\}$ with $M > 2$. The precise nature of the label set is not important as long as there exists one

Knowledge Discovery with Support Vector Machines, by Lutz Hamel
Copyright © 2009 John Wiley & Sons, Inc.

unique label for each class in the classification problem. For convenience we define the label set here as $\{1, 2, \ldots, M\}$.

In the one-versus-the-rest technique, given M classes, we construct M binary, support vector–based decision surfaces, say $g^1, \ldots, g^M$. Each decision surface is trained to separate one class from the rest. That is, the decision surface g^1 is trained to separate the class labeled 1 from all other classes, the decision surface g^2 is trained to separate the class labeled 2 from all other classes, and so on. To classify an unknown point we use a voting scheme based on which of the M decision surfaces returns the largest value for this unknown point. We then use the decision surface that returns the largest value for the unknown point to assign this point to a class.

Let us examine this construction in more detail. To train M decision surfaces we construct M binary training sets,

$$D^p = D^p_+ \cup D^p_-, \tag{11.2}$$

where

$$D^p_+ = \{(\overline{x}, +1) \mid (\overline{x}, y) \in D \wedge y = p\} \tag{11.3}$$

and

$$D^p_- = \{(\overline{x}, -1) \mid (\overline{x}, y) \in D \wedge y \neq p\}, \tag{11.4}$$

with $p = 1, \ldots, M$. The set D^p_+ contains all the observations in D that are members of the class p, and the set D^p_- contains all the remaining observations. For convenience we relabeled the training set D^p with labels in $\{+1, -1\}$. The label $+1$ is used for observations in class p, and the label -1 is used for observations that are not in class p. We train each decision surface g^p on the corresponding data set D^p, which gives rise to a decision surface of the form

$$g^p(\overline{x}) = \sum_{i=1}^{|D^p|} y_i \alpha_i^p k(\overline{x}_i, \overline{x}) - b^p, \tag{11.5}$$

with $(\overline{x}_i, y_i) \in D^p$. During the training of the M decision surfaces we use the same model parameters, such as the cost constant and kernel function for all the decision surfaces.

We know from Chapter 4 that the decision surface $g^p : \mathbb{R}^n \to \mathbb{R}$ returns a signed real value that can be interpreted as the distance of some point $\overline{x} \in \mathbb{R}^n$ to the decision surface. If the value returned is positive, the point $\overline{x}$ is above the decision surface and is considered to be a member of the class $+1$ with respect to the decision surface, and if the value returned is negative, the point is below the decision surface and is considered to be a member of the class -1 with respect to the decision surface. We can also interpret the value returned as a confidence value: The larger the value returned by a decision surface for some point, the more confident we are that this point belongs to the class $+1$ with respect to this decision surface. This means that if our decision surface returns a large negative value for some point, we are minimally confident that this point belongs to the class $+1$ (in fact, this implies that we are very confident that the point belongs to class -1). If, on the other hand, our decision surface returns a large positive value, we are very confident that the point belongs to the class $+1$. Now, since we laid out our training set D^p for the decision surface g^p in such a way that all observations in class p are considered positive examples [i.e., $(\overline{x}_i, p) \in D$ implies that $(\overline{x}, +1) \in D_+^p$], it follows that a decision surface g^m that returns the largest value for some point $\overline{x}$ among all other decision surfaces $g^1 \cdots g^M$ assigns this point to class m with $m \in \{1, \ldots, M\}$.

Given this, we can construct a decision function $\hat{f} : \mathbb{R}^n \to \{1, \ldots, M\}$ for our multiclass classification problem as follows:

$$\hat{f}(\overline{x}) = \underset{p}{\text{argmax}} \; g^p(\overline{x}), \tag{11.6}$$

where $p \in \{1, 2, \ldots, M\}$. The decision function returns the label of the decision surface that assigns some point $\overline{x} \in \mathbb{R}^n$ to its $+1$ class with the highest confidence.

To see how this technique works, let us look at a classification problem with three classes where the training set D is defined as

$$D = \{(\overline{x}_1, y_1), (\overline{x}_2, y_2), \ldots, (\overline{x}_l, y_l)\} \subset \mathbb{R}^2 \times \{1, 2, 3\},$$

with $l = 9$. Figure 11.1 is a graphical representation of this data set where each observation is represented by its corresponding label. There are three clearly distinct classes of observations, each labeled with the appropriate label. In the figure we also see a point $\overline{z}$ that we would like to classify.

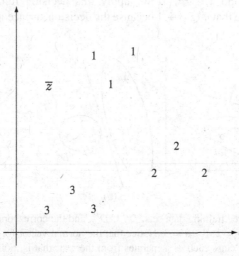

FIGURE 11.1 Multiclass classification problem with three classes. The question is: What should point $\overline{z}$ be classified as?

We proceed with the construction of the three training sets:

$$D^1 = D^1_+ \cup D^1_-,$$
$$D^2 = D^2_+ \cup D^2_-,$$
$$D^3 = D^3_+ \cup D^3_-,$$

where

$$D^1_+ = \{(\overline{x}, +1) \mid (\overline{x}, y) \in D \wedge y = 1\},$$
$$D^1_- = \{(\overline{x}, -1) \mid (\overline{x}, y) \in D \wedge y \neq 1\},$$
$$D^2_+ = \{(\overline{x}, +1) \mid (\overline{x}, y) \in D \wedge y = 2\},$$
$$D^2_- = \{(\overline{x}, -1) \mid (\overline{x}, y) \in D \wedge y \neq 2\},$$
$$D^3_+ = \{(\overline{x}, +1) \mid (\overline{x}, y) \in D \wedge y = 3\},$$
$$D^3_- = \{(\overline{x}, -1) \mid (\overline{x}, y) \in D \wedge y \neq 3\}.$$

We then train the decision surfaces, g^1, g^2, and g^3, on the corresponding data sets. Figure 11.2 illustrates these constructions. Part (a) shows the case for $p = 1$, part (b) for $p = 2$, and part (c) for $p = 3$. Notice that the normal vector for each decision surface always points to the class the decision surface g^p separates from the rest; that is, points that belong to that class are always considered to be above the decision surface. We are now in the position to construct the decision function $\hat{f} : \mathbb{R}^2 \to \{1, 2, 3\}$,

$$\hat{f}(\overline{x}) = \underset{p}{\mathrm{argmax}}\ g^p(\overline{x}), \qquad (11.7)$$

with $p = 1, 2, 3$ and $\overline{x} \in \mathbb{R}^2$. If we apply this decision function to point $\overline{z}$ in Figure 11.2, we see that $\hat{f}(\overline{z}) \mapsto 1$ because the decision surface g^1 returns the largest

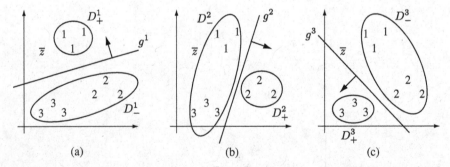

(a)　　　　　　　　(b)　　　　　　　　(c)

FIGURE 11.2　Three training data sets, $D^p_+ \cup D^p_-$, and the corresponding decision surfaces g^p: (a) $p = 1$; (b) $p = 2$; (c) $p = 3$. Notice that the normal vector for each decision surface always points to the class each g^p separates from the rest; that is, points that belong to that class are always considered to be above the decision surface. Here point $\overline{z}$ belongs to class 1 because the decision surface g^1 returns the largest value for this point.

value for this point. This is easily verified by inspecting Figure 11.2 carefully. This seems intuitive, since point $\bar{z}$ lies closest to the points of class 1 and therefore should be assigned to that class.

11.2 PAIRWISE CLASSIFICATION

Although the one-versus-the-rest classification technique has shown to be robust in real-world applications, the fact that the individual training sets for each decision surface are highly unbalanced could be a potential source of problems. Consider a classification problem with 10 classes, each with 1000 observations. Here the training set for each decision surface has 1000 observations labeled $+1$ and 9000 observations labeled -1. If we happen to train decision surfaces with extremely soft margins (i.e., decision surfaces with very small cost constants), it could happen that all observations labeled $+1$ fall into the margin and are potentially misclassified due to the unbalanced nature of the training set. The *pairwise classification* technique avoids this situation by constructing decision surfaces for each pair of classes. Classification of an unknown point is again achieved by a voting scheme.

Let us take a closer look at pairwise classification. Given a classification problem with the training set

$$D = \{(\bar{x}_1, y_1), (\bar{x}_2, y_2), \dots, (\bar{x}_l, y_l)\} \subset \mathbb{R}^n \times \{1, 2, \dots, M\}, \tag{11.8}$$

in pairwise classification we have to construct $M(M-1)/2$ decision surfaces: one decision surface for each possible pair of classes. We let $g^{p,q} : \mathbb{R}^n \to \{p, q\}$ denote the decision surface that separates the pair of classes p and q with $p \neq q$ and $\{p, q\} \subset \{1, 2, \dots, M\}$. We train each decision surface,

$$g^{p,q}(\bar{x}) = \sum_{i=1}^{|D^{p,q}|} y_i \alpha_i^{p,q} k(\bar{x}_i, \bar{x}) - b^{p,q}, \tag{11.9}$$

on the data set

$$D^{p,q} = D^p \cup D^q, \tag{11.10}$$

where

$$D^p = \{(\bar{x}, y) \mid (\bar{x}, y) \in D \wedge y = p\} \tag{11.11}$$

and

$$D^q = \{(\bar{x}, y) \mid (\bar{x}, y) \in D \wedge y = q\}. \tag{11.12}$$

The set D^p consists of all the observations in D with the label p and the set D^q consists of all the observations in D with the label q. The training set $D^{p,q}$ for the pair of classes p and q is simply the union of these two sets.

Once we have constructed all the pairwise decision surfaces $g^{p,q}$ using the corresponding training sets $D^{p,q}$, we can classify an unknown point by applying each of the $M(M-1)/2$ decision surfaces to this point, keeping track of how many times the point was assigned to what class label. The class label with the highest count is then considered the label for the unknown point.

Algorithm 11.1 summarizes these constructions. Here we are given a multiclass data set D together with a point $\overline{z}$ whose label is unknown. After initializing the label counter array cnt to zero for all labels, the algorithm proceeds with the construction of all possible pairwise training sets $D^{p,q}$ and the corresponding decision surfaces $g^{p,q}$. As soon as the decision surface $g^{p,q}$ is available, we apply it to the point $\overline{z}$. If this decision surface classifies this point as p [implied by the notation $g^{p,q}(\overline{z}) == p$], we increment the counter for class p; otherwise, we increment the counter for class q. Finally, once we have looped through all possible pairs of labels, we return the label with the highest count.

To demonstrate how this algorithm works, let us take a look at the data set from Section 11.1,

$$D = \{(\overline{x}_1, y_1), (\overline{x}_2, y_2), \ldots, (\overline{x}_l, y_l)\} \subset \mathbb{R}^2 \times \{1, 2, 3\},$$

with $l = 9$, as shown in Figure 11.1 with point $\overline{z}$, which we want to classify. In Figure 11.3 we demonstrate the construction and application of the three pairwise

Algorithm 11.1

```
// multiclass training set
let D = {(x̄₁, y₁), (x̄₂, y₂), ..., (x̄_l, y_l)} ⊂ ℝⁿ × {1, 2, ..., M}
// point to be classified
let z̄ ∈ ℝⁿ
// initialize the counter for the labels to zero
let cnt[1...M] = 0̄
// loop through all possible pairs of labels
for p = 1 to M - 1 do
   for q = p + 1 to M do
      // construct the decision surface for this pair of labels
      let D^{p,q} = Dᵖ ∪ Dᑫ  // see (11.11) and (11.12)
      train g^{p,q} on D^{p,q}
      // classify the unknown point with the current decision surface
      // and increment the appropriate counter
      if g^{p,q}(z̄) == p then
         cnt[p]++
      else
         cnt[q]++
      end if
   end for
end for
// return the label with the largest count
return argmax_{i=1,...,M} (cnt[i])
```

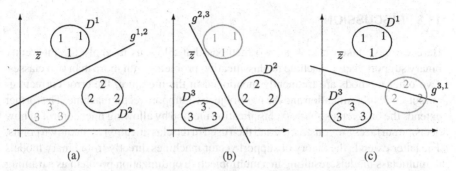

FIGURE 11.3 The three training data sets $D^p \cup D^q$ and the corresponding decision surfaces $g^{p,q}$ with $\{p, q\} \subset \{1, 2, 3\}$: (a) for $p = 1$ and $q = 2$; (b) for $p = 2$ and $q = 3$; (c) $p = 3$ and $q = 1$. Here point $\bar{z}$ belongs to class 1 because it is the largest score.

decision surfaces. In part (a) we show the decision surface $g^{1,2}$. When this decision surface is applied to point $\bar{z}$ it is clear that the decision surface will assign it to class 1. In part (b) we construct decision surface $g^{2,3}$ and then apply it to point $\bar{z}$. In this case $\bar{z}$ is assigned to class 3. Finally, in part (c) we construct decision surface $g^{3,1}$. When we apply this decision surface to point $\bar{z}$ it is assigned the label 1. Tallying up the scores for the individual classes gives us

Class 1	Class 2	Class 3
2	0	1

Therefore, we assign the label 1 to point $\bar{z}$. As before, this seems intuitive, since point $\bar{z}$ lies closest to the points of class 1 (see Figure 11.1) and therefore should be assigned to this class. It is nice to see that our one-versus-the-rest and pairwise classification agree here.

In the voting scheme of pairwise classification there is a possibility of a tie. We can break the tie by interpreting the actual values returned by the decision surfaces as confidence values. When we add up the absolute values of the confidence values assigned to each of the tied labels, we consider the winner to be the tied label with the largest sum of confidence values.

It seems that pairwise classification solves our problem of unbalanced data sets. However, it solves this problem at the expense of introducing a new complication: the fact that for M classes we have to construct $M(M-1)/2$ decision surfaces. For classification problems with a small number of classes the difference between the number of decision surfaces we have to build for the one-versus-the-rest and the pairwise classification is not that drastic. Consider a classification problem with $M = 4$. Here we have to construct four decision surfaces for the one-versus-the-rest classification and six decision surfaces in the pairwise classification. However, when considering classification problems with a large number of different classes, the difference can be quite drastic. In the case of $M = 10$, we need to construct 10 decision surfaces for one-versus-the-rest classification but 45 decision surfaces for pairwise classification.

11.3 DISCUSSION

Here we have taken a look at two methods that allow us to apply the inherently binary support vector machine to classification problems with more than two classes. Two other methods are frequently mentioned in the literature: the error-correcting-output-codes classification and the multiobjective support vector machine. The former extends the one-versus-the-rest classification method by allowing finer control of how decision surfaces are constructed and then used in the classification of unknown points. The latter extends the theory of support vector machines directly from binary models to multiclass models, resulting in a multiobjective optimization problem as a training algorithm. Both of these approaches have nice theoretical properties but are not often used in practice, due to their increased computational complexity.

We should mention that the WEKA GUI does not support multiclass classification for its SMO classifier. However, multiclass classification can be implemented using the Java SDK version of WEKA. On the other hand, the package we are using in R directly supports pairwise multiclass classification.

EXERCISES

11.1 Pick a support vector machine implementation from Chapter 8.

  (a) Extend this implementation to a multiclass setting using one-versus-the-rest classification (use R for your implementation).

  (b) Compare your implementation to the multiclass classification in the e1071 package in R using the iris data set [available in R using the data(iris) command].

11.2 Pick a support vector machine implementation from Chapter 8.

  (a) Extend this implementation to a multiclass setting using pairwise classification (use R for your implementation).

  (b) Compare your implementation with the implementation in the e1071 package in R using the iris data set [available in R using the data(iris) command].

11.3 Extend Algorithm 11.1 to include tie breaking.

11.4 [*challenging*] Implement a multiclass classification scheme for SMO using the WEKA Java SDK.

BIBLIOGRAPHIC NOTES

One-versus-the-rest classification is discussed in [1] and [65]. Pairwise classification for support vector machines is introduced in [47]. Dietterich and Bakiri introduced error-correcting output codes for support vector classifiers in [25]. The notion of a multiobjective support vector machine was suggested by a number of researchers (e.g., [11, 15, 71, 79]).

CHAPTER 12

REGRESSION WITH SUPPORT VECTOR MACHINES

Historically, support vector machines were developed in the context of classification problems. However, there exist another important class of problems: regression problems. Regression problems differ from classification problems in that the observations in a training set are not labeled with a label from a set of discrete labels but, instead, are associated with a number. Typically, that number is drawn from the set of real numbers. In this chapter we show how support vector machines can be adapted to deal with regression problems.

We begin the chapter with a definition of regression as a machine learning problem. We continue by taking a brief look at simple and multiple regression and how these problems are usually tackled in statistics. In the sections that follow we turn our attention to regression with support vector machines: first by developing linear support vector machines for regression in the primal setting, and then by deriving the dual formulation that will allow us to address nonlinear regression problems. We also take a brief look at model evaluation in the context of support vector regression models. We close the chapter by looking at some regression examples in both WEKA and R.

12.1 REGRESSION AS MACHINE LEARNING

In regression problems observations are associated with a numerical value rather than a label from a set of discrete labels. With this in mind, we can easily adapt our definition of machine learning (see Definition 1.1) to an instance of machine learning that deals with numerical training observations.

Knowledge Discovery with Support Vector Machines, by Lutz Hamel
Copyright © 2009 John Wiley & Sons, Inc.

Definition 12.1 (Machine Learning, Regression)
Given:

- *A data universe X*
- *A sample set S, where $S \subset X$*
- *Some target function $f : X \rightarrow \mathbb{R}$*
- *A training set D, where $D = \{(x, y) \mid x \in S \text{ and } y = f(x)\}$*

Compute a model $\hat{f} : X \rightarrow \mathbb{R}$ using D such that

$$\hat{f}(x) \cong f(x) \tag{12.1}$$

for all $x \in X$.

This definition differs from our original definition of machine learning only in the codomains of the target function and the model. That is, the original aim of machine learning persists, in that we are interested in computing a model that matches the output of the target function as best as possible over the entire data universe X. As in the case of classification, we typically choose X to be multidimensional, real data; that is, we choose X to be the set $\mathbb{R}^n$ with $n \geq 1$. Given this definition, the question remains: How does one compute the regression model $\hat{f}$?

12.2 SIMPLE AND MULTIPLE LINEAR REGRESSION

From a statistical perspective we can think of linear regression as fitting a hyperplane through a set of training points with a minimum error. This regression error is characterized by *residual terms*, which are defined as the difference between the output of the model and the actual value of the training observations. The goal in linear regression is to minimize these residuals.

To make this more concrete, assume a regression training set of the form

$$D = \{(\overline{x}_1, y_1), (\overline{x}_2, y_2), \ldots, (\overline{x}_l, y_l)\} \subset \mathbb{R}^n \times \mathbb{R}. \tag{12.2}$$

Let us assume that $\hat{f}(\overline{x})$ is a regression model on D; then the quantity

$$\rho_i = y_i - \hat{f}(\overline{x}_i) \tag{12.3}$$

for $(\overline{x}_i, y_i) \in D$, called a *residual*, measures the difference between model output and the actual observation. For a perfect model the residuals are all zero, that is, the output of the model matches exactly the values observed in the training set. However, it is overly optimistic to assume that we can construct such perfect models for real-world data sets. Therefore, we have to contend ourselves with constructing models where the residuals are minimized; that is, we construct models where the error between the model output and the values observed is minimized. In linear regression this is accomplished by computing the minimum *sum of squared errors*,

$$\min \sum_{i=1}^{l} \rho_i^2 = \min_{\hat{f}} \sum_{i=1}^{l} \left(y_i - \hat{f}(\overline{x}_i) \right)^2, \tag{12.4}$$

with $(\overline{x}_i, y_i) \in D$. Notice that the error depends on the model $\hat{f}$ we select to compute the residuals. This gives us an optimization problem that allows us to compute the optimal linear regression model $\hat{f}^*$ as

$$\hat{f}^* = \operatorname*{argmin}_{\hat{f}} \sum_{i=1}^{l} \left(y_i - \hat{f}(\overline{x}_i) \right)^2. \tag{12.5}$$

By taking advantage of the fact that we are constructing linear models, we can rewrite this equation as

$$(\overline{w}^*, b^*) = \operatorname*{argmin}_{\overline{w}, b} \sum_{i=1}^{l} (y_i - \overline{w} \bullet \overline{x}_i + b)^2, \tag{12.6}$$

where the optimal regression model is

$$\hat{f}^*(\overline{x}) = \overline{w}^* \bullet \overline{x} - b^*. \tag{12.7}$$

In simple linear regression, that is, regression problems where the observations in the training set have the form $(x, y) \in \mathbb{R} \times \mathbb{R}$, equation (12.6) can be solved analytically, yielding a slope w^* and an offset term b^* for a line that represents the linear model for the regression problem. Figure 12.1 illustrates a linear regression model for simple linear regression. Each point in the graph represents an observation $(x, y) \in \mathbb{R} \times \mathbb{R}$, and the vertical lines represent the residuals. The optimal model is constructed such that the residuals are minimized.

In multiple linear regression, that is, regression problems where the observations in the training set have the form $(\overline{x}, y) \in \mathbb{R}^n \times \mathbb{R}$, equation (12.6) can typically *not* be solved analytically unless the data fulfill certain collinearity conditions. Therefore, multiple linear regression problems are often solved using heuristics that guarantee that the collinearity conditions hold before applying an analytical approach.

Next we look at an example of simple linear regression in R. We use the built-in data set 'cars'. This data set gives measurements of the speed of a car (mph) as the independent variable versus the stopping distance (ft) as the dependent variable. The aim is to construct a linear model of this relationship. The following R code loads the data set, computes a linear model, plots the data set, and then plots the model over the

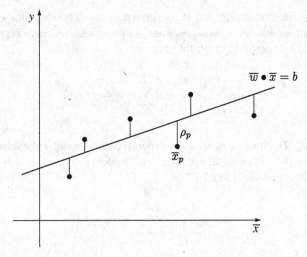

FIGURE 12.1   Linear regression with residuals. Here the point $\overline{x}_p$ is an observation and ρ_p is the residual at that observation given the model $\overline{w} \bullet \overline{x} = b$.

data set.

```
> data(cars)
> model <- lm(cars$dist ~ ., data = cars)
> plot(cars)
> abline(model)
```

Figure 12.2 shows the resulting plot.

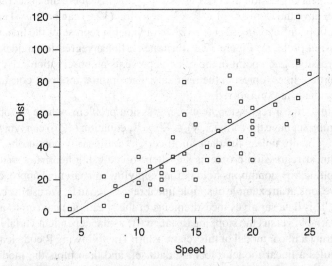

FIGURE 12.2   Simple linear regression model for the 'cars' data set.

12.3 REGRESSION WITH MAXIMUM-MARGIN MACHINES

A strong motivation for the development of support vector regression models is the straightforward extension from linear regression to nonlinear regression using the kernel trick. To develop support vector machines in the context of regression, we start with the primal setting of maximum-margin machines. In this case the underlying ideas are virtually the same as in the case of classification with maximum-margin machines: We are given a hyperplane and we would like to maximize the distances of the observations to that hyperplane.

Suppose that we have a regression problem where all the observations of the regression training set

$$D = \{(\overline{x}_1, y_1), (\overline{x}_2, y_2), \ldots, (\overline{x}_l, y_l)\} \subseteq \mathbb{R}^n \times \mathbb{R}$$

fit into a (hyper-) tube of width 2ε with $\varepsilon > 0$ (see Figure 12.3a). We can interpret this hypertube as a regression model by imagining that there is a hyperplane positioned right in the center of the tube that models the observations. Now, typically there are many different ways to position the hypertube of width 2ε and still have all the training observations contained within the tube. However, there exists an optimal hypertube alignment such that as many observations are pushed as close to the outer boundaries of the hypertube as possible. In other words, the optimal hypertube alignment is achieved when the distances of the observations from the center hyperplane are maximized. This is illustrated in Figure 12.3b, where the filled circles represent the observations that act as constraints to the optimization.

This is very similar to the problem of maximizing the margin of a decision surface (see Chapter 6) and it turns out that we can use the same optimization problem for finding the optimal hypertube alignment that we used for finding the maximum-margin

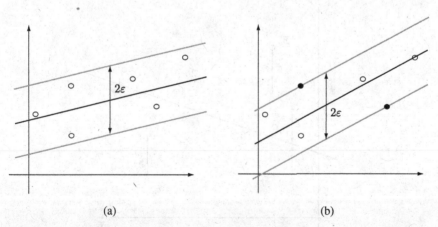

(a)   (b)

FIGURE 12.3 Solving regression problems with linear models using a ε hypertube: (a) regression model where all observations are within the hypertube depicted by the light gray lines; (b) optimal regression model with a maximum margin.

decision surface given in Proposition 6.1 by adjusting the constraints appropriately. We optimize the primal objective function,

$$\min \phi(\overline{w}, \overset{\circ}{b}) = \min_{\overline{w}, b} \tfrac{1}{2} \overline{w} \bullet \overline{w} \tag{12.8}$$

such that the constraints

$$y_i - \hat{f}(\overline{x}_i) \le \varepsilon, \tag{12.9}$$

$$\hat{f}(\overline{x}_i) - y_i \le \varepsilon, \tag{12.10}$$

are satisfied for $i = 1, \ldots, l$ and where $\hat{f}(\overline{x}) = \overline{w} \bullet \overline{x} - b$. The two constraint inequalities can also be captured with the single inequality, $|y_i - \hat{f}(\overline{x}_i)| \le \varepsilon$. It is perhaps in this form that it becomes most apparent that the constraints ensure that all observations have to be within the hypertube. This allows us to interpret the optimization as a computation where we adjust the rotation and offset term of the model until we maximize the distances of the observations to the central hyperplane with the constraint of keeping all the observations within the hypertube.

In the preceding development we made the assumption that it is possible to fit all observations into a hypertube of width 2ε. Of course, in real-world data sets this will hardly be the case. This can be seen in the cars data set of Section 12.2, where the ε value would need to be enormous to fit all the observations into a hypertube of width 2ε. For observations that fall outside the hypertube with a fixed value of ε, we introduce correction terms or *slack variables* that tell us how much of a correction is needed for these observations to be moved into the hypertube. Figure 12.4 illustrates this. For any observation $(\overline{x}_i, y_i)$ we use a pair of slack variables, ξ_i and ξ_i', that

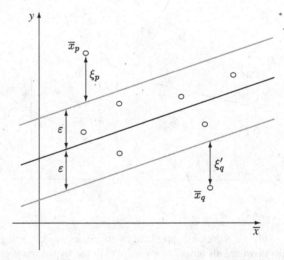

FIGURE 12.4   Linear maximum margin regression with slack variables.

capture the correction necessary for that observation. If no correction for the observation is necessary, both slack variables are set to zero. If the observation is above the hypertube, we set the slack variable ξ_i to the absolute value necessary to move the observation into the hypertube, and we set the other slack variable ξ_i' to zero. Conversely, if the observation is below the hypertube, we set the slack variable ξ_i' to the absolute value necessary to move the observation into the hypertube and we let the other slack variable ξ_i be zero. More precisely, we define the slack variables as

$$\xi_i = \begin{cases} 0 & \text{if } y_i - \hat{f}(\overline{x}_i) \le \varepsilon, \\ |y_i - \hat{f}(\overline{x}_i)| - \varepsilon & \text{otherwise,} \end{cases} \tag{12.11}$$

$$\xi_i' = \begin{cases} 0 & \text{if } \hat{f}(\overline{x}_i) - y_i \le \varepsilon, \\ |y_i - \hat{f}(\overline{x}_i)| - \varepsilon & \text{otherwise} \end{cases} \tag{12.12}$$

for $i = 1, \ldots, l$ with $(\overline{x}_i, y_i) \in D$. Here the slack variables ξ_i are zero except for observations that lie above the hypertube. Conversely, the slack variables ξ_i' are zero except for observations that lie below the hypertube. Given this, finding the optimal hyperplane then becomes a trade-off between maximizing the margin within the hypertube and minimizing the value of the slack variables. To express this as an optimization problem, we add the slack variables as a penalty term to our objective function in (12.8). We can now state regression with maximum-margin machines as follows:

Proposition 12.1 *Given a regression training set*

$$D = \{(\overline{x}_1, y_1), (\overline{x}_2, y_2), \ldots, (\overline{x}_l, y_l)\} \subseteq \mathbb{R}^n \times \mathbb{R},$$

we can compute the optimal regression model $\hat{f}^*(\overline{x}) = \overline{w}^* \bullet \overline{x} - b^*$ as the optimization

$$\min \phi(\overline{w}, b, \overline{\xi}, \overline{\xi}') = \min_{\overline{w}, b, \overline{\xi}, \overline{\xi}'} \frac{1}{2}\overline{w} \bullet \overline{w} + C \sum_{i=1}^{l}(\xi_i + \xi_i'), \tag{12.13}$$

such that the constraints

$$y_i - \hat{f}(\overline{x}_i) \le \xi_i + \varepsilon, \tag{12.14}$$

$$\hat{f}(\overline{x}_i) - y_i \le \xi_i' + \varepsilon, \tag{12.15}$$

$$0 \le \xi_i, \xi_i', \tag{12.16}$$

for $i = 1, \ldots, l$ hold with $\hat{f}(\overline{x}) = \overline{w} \bullet \overline{x} - b$.

In Proposition 12.1 the penalty constant C modulates the trade-off between margin maximization and the minimization of the slack variables.

12.4 REGRESSION WITH SUPPORT VECTOR MACHINES

Recall from Chapter 7 that we can derive the dual to maximum-margin optimization by constructing the Lagrangian optimization

$$\max_{\overline{\alpha}} \min_{\overline{x}} L(\overline{\alpha}, \overline{x}) = \max_{\overline{\alpha}} \min_{\overline{x}} \left(\phi(\overline{x}) - \sum_{i=1}^{l} \alpha_i g_i(\overline{x}) \right), \tag{12.17}$$

subject to the constraints

$$\alpha_i \geq 0 \tag{12.18}$$

for $i = 1, \ldots, l$. Here $g_i(\overline{x}) \geq 0$ are inequality constraints and the variables $\overline{\alpha}$ and $\overline{x}$ are called the *dual* and *primal variables* of the optimization problem, respectively.

As a first step in constructing the Lagrangian optimization we derive our inequality constraints. This is easily done by slightly rewriting the constraints appearing in the primal optimization problem in Proposition 12.1:

$$\xi_i + \varepsilon - y_i + \hat{f}(\overline{x}_i) \geq 0, \tag{12.19}$$

$$\xi_i' + \varepsilon - \hat{f}(\overline{x}_i) + y_i \geq 0, \tag{12.20}$$

$$\xi_i \geq 0, \tag{12.21}$$

$$\xi_i' \geq 0. \tag{12.22}$$

The four sets of inequality constraints imply that we have to introduce four sets of dual variables into our Lagrangian optimization. Substituting our objective function and the inequality constraints into the Lagrangian optimization above gives us the following:

$$\max_{\overline{\alpha}, \overline{\alpha}', \overline{\beta}, \overline{\beta}'} \min_{\overline{w}, b, \overline{\xi}, \overline{\xi}'} L(\overline{\alpha}, \overline{\alpha}', \overline{\beta}, \overline{\beta}', \overline{w}, b, \overline{\xi}, \overline{\xi}')$$

$$= \max_{\overline{\alpha}, \overline{\alpha}', \overline{\beta}, \overline{\beta}'} \min_{\overline{w}, b, \overline{\xi}, \overline{\xi}'} \left(\frac{1}{2} \overline{w} \bullet \overline{w} + C \sum_{i=1}^{l} (\xi_i + \xi_i') - \sum_{i=1}^{l} \alpha_i \left(\xi_i + \varepsilon - y_i + \hat{f}(\overline{x}_i) \right) \right.$$

$$\left. - \sum_{i=1}^{l} \alpha_i' \left(\xi_i' + \varepsilon - \hat{f}(\overline{x}_i) + y_i \right) - \sum_{i=1}^{l} \beta_i \xi_i - \sum_{i=1}^{l} \beta_i' \xi_i' \right), \tag{12.23}$$

subject to the constraints

$$\alpha_i, \alpha_i', \beta_i, \beta_i' \geq 0 \tag{12.24}$$

for $i = 1, \ldots, l$ and where $\hat{f}(\overline{x}) = \overline{w} \bullet \overline{x} - b$. Given a solution to the Lagrangian optimization

$$\max_{\overline{\alpha},\overline{\alpha}',\overline{\beta},\overline{\beta}'} \min_{\overline{w},b,\overline{\xi},\overline{\xi}'} L(\overline{\alpha},\overline{\alpha}',\overline{\beta},\overline{\beta}',\overline{w},b,\overline{\xi},\overline{\xi}') = L(\overline{\alpha}^*,\overline{\alpha}'^*,\overline{\beta}^*,\overline{\beta}'^*,\overline{w}^*,b^*,\overline{\xi}^*,\overline{\xi}'^*),$$

$$(12.25)$$

we know that it will satisfy the KKT conditions

$$\frac{\partial L(\overline{\alpha}^*,\overline{\alpha}'^*,\overline{\beta}^*,\overline{\beta}'^*,\overline{w}^*,b^*,\overline{\xi}^*,\overline{\xi}'^*)}{\partial \overline{w}} = \overline{0}, \qquad (12.26)$$

$$\frac{\partial L(\overline{\alpha}^*,\overline{\alpha}'^*,\overline{\beta}^*,\overline{\beta}'^*,\overline{w}^*,b^*,\overline{\xi}^*,\overline{\xi}'^*)}{\partial b} = 0, \qquad (12.27)$$

$$\frac{\partial L(\overline{\alpha}^*,\overline{\alpha}'^*,\overline{\beta}^*,\overline{\beta}'^*,\overline{w}^*,b^*,\overline{\xi}^*,\overline{\xi}'^*)}{\partial \xi_i} = 0, \qquad (12.28)$$

$$\frac{\partial L(\overline{\alpha}^*,\overline{\alpha}'^*,\overline{\beta}^*,\overline{\beta}'^*,\overline{w}^*,b^*,\overline{\xi}^*,\overline{\xi}'^*)}{\partial \xi_i'} = 0, \qquad (12.29)$$

$$\alpha_i^* \left(\xi_i^* + \varepsilon - y_i + \hat{f}^*(\overline{x}_i) \right) = 0, \qquad (12.30)$$

$$\alpha_i'^* \left(\xi_i'^* + \varepsilon - \hat{f}^*(\overline{x}_i) + y_i \right) = 0, \qquad (12.31)$$

$$\beta_i^* \xi_i^* = 0, \qquad (12.32)$$

$$\beta_i'^* \xi_i'^* = 0, \qquad (12.33)$$

$$\xi_i^* + \varepsilon - y_i + \hat{f}^*(\overline{x}_i) \geq 0, \qquad (12.34)$$

$$\xi_i'^* + \varepsilon - \hat{f}^*(\overline{x}_i) + y_i \geq 0, \qquad (12.35)$$

$$\xi_i^*, \xi_i'^* \geq 0, \qquad (12.36)$$

$$\alpha_i, \alpha_i' \geq 0, \qquad (12.37)$$

$$\beta_i^*, \beta_i'^* \geq 0, \qquad (12.38)$$

where $i = 1, \ldots, l$ and $\hat{f}^*(\overline{x}) = \overline{w}^* \bullet \overline{x} - b^*$ is the optimal regression function. Using the KKT conditions, it is not difficult to show that the following proposition holds.

Proposition 12.2 *Given a regression training set*

$$D = \{(\overline{x}_1, y_1), (\overline{x}_2, y_2), \ldots, (\overline{x}_l, y_l)\} \subseteq \mathbb{R}^n \times \mathbb{R},$$

we can compute the optimal support vector regression model $\hat{f}^*(\overline{x}) = \overline{w}^* \bullet \overline{x} - b^*$
with the dual optimization problem

$$\max_{\overline{\alpha},\overline{\alpha}'} \phi'(\overline{\alpha}, \overline{\alpha}') = \max_{\overline{\alpha},\overline{\alpha}'} \left(-\frac{1}{2} \sum_{i=1}^{l} \sum_{j=1}^{l} (\alpha_i - \alpha_i')(\alpha_j - \alpha_j')\overline{x}_i \bullet \overline{x}_j \right.$$

$$\left. + \sum_{i=1}^{l} y_i(\alpha_i - \alpha_i') - \varepsilon \sum_{i=1}^{l} (\alpha_i + \alpha_i') \right), \qquad (12.39)$$

subject to the constraints

$$\sum_{i=1}^{l}(\alpha_i - \alpha_i') = 0, \tag{12.40}$$

$$C \geq \alpha_i, \alpha_i' \geq 0 \tag{12.41}$$

for $i = 1, \ldots, l$, where

$$\overline{w}^* = \sum_{i=1}^{l}(\alpha_i^* - \alpha_i'^*)\overline{x}_i, \tag{12.42}$$

$$b^* = \frac{1}{l}\sum_{i=1}^{l}\overline{w}^* \bullet \overline{x}_i - y_i. \tag{12.43}$$

In support vector regression models we can interpret an observation $(\overline{x}_i, y_i)$ for which the coefficient $(\alpha_i - \alpha_i')$ is nonzero as a support vector. Notice that the solution to the optimal regression model

$$\hat{f}^*(\overline{x}) = \overline{w}^* \bullet \overline{x} - b^*$$

$$= \sum_{i=1}^{l}(\alpha_i^* - \alpha_i'^*)\overline{x}_i \bullet \overline{x} - \frac{1}{l}\sum_{i=1}^{l}\sum_{j=1}^{l}(\alpha_i^* - \alpha_i'^*)\overline{x}_i \bullet \overline{x}_j - y_j \tag{12.44}$$

depends only on the support vectors. Therefore, we can refer to this model as a *support vector regression machine.*

As a last observation, consider the fact that linear regression with support vector machines can be extended to nonlinear regression by applying the kernel trick to both the optimization and the model. That is, we can replace the dot product in the optimization and in the model with an appropriate kernel function to extend support vector regression to the nonlinear setting.

12.5 MODEL EVALUATION

Similar to support vector classification models, support vector regression models also have a number of free parameters that need to be tuned. These are the kernel k with its corresponding parameters λ, the ε parameter, and the cost constant C. Our techniques of hold-out and cross-validation testing as well as bootstrapping carry over to support vector regression models, with the difference that the 0–1 loss function is replaced by a loss function that computes how well the model fits the observations. That is, rather than measuring misclassification, we measure how different the predicted value is from the observed value.

The most common error estimate for regression functions is the *mean-squared error*. We define a loss function called $\mathcal{L}_2$ that computes the squared residual at an observation $(\overline{x}, y)$ given a model $\hat{f}$,

$$\mathcal{L}_2(y, \hat{f}(\overline{x})) = \left(y - \hat{f}(\overline{x})\right)^2. \tag{12.45}$$

Now, given a regression training set

$$D = \{(\overline{x}_1, y_1), (\overline{x}_2, y_2), \ldots, (\overline{x}_l, y_l)\} \subseteq \mathbb{R}^n \times \mathbb{R},$$

we define the mean-squared error computed on D as

$$\mathrm{mse}_D\left[\hat{f}_D[k, \lambda, \varepsilon, C]\right] = \frac{1}{l} \sum_{i=1}^{l} \mathcal{L}_2\left(y_i, \hat{f}_D[k, \lambda, \varepsilon, C](\overline{x}_i)\right), \tag{12.46}$$

with $(\overline{x}_i, y_i) \in D$. Here we use the model $\hat{f}_D$, where the subscript indicates that it was constructed using set D. In this case we can interpret the mean-squared error as the average loss $\mathcal{L}_2$ of model $\hat{f}_D$ over the data set D.

We can generalize this to the hold-out testing technique by splitting the set D into two nonoverlapping partitions P and Q such that

$$D = P \cup Q, \tag{12.47}$$

where we use P as a training set and Q as a test set. The hold-out error can then be computed as

$$\mathrm{mse}_Q\left[\hat{f}_P[k, \lambda, \varepsilon, C]\right] = \frac{1}{|Q|} \sum_{(\overline{x}_i, y_i) \in Q} \mathcal{L}_2\left(y_i, \hat{f}_P[k, \lambda, \varepsilon, C](\overline{x}_i)\right). \tag{12.48}$$

For the hold-out error we compute the average loss over the set Q of a model trained on P. An optimal model will minimize the mean-squared error over the test set Q.

Given the $\mathcal{L}_2$ loss function, it is straightforward to derive the corresponding expression for the cross-validated error (see the exercises). It should also not be any problem to generalize the computation of the confidence interval based on the bootstrap from classification to regression (see the exercises).

As a final note we should mention that another popular method of determining the error of a regression model is the *root-mean-squared error* derived from the mean-squared error simply by taking its square root. This is one of the error metrics reported in WEKA.

12.6 TOOL SUPPORT

Regression with support vector machines is available in both WEKA and R. Here we demonstrate regression in both systems using the cars data set used at the beginning of this chapter. We assume that this data set is available as the file "cars.csv".

12.6.1 WEKA

As usual, we load the data file into WEKA from the *Preprocess* tab. Notice that both the independent attribute 'speed' and the dependent attribute 'dist' are numeric attributes, and WEKA displays the appropriate data summaries in its *Selected Attribute* panel. Once the data set is loaded, we switch to the *Classify* tab (in WEKA regression models are grouped together with the classification models). To construct a support vector regression model, we press the *Choose* button and navigate to the SMOreg model,

$$\text{weka} \rightarrow \text{classifiers} \rightarrow \text{functions} \rightarrow \text{SMOreg}.$$

For our first regression model we select the training set as the test option and make sure that the dist attribute is the target attribute. We use the default linear kernel for our regression model. However, to compare the model to the linear model constructed in Section 12.2 we need to change the *filterType* to no normalization and standardization. Now you can press the *Start* button in order to train the model. WEKA constructs the linear regression model

$$\hat{f}(x) = 3.4x - 11.6, \tag{12.49}$$

with a root-mean-squared error of 15.48. We can compare this model to the model constructed using simple linear regression by plotting the models side by side (see Figure 12.5). Here we plotted the simple linear regression model as a dashed line and the model computed by WEKA as a solid line. Although the support vector

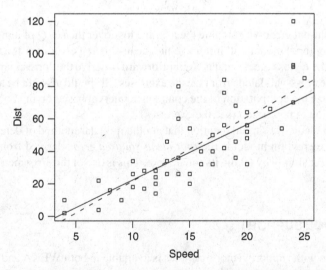

FIGURE 12.5 Comparing the simple linear regression model (dashed line) for the 'cars' data set with the support vector regression model (solid line) computed by WEKA.

regression model seems pretty good, recall that we used the training set as the test set. This means that there might be some overfitting. We leave it as an exercise for the reader to apply the hold-out or cross-validation technique to construct an optimal regression model.

12.6.2 R

In contrast to WEKA, R provides a substantial amount information about the underlying support vector model. In this case the function svm returns an object that contains the support vector model. The model is given in the standard support vector machine format,

$$\hat{f}(\overline{x}) = \overline{w} \bullet \overline{x} - b. \tag{12.50}$$

In the case of regression the normal vector $\overline{w}$ is given as

$$\overline{w} = \sum_{i=1}^{l} (\alpha_i - \alpha_i')\overline{x}_i. \tag{12.51}$$

Concretely, the object returned holds an index vector that points to all observations in the training set that represent support vectors. It also holds a vector with the coefficient $\alpha_i - \alpha_i'$ for each support vector. In addition, it holds the offset term $-b$ of the regression model.

To demonstrate the capabilities of R, we use the following R program.

```
# load our svm library
library(e1071)

# get the epsilon svm parameter from the user
e <- as.integer(readline(prompt="Enter epsilon value: "))

# plot cars data set on new canvas
# data points are plotted as circles
quartz(height=4,width=4,pointsize=8)
data(cars)
plot(cars,pch=22,cex=.5)

# build svm regression model
svm.model <- svm(cars$dist ~.,
                data=cars,
                type="eps-regression",
                kernel="linear",
                scale=FALSE,
                cost=1,
                epsilon=e)
```

```
# plot the regression line with the epsilon tube
w <- sum(cars$speed[svm.model$index]*svm.model$coefs)
offset <- (- svm.model$rho)
abline(a=offset,b=w)
abline(a=offset+e,b=w,lty=2)
abline(a=offset-e,b=w,lty=2)

# plot the support vectors as solid squares
x <- cars$speed[svm.model$index]
y <- cars$dist[svm.model$index]
points(x,y,type="p",pch=22,cex=.5,bg="black")
```

This program prompts the user for an ε value, plots the cars data set, and builds a linear support vector regression model. Once the model is constructed, the program continues to extract the slope and the offset term from the object returned. The slope is easily calculated with equation (12.51). With this it is possible to plot the regression line together with its ε tube. The last set of computations in the program highlight as solid squares precisely those observations in the data set that are support vectors.

We use this R program to compute two support vector regression models. The first model we train with $\varepsilon = 5$, as shown in Figure 12.6. In this case the tube is very narrow, which implies that not all observations can fit into it. As we would expect, the observations outside the hypertube are considered support vectors, indicated by the solid squares. If we were to investigate the coefficient $\alpha_i - \alpha_i'$ for each of these observations, we would find that the value would be bound by the cost constant C. Also notice that there are a number of support vectors right on the ε boundaries.

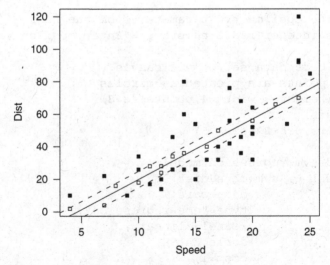

FIGURE 12.6   Linear support vector regression model of the cars data set with $\varepsilon = 5$.

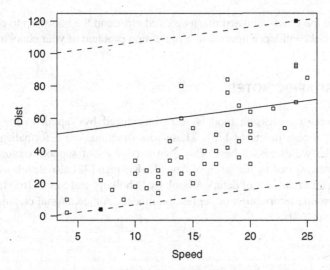

FIGURE 12.7   Linear support vector regression model of the cars data set with $\varepsilon = 50$.

Those support vectors are due to the maximum-margin optimization. This aspect of the optimization becomes clear if we make ε big enough so that all observations fall within the hypertube. To see this, we let $\varepsilon = 50$. The resulting regression model is shown in Figure 12.7. Here we do not have any support vectors due to slack variables, but we have two support vectors that are due to the maximum margin optimization. The alignment of the regression line has been optimized such that it maximizes the distance of the observations to the regression line under the constraint that all observations stay within the tube.

EXERCISES

12.1 Find a regression data set and build a regression model in R using the statistical linear regression models available through the function 1m.

    (a) If your training set is of type $\mathbb{R}^2 \times \mathbb{R}$ or $\mathbb{R} \times \mathbb{R}$, use R to plot the regression model.

    (b) Determine the average of the residuals of the model.

12.2 Construct a linear regression model for the cars data set in WEKA and compare it to the linear model constructed with R in Section 12.2.

12.3 Derive equation (12.42).

12.4 Derive equation (12.39).

12.5 Explain equation (12.43) informally.

12.6 Derive an expression for the cross-validated mean-squared error [see equation (9.30)].

12.7 Use the cross-validated mean-squared error and the bootstrap to compute the model confidence interval of a regression problem of your choosing.

BIBLIOGRAPHIC NOTES

Support vector regression models were introduced by Vapnik in the context of ε-insensitive loss functions [73]. These loss functions are a formalization of the ε-hypertube we discussed here. Our own exposition of support vector regression models was inspired by the work of Abe [1]. Kecman [42] also develops regression models in a fair amount of detail. A book by Schölkopf and Smola [65] has substantial background information on regression models. A nice tutorial on support vector regression is [68].

CHAPTER 13

NOVELTY DETECTION

An interesting application of support vector machines is in the area of data description. What is different about the application of support vector machines in data description compared to classification is that we are considering unlabeled data and our goal is to construct models that give us some insight into the nature of this unlabeled data. For instance, we might be interested in finding out if the data are evenly distributed throughout the space spanned by the attributes or if there are data points that can be considered outliers. This particular view of data description, where a data point that does not conform to the distribution pattern of the other data points in the data set is considered an outlier or novelty, is usually referred to as *novelty detection*.

An important aspect of novelty detection is that the models we construct can be used for both the description of the training data and for data points not in the training data. Consider an application of such data description models on a factory floor where some sort of widget is being produced. Suppose that we train a model on a factory run of a couple of thousand widgets in such a way that it detects defective widgets as outliers. We can then deploy the model with a suitable set of sensors on the factory floor to reject defective widgets automatically. That is, we can deploy the model to reject widgets that do not conform to the characteristics of the majority of widgets in the training set.

We begin this chapter by developing the theoretical underpinnings of novelty detection with maximum-margin machines. We then discuss the dual setting for these machines together with the implication of nonlinearity due to kernel functions. We close the chapter by looking at some examples in R.

Knowledge Discovery with Support Vector Machines, by Lutz Hamel
Copyright © 2009 John Wiley & Sons, Inc.

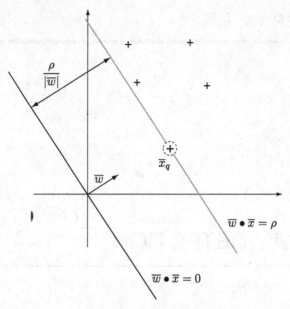

FIGURE 13.1   Novelty detection with maximum-margin machines.

13.1 MAXIMUM-MARGIN MACHINES

The central idea in novelty detection with maximum-margin machines is to construct a hyperplane through the origin of the input space whose margin separates the unlabeled training points from the origin in some optimal way. Figure 13.1 demonstrates this. Notice here that we rotated the hyperplane in such a way that the margin $\rho/|\overline{w}|$ is maximized and is limited by the point $\overline{x}_q$.

Assume that we have an unlabeled training set,

$$D = \{\overline{x}_1, \overline{x}_2, \ldots, \overline{x}_l\} \subset \mathbb{R}^n, \tag{13.1}$$

whose elements are located only in the first hyperoctant (the components of all vectors are positive) and can be linearly separated from the origin. In this case maximizing the margin of a hyperplane going through the origin gives rise to the following convex optimization problem:

$$\min \phi(\overline{w}, \rho) = \min_{\overline{w}, \rho} \tfrac{1}{2}\overline{w} \bullet \overline{w} - \rho, \tag{13.2}$$

subject to the constraints

$$\overline{w} \bullet \overline{x}_i \geq \rho, \tag{13.3}$$

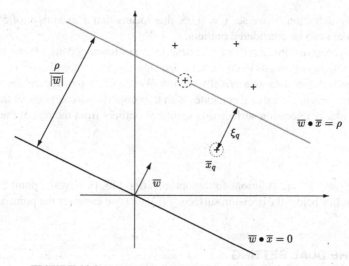

FIGURE 13.2 Novelty detection with soft-margin machines.

where $\overline{x}_i \in D$. The optimization specifies that we rotate the hyperplane $\overline{w} \bullet \overline{x} = 0$ until we have maximized the margin $\rho/|\overline{w}|$ under the constraint that all data points lie on or outside the margin.

The key insight to novelty detection is the introduction of slack variables into our optimization problem. Consider the case above, where we computed the optimal hyperplane but now we continue to push the margin beyond the points that constrain it. Figure 13.2 illustrates this and as in the case of soft-margin classifiers, we introduce slack variables ξ_i which are nonzero for any data points that fall into the margin. We are now faced with the by now familiar optimization problem that needs to trade off the size of the slack variables against the size of the margin,

$$\min \phi(\overline{w}, \rho) = \min_{\overline{w}, \rho} \frac{1}{2} \overline{w} \bullet \overline{w} - \rho + \frac{1}{vl} \sum_{i=1}^{l} \xi_i, \qquad (13.4)$$

subject to the constraints

$$\overline{w} \bullet \overline{x}_i \geq \rho - \xi_i, \qquad (13.5)$$

$$\xi_i \geq 0 \qquad (13.6)$$

for $i = 1, \ldots, l$. Here we introduced a new penalty constant $0 < v \leq 1$ that modulates the trade-off between the size of the slack variables and the size of the margin. In this formulation the penalty constant v acts as an upper bound on the number of support vectors with nonzero slack variables. For instance, if we let $v = 0.2$, a maximum of 20% of the training points are allowed to have nonzero slack variables. In the case of novelty detection, if we set $\nu = 0.05$, this means that a maximum of 5% of the training data can be considered outliers.

So far we have considered only the description of training data. We can perform a simple trick that allows us to construct a decision surface that will classify any point not in the training data as a novelty or not: We translate the hyperplane that runs through the origin such that it coincides with the supporting hyperplane of the margin and consider it a decision surface that separates outliers from the rest of the data:

$$\hat{f}(\overline{x}) = \overline{w}^* \bullet \overline{x} - \rho^*, \tag{13.7}$$

where $\overline{w}^*$ and ρ^* are solutions to the optimization (13.4). Given a point $\overline{z} \in \mathbb{R}^n$, if that point lies below the decision surface, $\hat{f}(\overline{z}) < 0$, we consider the point an outlier.

13.2 THE DUAL SETTING

In Section 13.1 we made some strong assumptions on the structure of the training data D; we assumed that all the training points are located in the first hyperoctant of the space $\mathbb{R}^n$, and furthermore, we assumed that the training points can be linearly separated from the origin. By constructing the dual optimization problem we can relax these restrictions because the introduction of appropriate kernel functions will allow us to consider training points located in arbitrary hyperoctants and we are not restricted to linear decision surfaces.

We begin by constructing the Lagrangian from our primal optimization problem (13.4) and its constraints (13.5) and (13.6):

$$L(\overline{\alpha}, \overline{\beta}, \overline{w}, \rho, \overline{\xi}) = \frac{1}{2}\overline{w} \bullet \overline{w} - \rho + \frac{1}{\nu l}\sum_{i=1}^{l}\xi_i$$

$$-\sum_{i=1}^{l}\alpha_i\,(\overline{w} \bullet \overline{x}_i - \rho + \xi_i) - \sum_{i=1}^{l}\beta_i\xi_i. \tag{13.8}$$

It is straightforward to construct the KKT conditions for the optimization problem

$$\max_{\overline{\alpha}, \overline{\beta}}\ \min_{\overline{w}, \rho, \overline{\xi}}\ L(\overline{\alpha}, \overline{\beta}, \overline{w}, \rho, \overline{\xi}) \tag{13.9}$$

subject to the constraints

$$\alpha_i \geq 0, \tag{13.10}$$

$$\beta_i \geq 0 \tag{13.11}$$

for $i = 1, \ldots, l$. We leave this as an exercise for the reader. From the KKT conditions and the Lagrangian optimization (13.9) we can derive the dual to our primal optimization problem (13.4),

$$\max \phi'(\overline{\alpha}) = \max_{\overline{\alpha}} \left(-\frac{1}{2} \sum_{i=1}^{l} \sum_{j=1}^{l} \alpha_i \alpha_j \overline{x}_i \bullet \overline{x}_j \right), \qquad (13.12)$$

subject to the constraints

$$\frac{1}{\nu l} \geq \alpha_i \geq 0, \qquad (13.13)$$

$$\sum_{i=1}^{l} \alpha_i = 1 \qquad (13.14)$$

for $i = 1, \ldots, l$. From our work on soft-margin classifiers we know that training points with coefficients $\alpha_i = 1/\nu l$ are training points inside the margin; that is, these training points are considered outliers. Thus, in the dual formulation, any training point whose coefficient is bounded by the constant $1/\nu l$ can be considered an outlier.

The model that allows us to classify data points that are not in the training set as outliers is the decision surface running through the origin translated to coincide with the supporting hyperplane of the margin:

$$\hat{f}(\overline{x}) = \overline{w}^* \bullet \overline{x} - \rho^*$$
$$= \sum_{i=1}^{l} \alpha_i^* \overline{x}_i \bullet \overline{x} - \rho^*, \qquad (13.15)$$

where $\overline{\alpha}^*$ is the solution to the optimization (13.12). We can compute ρ^* from any support vector not in the margin, that is, we can compute ρ^* from any training point $\overline{x}_i$ whose coefficient is $0 < \alpha_i^* < 1/\nu l$ and therefore lies on the margin:

$$\rho^* = \sum_{j=1}^{l} \alpha_j^* \overline{x}_j \bullet \overline{x}_i. \qquad (13.16)$$

As in our previous approaches to dual maximum-margin machines, data points appear only in the context of dot products in (13.12) and (13.15). This implies that we can perform the kernel trick and replace the dot products by an appropriate kernel function. The kernel trick lifts the restrictions that we imposed on the training data in Section 13.1 because we can always select a kernel function that maps the training data into the first hyperoctant in the feature space. From our previous work with kernel functions, we know that the transformation from input space into a feature space allows us to consider nonlinear decision surfaces in the input space.

13.3 NOVELTY DETECTION IN R

Let us look at novelty detection in R using the e1071 package. The first exercise is an illustration of the linear separation of the training points from the origin. Here we construct a hyperplane through the origin and then maximize the margin of this hyperplane given some penalty constant ν. The following R code accomplishes this:

```
library(e1071)
# set up our output device
quartz(height=4,width=4,pointsize=8)

# create a 2D data set and plot as squares
x1 <- rnorm(10,mean=4)
x2 <- rnorm(10,mean=4)
x <- data.frame(x1,x2)
plot(x,pch=22,cex=.5,xlim=c(-2,8),ylim=c(-2,8))

# build the novelty detection model
model <- svm(x,
             type="one-classification",
             kernel="linear",
             nu=0.1,
             scale=FALSE)

# plot the support vector outliers as filled squares
ix <- model$index[model$coefs == 1.0]
x1 <- x$x1[ix]
x2 <- x$x2[ix]
sv <- data.frame(x1,x2)
points(sv,type="p",pch=22, col=2)

# plot the hyperplane together with the
# margin that constitutes the novelty decision surface
w1 <- sum(x$x1[model$index]*model$coefs)
w2 <- sum(x$x2[model$index]*model$coefs)
slope <- -(w1/w2)
offset <- (model$rho/w2)
abline(a=offset,b=slope,lty=2)
abline(a=0,b=slope)
```

Running the code will plot the outliers as large black squares, the hyperplane as a solid line, and the margin as a dashed line. The resulting plot is shown in Figure 13.3. Notice how the margin separates the outlier from the rest of the training set.

As a second example we apply a nonlinear support vector machine with a Gaussian kernel to a randomly generated data set in $\mathbb{R}^2$. Here we let $\nu = 5\%$. The R code that

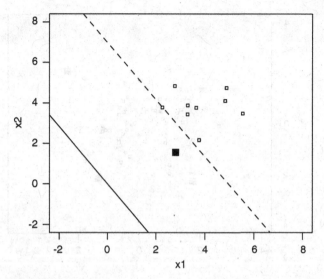

FIGURE 13.3 Demonstrating novelty detection with a linear kernel.

accomplishes this is

```
library(e1071)
# set up our output device
quartz(height=4,width=4,pointsize=8)

# create a 2D data set and plot as squares
x1 <- rnorm(100)
x2 <- rnorm(100)
x <- data.frame(x1,x2)
plot(x,pch=22,cex=.5,xlim=c(-4,4),ylim=c(-4,4))

# build the novelty detection model
model <- svm(x,
             type="one-classification",
             kernel="radial",
             gamma=0.1,
             nu=0.05)

# plot the support vectors as filled squares
ix <- model$index[model$coefs == 1.0]
x1 <- x$x1[ix]
x2 <- x$x2[ix]
sv <- data.frame(x1,x2)
points(sv,type="p",pch=22, col=2)
```

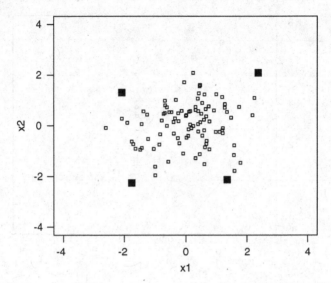

FIGURE 13.4 Demonstrating novelty detection with a nonlinear kernel.

This R code generates the plot given in Figure 13.4. The solid black squares are the support vectors, which we consider outliers. This data set is nonlinear and has points in all four quadrants and therefore illustrates very nicely that through the use of appropriate kernels, we are no longer restricted to linear separability from the origin, nor are we restricted to data points only in the first hyperoctant.

. As the final experiment we take a look at the 'cars' data set. Here we treat each training point as an unlabeled point in $\mathbb{R}^2$. We construct a novelty detection model with the penalty constant $\nu = 10\%$. The R code is given as

```
library(e1071)
data(cars)
# set up our output device
quartz(height=4,width=4,pointsize=8)

# build model
m <- svm(cars,gamma=.1,nu=0.10,kernel="radial")

# visualize - black training point, solid outliers
ix <- m$index[m$coefs == 1.0]
plot(cars,col = (1:50 %in% ix) + 1,pch=22,cex=.5)
```

The plot generated by the R code is given in Figure 13.5. We see three outliers identified. The top right outlier is perhaps intuitive. However, the other two outliers seem kind of odd. This is due to the fact that novelty detection using support vector machines does not take the underlying linear relationship of the training points into account.

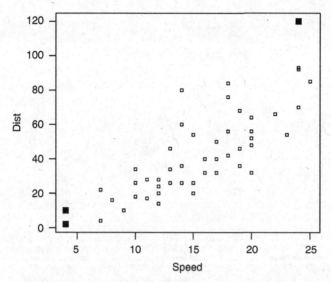

FIGURE 13.5   Novelty detection on the 'cars' data set.

EXERCISES

13.1   Give the KKT conditions for the optimization problem (13.9).

13.2   Derive expression (13.12) together with its constraints.

13.3   Construct a three-dimensional unlabeled data set and find the $\nu = 5\%$ outliers. Plot the results. (Do this work using R.)

BIBLIOGRAPHIC NOTES

Our development of novelty detection using support vector machines is based largely on the material published in [66]. An alternative approach to novelty detection using hyperspheres instead of hyperplanes is given in [70] and is also discussed in [65].

APPENDIX A

NOTATION

X	Sets are denoted by capital letters in italic type.
$A \times B$	The *cross product* of sets A and B. Let $A = \{a, b\}$ and $B = \{c, d\}$; then $A \times B = \{(a, c), (a, d), (b, c), (b, d)\}$.
$\overline{v}$	A vector in $\mathbb{R}^n$ where $\overline{v} = (v_1, v_2, \ldots, v_n)$ and v_i is called a *component*.
$|\overline{v}|$	The length of $\overline{v}$, defined as $\sqrt{v_1^2 + v_2^2 + \cdots + v_n^2}$.
iff	Shorthand for "if and only if."
$\overline{a} \bullet \overline{b}$	The dot product of two vectors defined as $\overline{a} \bullet \overline{b} = a_1 b_1 + \cdots + a_n b_n = |\overline{a}||\overline{b}| \cos \gamma$.
$|A|$	The cardinality of set A.
min	Optimization operator; $f(x^*) = \min f(x)$, where x^* is considered an optimal solution that minimizes the objective function f.
argmin	Optimization operator that returns the solution that minimizes the objective function, $x^* = \mathrm{argmin}\, f(x)$.
$\mathbf{M}$	Matrices are denoted by uppercase symbols written in bold face type.
$X^{\mathrm{T}}, \overline{v}^{\mathrm{T}}$	The transpose of a matrix and vector, respectively.
$\phi(\overline{x})$	Primal objective function.
$\phi'(\overline{\alpha})$	Dual objective function.
$L(\overline{\alpha}, \overline{x})$	The Lagrangian, with the primal variable $\overline{x}$ and the dual variable $\overline{\alpha}$.
$k(\overline{x}, \overline{y})$	Kernel function, defined as $k(\overline{x}, \overline{y}) = \Phi(\overline{x}) \bullet \Phi(\overline{y})$.
$k(\cdot, \overline{x})$	Partially evaluated kernel at point $\overline{x}$.
$\mathrm{sgn}(k)$	The *sign* function, defined as $+1$ if $k \geq 0$, otherwise, -1.
ξ_j	Slack variable for point $\overline{x}_j$.
$\mathrm{err}_D[\hat{f}_D]$	Training error of model $\hat{f}_D$.
$R[\hat{f}]$	Expected risk of model $\hat{f}$.
$\mathcal{L}$	Loss function.
ε	Tolerance band for support vector regression.
C	Cost constant.

Knowledge Discovery with Support Vector Machines, by Lutz Hamel
Copyright © 2009 John Wiley & Sons, Inc.

TUTORIAL INTRODUCTION TO R

R is a programming language designed to support data analysis and model building. It is an open-source reimplementation of the commercial statistical computing environment S-Plus.[1] R supports all traditional programming constructs, such as expressions, assignments, conditionals, loops, and functions. In addition to scalar arithmetic, R also supports vector arithmetic. This is a very powerful extension to the standard scalar programming paradigm, and using vector arithmetic is the preferred way of accomplishing things in R. R possesses a straightforward object system that supports high-level concepts such as statistical models very nicely. Object instantiation and inheritance are based on a prototyping mechanism. In addition to the programming language constructs, R incorporates a powerful graphics engine that supports many built-in graphical techniques, such as scatterplots, histograms, and simple linear regression plots, among many others. Because R is an open-source project, many extension modules have been written for it, implementing everything from basic statistics to microarray analysis and in our case, support vector machines.

R is an interactive environment that allows the user to type in a program or expression at the command line prompt and have R evaluate the program or expression immediately. Figure B.1 shows perhaps the simplest interactive session possible with R. In this case the user typed in the expression 2+2 at the prompt, then hit the return key, and the system responded with the result 4.

---

[1] R is available on the Web site http://www.r-project.org, and information on S-Plus may be found on the Web site of the Insightful Corporation, http://www.insightful.com.

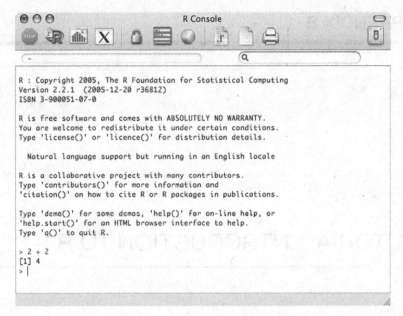

FIGURE B.1 Simple session in the command line console of R.

B.1 PROGRAMMING CONSTRUCTS

The fundamental programming construct in R is the assignment of a value to a variable using the < - operator, and as can be expected in a programming language, variables can then appear in expressions:

```
> x <- 2
> 2 * x
[1] 4
```

As part of its vector arithmetic facility, R allows the user to construct vectors using the constructor function c:

```
> v <- c(1,2,3)
> v
[1] 1 2 3
> v[2]
[1] 2
> v[2:3]
[1] 2 3
> v[v >= 2]
[1] 2 3
```

Here the function call c(1,2,3) constructs a vector with the components 1, 2, and 3, and then assigns this vector to the variable v. Just typing a variable name at the command line prompt displays the contents of that variable, which in this case is the vector. Components of a vector can be accessed with the standard bracket operator, where the value in the bracket is the component index. R differs from many other programming languages in that it allows for fairly complex index expressions. For example, we can extract components two through three of vector v with the index expression 2:3. We can extract all components whose value is greater or equal to 2 with the index expression v >= 2.

R allows the user to perform vector arithmetic on vector variables such as

```
> v + 1
[1] 2 3 4
```

or in a more complicated example,

```
> v
[1] 1 2 3
> w <- v + 1
> q <- w + v
> q
[1] 3 5 7
```

We can also define functions in R:

```
> add1 <- function(x) { x + 1 }
> add1
function(x) { x + 1 }
> add1(2)
[1] 3
```

Here we define a function using the function constructor that increments its argument by one and returns this incremented value. Returning a value from a R function is accomplished simply by stating the value as the last statement of the function itself. In this case it is the expression x + 1. We give our function a name by assigning it to the variable add1. We can then use the variable name as the function name to call the function.

There is an interesting observation with respect to the vector constructor: Nested calls to the constructor will still construct a single vector:

```
> c(c(1,2),3)
[1] 1 2 3
> v <- c(1,2)
> v
[1] 1 2
> w <- c(v,3)
> w
[1] 1 2 3
```

We make use of this property in the following function, which accepts a vector of values and returns a vector whose components are the values of the input vector incremented by one:

```
> addv1 <- function(v)
    {
        y <- c()
        for (x in v) {
            x1 <- x + 1
            y <- c(y,x1)
        }
        y
    }
> w
[1] 2 3 4
> addv1(w)
[1] 3 4 5
```

The function first constructs an empty vector in y; then it loops through all components of the input vector v, incrementing each by one and adding the newly calculated value to the end of the vector y. Once the function has iterated over all the input components, it returns the newly constructed vector y. In the code above we also show a simple example of the use of the function. This function performs the same operation as the vector operation w + 1. From a performance point of view it is always desirable to use the built-in vector operations; explicit iteration over vector elements is extremely slow.

B.2 DATA CONSTRUCTS

R is about programming with data; therefore, it is not unexpected that R provides many different ways to represent data. We have already seen scalar and vector values. R supports a special type of vector called a list, which acts just like a vector but allows for the addition of metadata such as field names. Consider

```
> lp <- list(name="joe",
             profession="cook",
             marital.status="married")
> lp
$name
[1] "joe"

$profession
[1] "cook"
```

```
$marital.status
[1] "married"

> lp[1]
$name
[1] "joe"
> lp$name
[1] "joe"
```

Here we construct a list of attributes for a person called `joe`. The list acts as a vector in the sense that we can extract information with the standard indexing operator but we can also extract information from the list via the names of the elements in the list using the $ operator.

In addition to one-dimensional vectors, R also provides a facility to build multidimensional arrays:

```
> aa <- array(0,dim=c(3,3))
> aa[2,2] <- 1
> aa
      [,1]  [,2]  [,3]
[1,]    0    0    0
[2,]    0    1    0
[3,]    0    0    0
> aa[,2]
[1] 0 1 0
```

An example of a three-dimensional array is

```
> aaa <- array(0,dim=c(3,3,3))
> aaa[2,2,] <- 1
> aaa
, , 1

      [,1]  [,2]  [,3]
[1,]    0    0    0
[2,]    0    1    0
[3,]    0    0    0

, , 2

      [,1]  [,2]  [,3]
[1,]    0    0    0
[2,]    0    1    0
[3,]    0    0    0
```

```
, , 3

      [,1] [,2] [,3]
[1,]    0    0    0
[2,]    0    1    0
[3,]    0    0    0
```

The `matrix` constructor allows the user to construct two-dimensional arrays that incorporate metadata in the form of row and column names:

```
> ma <- matrix(0,nrow=3,ncol=3,
                dimnames=list(c("row1","row2","row3"),
                              c("col1","col2","col3")))
> ma[2,2] <- 1
> ma
     col1 col2 col3
row1    0    0    0
row2    0    1    0
row3    0    0    0
> ma[,2]
row1 row2 row3
   0    1    0
```

One of the most often used data structures in R is the data frame. This is a two-dimensional array that assigns names to the columns. What distinguishes data frames from the other multidimensional structures is the fact that we can access the columns in a data frame by their names using the $ operator. This makes programs written with data frames much more transparent and easier to understand. Here is a small snippet of R code using a data frame:

```
> x <- rnorm(5)
> y <- rnorm(5)
> df <- data.frame(x,y)
> df
           x            y
1 -1.32671927 -0.8523517
2 -0.01688355  0.7543477
3  1.53489098  0.4770785
4 -2.01491992 -0.4205267
5 -0.37707736  0.1549296
> dist <- sqrt(df$x^2 + df$y^2)
> dist
[1] 1.5769234 0.7545366 1.6073252 2.0583355 0.4076647
> plot(df,xlim=c(-3,3),ylim=c(-1,1))
```

The last line in the code above plots the data frame as shown in Figure B.2. Furthermore, data frames are structures that many facilities in R, such as the `plot`

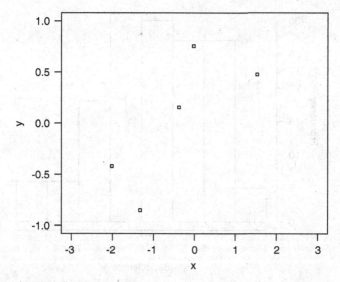

FIGURE B.2 Plot of a data frame with the columns x and y.

and `write.csv` functions, can interpret directly . The `read.csv` function returns a data frame constructed from a given CSV file.

B.3 BASIC DATA ANALYSIS

R's basic data analysis capabilities are best demonstrated with an example. Here we use the built-in data frame for the iris data set:

```
> data(iris)
> summary(iris)
  Sepal.Length       Sepal.Width       Petal.Length
 Min.   :4.300     Min.   :2.000     Min.   :1.000
 1st Qu.:5.100     1st Qu.:2.800     1st Qu.:1.600
 Median :5.800     Median :3.000     Median :4.350
 Mean   :5.843     Mean   :3.057     Mean   :3.758
 3rd Qu.:6.400     3rd Qu.:3.300     3rd Qu.:5.100
 Max.   :7.900     Max.   :4.400     Max.   :6.900
  Petal.Width           Species
 Min.   :0.100     setosa    :50
 1st Qu.:0.300     versicolor:50
 Median :1.300     virginica :50
 Mean   :1.199
 3rd Qu.:1.800
 Max.   :2.500
```

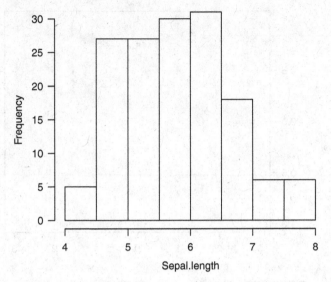

FIGURE B.3 Histogram of `Sepal.Length`.

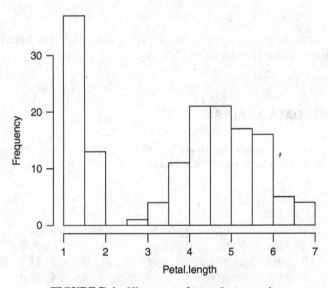

FIGURE B.4 Histogram of `Petal.Length`.

Examining the summary data, we find that we have four independent numerical attributes and one dependent categorical attribute, `Species`, with three labels.

We might wish to inspect the data distribution of some of the independent variables:

```
> hist(iris$Sepal.Length)
> hist(iris$Petal.Length)
```

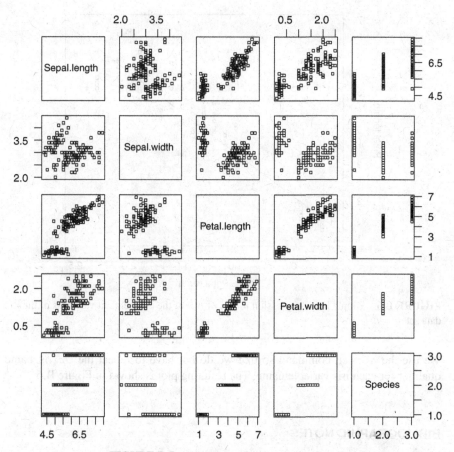

FIGURE B.5   Scatterplots for the iris data set.

The resulting plots are shown in Figures B.3 and B.4, respectively.

We can also obtain scatterplots for the iris data set:

```
> plot(iris)
```

The plots are shown in Figure B.5.

To illustrate model construction in R, we build a simple linear regression model for the Petal.Length and Petal.Width of the iris data set:

```
> attach(iris)
> model <- lm(Petal.Length ~ Petal.Width)
> plot(Petal.Width,Petal.Length)
> abline(model)
```

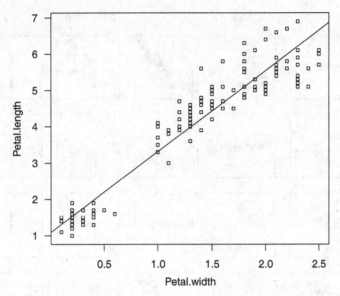

FIGURE B.6 Simple linear regression model of two of the independent variables of the iris data set.

We use the `attach` command so that we do not have to repeat the `iris$` name qualifier for each iris variable name. The resulting plot is shown in Figure B.6.

BIBLIOGRAPHIC NOTES

Perhaps the gentlest introduction to R is the book by Dalgaard [24]. Another nice introduction to R is [77]. A more comprehensive treatment of data analysis and statistics using R is [76]. The two de facto standard references for the R language are [4] and [19]. The graphics capabilities of R are described in [55].

REFERENCES

1. S. Abe. *Support Vector Machines for Pattern Classification*. Springer-Verlag, New York, 2005.

2. P. Adriaans and D. Zantinge. *Data Mining*. Addison-Wesley Longman, Reading, MA, 1997.

3. M.A. Aizerman, E.M. Braverman, and L. Rozonoer. Theoretical Foundations of the Potential Function Method in Pattern Recognition Learning. *Automation and Remote Control*, 25(17): (821–837), 1964.

4. R.A. Becker, J.M. Chambers, and A.R. Wilks. *The New S Language*. Wadsworth & Brooks, Pacific Grove, CA, 1988.

5. K.P. Bennett and E.J. Bredensteiner. Duality and Geometry in SVM Classifiers. In *Proceedings of the 17th International Conference on Machine Learning*, pages 57–64, 2000.

6. K.P. Bennett and C. Campbell. Support Vector Machines: Hype or Hallelujah? *ACM SIGKDD Explorations Newsletter*, 2(2):1–13, 2000.

7. L.D. Berkovitz. *Convexity and Optimization in $\mathbb{R}^n$*. Wiley, Hoboken, NJ, 2002.

8. M.J.A. Berry and G.S. Linoff. *Data Mining Techniques: For Marketing, Sales, and Customer Relationship Management*. Wiley, Hoboken, NJ, 2004.

9. C. Bishop. *Neural Networks for Pattern Recognition*. Oxford University Press, New York, 1995.

10. C. Bishop. *Pattern Recognition and Machine Learning*. Springer-Verlag, New York, 2006.

11. S. Borer and W. Gerstner. Support Vector Representation of Multi-categorical Data. In *Proceedings of the International Conference on Artificial Neural Networks*, pages 733–738, 2002.

12. B.E. Boser, I.M. Guyon, and V.N. Vapnik. A Training Algorithm for Optimal Margin Classifiers. In *Proceedings of the 5th Annual Workshop on Computational Learning Theory*, pages 144–152, 1992.

13. L. Bottou, O. Chapelle, D. DeCoste, and J. Weston. *Large-Scale Kernel Machines*. MIT Press, Cambridge, MA, 2007.

14. S.P. Boyd and L. Vandenberghe. *Convex Optimization*. Cambridge University Press, New York, 2004.

15. E.J. Bredensteiner and K.P. Bennett. Multicategory Classification by Support Vector Machines. *Computational Optimization and Applications*, 12(1):53–79, 1999.

16. L. Breiman, J.H. Friedman, R.A. Olshen, and C.J. Stone. *Classification and Regression Trees*. Wadsworth Statistics/Probability Series, Wadsworth, Belmont, CA, 1984.

17. C.J.C. Burges. A Tutorial on Support Vector Machines. *Data Mining and Knowledge Discovery*, 2(2):121–167, 1998.

18. C. Campbell and N. Cristianini. Simple Learning Algorithms for Training Support Vector Machines. Technical report. University of Bristol, UK, 1999.

19. J.M. Chambers. *Programming with Data: A Guide to the S Language*. Springer-Verlag, New York, 1998.

20. C. Chang and C. Lin. *LIBSVM: A Library for Support Vector Machines*, 2001. Software available at http://www.csie.ntu.edu.tw/~cjlin/libsvm.

21. M.E. Cohen and D.L. Hudson. *Neural Networks and Artificial Intelligence for Biomedical Engineering*. Wiley-IEEE Press, New York, 1999.

22. C. Cortes and V. Vapnik. Support-Vector Networks. *Machine Learning*, 20(3):273–297, 1995.

23. N. Cristianini and J. Shawe-Taylor. *An Introduction to Support Vector Machines and Other Kernel-Based Learning Methods*. Cambridge University Press, New York, 2000.

24. P. Dalgaard. *Introductory Statistics with R*. Springer-Verlag, New York, 2002.

25. T.G. Dietterich and G. Bakiri. Solving Multiclass Learning Problems via Error-Correcting Output Codes. *Journal of Artificial Intelligence Research*, 2:263–286, 1995.

26. R.O. Duda and P.E. Hart. *Pattern Classification and Scene Analysis*. Wiley, New York, 1973.

27. B. Efron. Bootstrap Methods: Another Look at the Jackknife. *Annals of Statistics*, 7(1):1–26, 1979.

28. B. Efron and R. Tibshirani. Statistical Data Analysis in the Computer Age. *Science*, 253(5018):390–395, 1991.

29. B. Efron and R. Tibshirani. *An Introduction to the Bootstrap*. Chapman & Hall/CRC Press, Boca Raton, FL, 1993.

30. R.E. Fan, P.H. Chen, and C.J. Lin. Working Set Selection Using Second Order Information for Training Support Vector Machines. *Journal of Machine Learning Research*, 6:1889–1918, 2005.

31. U.M. Fayyad, G. Piatetsky-Shapiro, P. Smyth, and R. Uthurusamy. *Advances in Knowledge Discovery and Data Mining*. MIT Press, Cambridge, MA, 1996.

32. Y. Freund and R.E. Schapire. Large Margin Classification Using the Perceptron Algorithm. *Machine Learning*, 37(3):277–296, 1999.

33. T. Friess, N. Cristianini, and C. Campbell. The Kernel-Adatron Algorithm: A Fast and Simple Learning Procedure for Support Vector Machines. In J. Shavlik, editor, *Proceedings of the 15th International Conference on Machine Learning*. Morgan Kaufmann, San Francisco, 1998.

34. J.E. Gentle. *Elements of Computational Statistics*. Springer-Verlag, New York, 2002.

35. P.R. Halmos. *Finite-Dimensional Vector Spaces*. Springer-Verlag, New York, 1974.

36. T. Hastie, R. Tibshirani, and J.H. Friedman. *The Elements of Statistical Learning: Data Mining, Inference, and Prediction*. Springer-Verlag, New York, 2001.

37. J. Hefferon. Linear Algebra. http://joshua.smcvt.edu/linalg.html.

38. R. Herbrich. *Learning Kernel Classifiers: Theory and Algorithms*. MIT Press, Cambridge, MA, 2002.

39. R.V. Hogg, A. Craig, and J.W. McKean. *Introduction to Mathematical Statistics*. Prentice Hall, Upper Saddle River, NJ, 2004.

40. A. Karatzoglou, D. Meyer, and K. Hornik. Support Vector Machines in R. *Journal of Statistical Software*, 15(9):9, 2006.

41. W. Karush. Minima of Functions of Several Variables with Inequalities as Side Constraints. Master's thesis, Dept. of Mathematics, University of Chicago, 1939.

42. V. Kecman. *Learning and Soft Computing: Support Vector Machines, Neural Networks, and Fuzzy Logic Models*. MIT Press, Cambridge, MA, 2001.

43. R. Kimball. *The Data Warehouse Toolkit*. Wiley, Hoboken, NJ, 2002.

44. M. Kirby. *Geometric Data Analysis: An Empirical Approach to Dimensionality Reduction and the Study of Patterns*. Wiley, Hoboken, NJ, 2000.

45. D. Klein. Lagrange Multipliers Without Permanent Scarring, 2007. http://www.cs.berkeley.edu/~klein/papers/lagrange-multipliers.pdf.

46. R. Kohavi. A Study of Cross-Validation and Bootstrap for Accuracy Estimation and Model Selection. In *Proceedings of the 14th International Joint Conference on Artificial Intelligence*, pages 1137–1143. Morgan Kaufmann, San Francisco, 1995.

47. U. Kressel. Pairwise Classification and Support Vector Machines, in *Advances in Kernel Methods: Support Vector Learning* pages 255–268. MIT Press, Cambridge, MA, 1999.

48. E. Kreyszig. *Advanced Engineering Mathematics*. Wiley, New York, 1993.

49. H.W. Kuhn and A.W. Tucker. Nonlinear Programming. In *Proceedings of the 2nd Berkeley Symposium on Mathematical Statistics and Probability*. University of California Press; Berkeley, CA, and Cambridge University Press, Cambridge, UK, 1951.

50. G. Mak. The Implementation of Support Vector Machines using the Sequential Minimal Optimization Algorithm. Ph.D. dissertation, McGill University, 2000.

51. T. Masters. *Practical Neural Network Recipes in C++*. Academic Press, New York, 1993.

52. D. Miller. Bootstrap 101: Obtain Robust Confidence Intervals for Any Statistic. In *Proceedings of the SAS User Group Conference*, 2004.

53. M. Minsky and S. Papert. *Perceptrons: An Introduction to Computational Geometry*. MIT Press, Cambridge, MA, 1988.

54. T.M. Mitchell. *Machine Learning*. McGraw-Hill, New York, 1997.

55. P. Murrell. *R Graphics*. Chapman & Hall/CRC Press, Boca Raton, FL, 2005.

56. Y. Nesterov. *Introductory Lectures on Convex Optimization: A Basic Course.* Kluwer Academic, Norwell, MA, 2004.

57. E. Osuna, R. Freund, and F. Girosi. Improved Training Algorithm for Support Vector Machine. Presented at NNSP'97, 1997.

58. C.J. Platt. Sequential Minimal Optimisation: A Fast Algorithm for Training Support Vector Machines. Microsoft Research Technical Report MSR-TR-98-14, 1998.

59. T. Poggio and S. Smale. The Mathematics of Learning: Dealing with Data. Presented at the International Conference on Neural Networks and Brain, 2005.

60. K.R. Popper. *The Logic of Scientific Discovery.* Routledge, New York, 2002. Originally published as "Logik der Forschung" in 1935.

61. D. Pyle. *Data Preparation for Data Mining.* Morgan Kaufmann, San Francisco, 1999.

62. J.R. Quinlan. *C4.5: Programs for Machine Learning.* Morgan Kaufmann, San Francisco, 1993.

63. J. Renegar. *A Mathematical View of Interior-Point Methods in Convex Optimization.* SIAM, Philadelphia, 2001.

64. F. Rosenblatt. The Perceptron: A Perceiving and Recognizing Automaton. Cornell Aeronautical Laboratory Report, pages 85–460, 1957.

65. B. Schölkopf and A.J. Smola. *Learning with Kernels: Support Vector Machines, Regularization, Optimization, and Beyond.* MIT Press, Cambridge, MA, 2002.

66. B. Schölkopf, R. Williamson, A.J. Smola, J. Shawe-Taylor, and J. Platt. Support Vector Method for Novelty Detection. *Advances in Neural Information Processing Systems*, 12:582–588, 2000.

67. J. Shawe-Taylor and N. Cristianini. *Kernel Methods for Pattern Analysis.* Cambridge University Press, New York, 2004.

68. A.J. Smola and B. Schölkopf. A Tutorial on Support Vector Regression. *Statistics and Computing*, 14(3):199–222, 2004.

69. J.A. Snyman. *Practical Mathematical Optimization: An Introduction to Basic Optimization Theory and Classical and New Gradient-Based Algorithms.* Springer-Verlag, New York, 2005.

70. D.M.J. Tax and R.P.W. Duin. Support Vector Data Description. *Machine Learning*, 54(1):45–66, 2004.

71. V.N. Vapnik. *Statistical Learning Theory.* Wiley, New York, 1998.

72. V.N. Vapnik. An Overview of Statistical Learning Theory. *IEEE Transactions on Neural Networks*, 10(5):988–999, 1999.

73. V.N. Vapnik. *The Nature of Statistical Learning Theory.* Springer-Verlag, New York, 2000.

74. V.N. Vapnik. *Estimation of Dependences Based on Empirical Data.* Springer-Verlag, New York, 2006.

75. V.N. Vapnik and A.Y. Chervonenkis. On the Uniform Convergence of Relative Frequencies of Events to Their Probabilities. *Theory of Probability and Its Applications*, 16:264, 1971.

76. W.N. Venables and B.D. Ripley. *Modern Applied Statistics with S.* Springer-Verlag, New York, 2002.

77. W.N. Venables and D.M. Smith. *An Introduction to R.* Network Theory, 2001.

78. R.E. Walpole, K. Ye, R.H. Myers, and S.L. Myers. *Probability and Statistics for Engineers and Scientists*. Prentice Hall, Upper Saddle River, NJ, 2002.

79. J. Weston and C. Watkins. Multi-Class Support Vector Machines. In *Proceedings ESANN*, 1999.

80. I.H. Witten and E. Frank. *Data Mining: Practical Machine Learning Tools and Techniques*. Morgan Kaufmann, San Francisco, 2005.

INDEX

Knowledge Discovery with Support Vector Machines, by Lutz Hamel
Copyright © 2009 John Wiley & Sons, Inc.

WILEY SERIES ON METHODS AND APPLICATIONS IN DATA MINING

Series Editor: **Daniel T. Larose**

Discovering Knowledge in Data: An Introduction to Data Mining • Daniel T. LaRose

Data-Mining on the Web: Uncovering Patterns in Web Content, Structure, and Usage • Zdravko Markov and Daniel Larose

Data Mining Methods and Models • Daniel Larose

Practical Text Mining with Perl • Roger Bilisoly

Knowledge Discovery with Support Vector Machines • Lutz Hamel